GRAMERCY PARK

GRAMERCY PARK

PARK

An American Bloomsbury

✦

CAROLE KLEIN

The Johns Hopkins University Press
Baltimore and London

Originally published in hardcover by Houghton Mifflin Company
Johns Hopkins Paperbacks edition, 1999
2 4 6 8 9 7 5 3 1

The Johns Hopkins University Press
2715 North Charles Street
Baltimore, Maryland 21218-4363
www.press.jhu.edu

Library of Congress Cataloging-in-Publication Data will be found
at the back of this book.

A catalog record for this book is available from the British Library.

ISBN 0-8018-6297-3

A friend is . . . a second self.

— Cicero
De Amicitia XXI, 50 B.C.

FOR BARBARA LINDEMAN

ACKNOWLEDGMENTS

———————◆———————

I am delighted to have the opportunity to acknowledge the assistance of a number of people and sources in researching and writing this book.

The Elmer Holmes Bobst Library of New York University was a primary resource for my research, and its staff of librarians was unfailingly helpful.

Ellen Wallenstein of the Museum of the City of New York, and Katherine Naylor of The New-York Historical Society, were infinitely patient and helpful in locating the photographs that so enrich my text. Louis A. Rachow, curator of the Hampden-Booth Theatre Library of The Players Club, graciously allowed me to use that unique collection, and served as an imaginative guide to its contents. Raymond Wemmlinger, librarian of the Hampden-Booth Library, unstintingly offered his assistance in my efforts to gather photographs and was equally willing to respond to ongoing questions about theatrical history.

Many people shared their private collections of pictures and other material with me. I want especially to thank Dr. Eugene Weise of New York City for his generous invitation to borrow from his impressive store of photographs of Gramercy Park, and also Ms. Janet Le Clair, who allowed me to use the rare portrait of Robert Henri that is part of the Robert Henri estate. Mr. O. Aldon James, Jr., president of the National Arts Club, was always willing to direct me to a source of information, and my visits to the club were invariably regenerating to my project.

A number of friends provided unwavering encouragement for my work, and my affection reaches out to them all. I want specifically to thank Ms. Marjory Bassett, who never lost an opportunity to express her enthusiasm for this project and to bring it to other people's attention.

My participation in the Biography Seminar of The New York Institute for the Humanities during the course of writing my book was a source of both concrete help and creative renewal. First under the direction of Aileen Ward, and then of Joan Peyser and John Maynard, the meetings became vital wellsprings of thought and energy.

Katia Spieglman was a thorough and resourceful researcher, whose efforts very much accelerated my writing schedule.

Jane Hanna Auch deserves all the appreciation I can summon for her supportive friendship and for her extraordinary skill in finding obscure photographic material. She seemed to transform herself into a determined wizard, capable of pulling just the right picture out of the air.

Finally, I thank Cameron Barry. The amount of material that went into writing this book was so vast that resolute attention had to be paid to maintaining the narrative thread. Cameron, who is gifted with both great literary taste and acute critical skills, helped me stay on course. She quickly became an absolutely crucial other eye. Her brilliant feedback is woven into all my efforts, and I am eternally grateful.

CONTENTS

IV

HOW BRIGHT THE NIGHT,
HOW BLEAK THE MORNING: 1920–1939

ILLUSTRATIONS

———◆———

AUTHOR'S NOTE

❖

SEVERAL YEARS AGO, I wrote a biography of Aline Bernstein, the famous stage designer. Aline was born in Manhattan in 1880, and my research on her early life introduced me to a city I had never known, although vestiges of it remain here and there in a historical street name, a hidden courtyard, or the elaborate façade of an iron building.

New York is a city that continuously and impatiently moves ahead. Because of this, its rich past is often neglected, and I was captivated by Aline's Manhattan of cobblestone streets, horse-drawn carriages, and the gaslit theaters where her father performed Shakespeare with famed stars like Edwin Booth.

As a middle-aged woman, in the 1920s, Aline fell in love with Thomas Wolfe, who was twenty-five. The fledgling southern author was determined to make his mark in a city that he saw as "far-shining, glorious, time-enchanted." I began to think about how the magnetism of New York has always drawn to itself impassioned dreamers, and I wanted to understand the forces that had made the city a symbol of infinite expectation and possibility.

New Yorkers walk, and I am no exception. One day, on a stroll uptown from my home in Greenwich Village, I turned east from bustling Park Avenue South at Twentieth Street, and I came to one of my favorite places — Gramercy Park, an unspoiled reminder of the city's origins, but with a rich history all its own that I wanted to examine.

As Paul Goldberger, architecture critic for the *New York Times*, has commented, Gramercy Park "is probably the only quarter in New York in which one might still today, at least for a fleeting moment, actually sustain the illusion of being in London." And, indeed, what Gramercy Park most resembles is a nineteenth-century London square. The graceful rows of red brick and brownstone houses, with their lacy wrought-iron grillwork, magnificent mahogany doors, and brass lanterns, project an air of civility and serenity more often associated with England than with America.

In the center of this stately square is the small private park that gives the area its name. For 150 years, the park, quietly protected by elegant iron gates, has opened only to the keys of Gramercy Park residents. In fact, those keys were once golden. Inside the gates, one's sense of timelessness is heightened. Carefully tended flowers line immaculate gravel paths, wooden benches are set out at discreet distances so that one conversation does not intrude on another; even the children who play on the lawn seem calmed by their surroundings. It would not surprise a visitor to see a little girl dressed in a long crinoline skipping down the path and rolling a hoop. No wonder, then, that the air seems shadowy with ghosts.

As soon as I began to do research on the neighborhood, I found that the ghosts of Gramercy Park were people whose lives and accomplishments had been absolutely dazzling. I also realized that Gramercy Park's connection to London goes beyond the genteel dimensions of the square. I discovered that it is the closest thing America has ever had to a Bloomsbury, a rich mix of talents living and working together in a circumscribed area. And, because the neighborhood remained virtually unchanged as the city grew up around it, this atmosphere prevailed from decade to decade. The cast of important people changed, but the interactions and sense of shared purpose continued. If New York City was the best place to test one's talent, Gramercy Park was, for many, the environment in which to nourish it.

My book ends with the 1930s, which marks a century of growth from the first flowering of Gramercy Park. More important, it seems to me that since then we have experienced an intensification of the amazing innovations that marked New York's earlier periods. And it is the innovations themselves that I wanted to trace and explore. Inevitably, I have chosen to highlight some people and events and to omit others.

Some of the names will be familiar, although they are often remembered more as symbols of historical events than as living human beings. Others, like those of the two remarkable men who begin this story — Samuel Ruggles, the visionary who created Gramercy Park, and George Templeton Strong, his son-in-law — are perhaps less likely to be recognized. Their influence on our history is so significant that you will no doubt be astonished — as I was — that they have stayed so long in the shadows.

Gramercy Park is not a traditional historical or cultural study, but it is historically accurate in its recounting of places and events. My principal goal is to share with you the richness of Gramercy Park, a dynamic and distinctive cultural landmark in a city that remains a source of energy for all America.

NEW YORK CITY

1987

I

The London of America

———◆———

1822-1860

Samuel Ruggles as a young man

I

THE BIRTH
OF
GRAMERCY PARK

SAMUEL RUGGLES arrived in New York early in the year 1822. It was the beginning of a decade of phenomenal change for the city that Walt Whitman would later describe as "the great place of the western continent, the heart, the brain, the focus, the main spring, the pinnacle, the extremity, the no more beyond of the New World."

New York was the "London of America," wrote the native New Yorker John Pintard in 1826, but, unlike London, it had no cultural history or architectural traditions to maintain. New York's growth was dictated largely by commerce, which also guided its citizens' values and tastes. Without the restraints of tradition, new rules could be made by anyone forceful enough to make himself heard. And, because the mercantile spirit was the core of city life, fortunes could be made by anyone, almost overnight. "Rich men spring up like mushrooms," observed one wag. Small wonder, then, that the lure of New York City attracted young men like Samuel Ruggles, who would leave his mark on its miraculous life.

Samuel Bulkley Ruggles was born in Connecticut in 1800, a descendent of John Ruggles, who had emigrated to America from

Essex, England, in 1635. Sam's parents, both raised in New England, moved to New York State when Sam was still a small boy. The family was financially and socially prominent; music and books filled the large, graceful home in Poughkeepsie, and Sam, a precocious child, seemed destined to follow his father's footsteps into law. The boy was immensely curious about a broad range of subjects and was capable of sophisticated thinking at an early age. No greater proof of this precocity is needed than his acceptance into Yale's sophomore class when he was only twelve years old.

Timothy Dwight, then president of Yale, offered his students an education that exceeded the scope of much early-nineteenth-century higher learning. When he graduated on an April morning in 1814, the youngest member of his class, Samuel Ruggles was aware that the interests that had fired his imagination at Yale would actively engage him for the rest of his life.

As soon as he was licensed to practice law, Sam made up his mind to go to New York City. He was not ashamed to say that he felt he was a match for Manhattan. Restless and confident, he was ready for any challenge New York could offer, and it excited him to know that he could not even surmise what those challenges would be.

As he walked the streets, his eyes devoured the landscape. Steeples from New York's ninety churches and secular buildings of varying size and shape — the graceful marble of City Hall, a Masonic hall, Columbia College, New York and Bellevue hospitals — seemed to fill the sky above the city's built-up portion, which spread outward and upward from the Battery to Astor Place. There were small manufacturing buildings, printing establishments for thirty-five daily and weekly newspapers, eleven public markets, five prisons, and the magnificent Park Theater, which held twenty-five hundred people. Plans were already being laid for an even grander theater, the Bowery, not to mention an amazing pleasure garden at the corner of Broadway and Prince Street. Called Niblo's, it would have fountains and fireworks to amuse the child in every visitor.

Perhaps most wondrous of all were the boldly beautiful, elegantly dressed young women who walked confidently through these busy streets. Who in Poughkeepsie, or even New Haven, would dress herself at ten in the morning in a pink satin dress, a flowered silk

*Manhattan's uneven landscape is made level as the city moves
uptown. Broadway and the Bowery, 1831.*

*Niblo's, the city's most
fashionable pleasure garden,
where New Yorkers went
to promenade, find
refreshment, and be amused
and entertained*

*Broadway and its chief embellishment: the six-story,
six-hundred-bed Astor House Hotel in the 1840s*

bonnet, and such delicate laced boots? Where did they find the money to pay for such finery? Sam wondered. Inquiring at a shop out of curiosity, he was amazed to discover that a morning bonnet might cost $60, and the lace-and-silk shawl that draped the shoulders of a tradesman's daughter sold for nearly half that sum.

Sam's own clothes, meticulously tailored to his six-foot frame, were as fine as anything he saw along Wall Street and Broadway. His family connections to early Knickerbocker aristocracy and his years at Yale had taught him the conventions of elegance. His head of lustrous brown hair held high, his blue eyes flashing, and his mouth looking unmistakably sensual, Sam could hold his own in the most august circles.

In lesser company, Sam's manners were never smug or patrician, for he combined diverse qualities with disarming grace and ease. Both pragmatist and idealist, Sam had a natural optimism that could give way to hard-eyed realism. He lived fully in every moment, yet he had an uncanny sense of the future. His passion for many fields — law, art, music, politics, and public service — kept alive the fires of his imagination. Hamilton Fish, who became secretary of state following his career as mayor and governor of New York, once attempted to describe his dynamic friend; he said, "Samuel Ruggles could throw off more brilliant and pregnant ideas in a given moment than any man I ever saw."

There was much to think about in this exciting period of New York history. Almost daily, the city seemed to be reshaping itself in size and potential. The 1820 census had numbered 123,706 citizens. It was obvious that this figure would double before the decade ended. Ten to twenty thousand more people took up temporary residence almost every season. Although more than a thousand new homes were constructed each year, housing was in short supply and forced many New Yorkers — even whole families — to live in hotels or boarding houses.

Samuel preferred the more intimate boarding houses to the grandly proportioned City Hotel, where he had stayed on first arriving in New York, and which took up the entire block between Cedar and Thames streets. It was common practice there to have a public breakfast and dinner, but companionship was limited for both guests and neighborhood businessmen. Meals were generally eaten in silence and with such dispatch that it seemed the diners begrudged any time spent away from the teeming life outdoors.

Sam quickly established himself in the city as a lawyer, opening an office on Pine Street, but he was eager to get into commerce. And there was something he wanted even more: to establish an emotional base in Manhattan.

Being a bachelor in New York was admittedly great sport. He could go out every night in the week to some new performance or entertainment, and there were concerts and balls in the ladies' dining room of the City Hotel. The huge Park Theater offered plays starring the most distinguished actors of the day — Edmund Kean and Junius Booth among them — as well as dancers and singers in elaborate costume. On pleasant evenings, Sam and his friends gathered in Contoit's Garden, on Broadway near Franklin Street, where they sat at small tables under the light of tiny candles swinging in glass globes, eating ice cream and pound cake and drinking cold lemonade. There were also social gatherings at people's homes, where the guests sang, played whist, or danced a modest minuet.

Lately, however, Samuel had found himself looking wistfully at couples strolling arm in arm as they promenaded along Broadway on warm Sunday afternoons, or at children playing under the watchful eyes of their parents, who sat companionably on benches bordering the graveled paths and green lawns of Battery Park.

Clearly, Sam was ready to respond to the charms of the young woman who was introduced to him one evening. Mary Rosalie Rathbone was the quiet, winsome daughter of a leading New York merchant. To Sam's friends, like Hamilton Fish and William Seward, Mary may have seemed less vivacious than the woman they imagined him being drawn to, but his obvious happiness in her company quelled their doubts. Sam and Mary were married in May 1822, and from that day on Mary was content to stand amiably in Samuel's shadow.

In 1834, after living in rented quarters, Sam and Mary moved with their two sons and daughter to fashionable Bond Street, where some of the city's most renowned citizens, such as Albert Gallatin, secretary of the treasury under Presidents Jefferson and Madison, also had homes. Samuel loved the quiet, graceful street, secluded from urban hustle and bustle, but he could see signs that the city would continue to expand and that commerce would soon encroach on family life.

Wall Street, once an area of many private homes, was by 1825 the site of many of the banking firms and money exchanges that came to define it. These commercial beginnings were bolstered by the chartering of the New York Gas Light Company in 1823. A year later, the company held an awesome public exhibition of its works at 286 Water Street, the first house in New York City to be lit by gas. This miracle of invention soon illuminated all the rapidly multiplying financial transactions of lower Manhattan.

Pearl Street, winding a narrow path around Wall Street, was populated largely by wholesalers dealing in dry goods. Broadway, already well established as the city's most magnificent thoroughfare, cut an elegant path eighty feet wide and almost three miles long through the city. Many of the homes on it were being replaced by cosmopolitan shops, some so grand that English visitors called them the equal of any on London's Regent Street.

There were many eyesores as well, particularly the clutter of placards suspended from beams that jutted out over pedestrians' heads, advertising the wonders to be found inside each shop. Some vendors wove their way through the crowds on Broadway and the Bowery, hawking a bewildering array of products, from limestone for new homes to new pairs of shoes. A steady stream of boys carried saws and wooden horses through the crowds, offering cords of wood they would cut into suitable lengths for the family fireplace. Licensed porters, stationed at busy corners, would carry such heavy purchases home on their handcarts — anything for a price.

There was also plenty of food available for the potential customer, particularly along the relatively rural Bowery. Families, enjoying the fresh air from their porches or stoops, might bid a child to stop rolling his hoop and go to one of the spots where Negro women dispensed ears of corn from pails of hot water. These colorfully garbed ladies, in their red aprons and yellow bandannas, sometimes walked up and down the streets, carrying trays of baked pears, moist and sweet with molasses.

At the turn of the century, Negroes had accounted for almost 10 percent of the city's population, although there were fewer than thirty-five hundred living in New York. Thirty-five years later, they represented only 5 percent of the population, but their number had swelled to sixteen thousand. There were no slaves in New York after 1827, but there was ample evidence of continuing segregation in public places and in the kinds of work available to this group of immigrants. Most colored people (as they were called) worked as servants, managed small stores, ran oyster stands, or, like the female vendors, sold food to the passing gentry. Other immigrants and visitors found these New Yorkers to be more self-assured and better established than the Negroes in their own countries or states.

A Swedish writer, Carl Arfwedson, who visited New York in 1832, was mesmerized by the bold style of dress of the colored people as they promenaded along the Battery on Sunday afternoons. The women in their bonnets, all "decorated with ribbons, plumes, and flowers, of a thousand different colors"; the men, with their yellow gloves, jaunty hats, and vests in "all colors of the rainbow," amazed and delighted him. Even the formidable Mrs. Trollope, whose book *The Domestic Manners of the Americans* was filled with biting criticisms of American life, found much to admire in the "air of confidence" projected by Negroes in New York City. She felt it to be very different from the attitude of blacks in the other American cities she had visited.

Farmers from Long Island also joined in the commerce of lower Manhattan. Some yoked tin cans of milk to their shoulders with a pole and thick leather straps; others, "sandmen," dressed in long white coats, wheeled their carts in and out of taverns, replenishing the sandy floors with fresh supplies from the beaches of Rockaway.

Because the contamination of Manhattan's water supply was a growing problem, street-corner commerce invariably included pure spring water from the pristine suburbs, along with an "artificial soda water" that compensated for the brackish city water piped to residents through hollowed wooden logs. By 1835 there was great agitation over the need to build a municipal waterworks, and Samuel Ruggles's name was closely associated with plans to bring water to New York City from the Croton River, twenty-two miles north. But it was not until 1842 that the distributing reservoir would open at Forty-second Street and Fifth Avenue, where the New York Public Library now stands.

Day and night, along the Battery, Broadway, or Wall Street, the commercial din was so intense that even the most devoted New Yorker could feel overwhelmed by noise. As Walt Whitman would later ask, "Amid this universal clatter, the incessant din of business, the all-swallowing vortex of the great money whirlpool . . . who has any . . . idea . . . of silence?"

And this noisy city was not very clean. There were no city ordinances to regulate the control of garbage. As new buildings hastily went up to accommodate Broadway's commercial expansion, wagons of building materials dumped their contents in front of the building sites, filling the air with dust and particles of stone. Added to these heaps of debris were food scraps and other refuse that shopkeepers piled in the streets, where it was happily foraged by the scavenging pigs that were a permanent part of the Manhattan landscape. This mecca of the New World took some getting used to. A visiting Scottish printer cautioned friends considering a similar visit that "the streets of New York are not to be perambulated with impunity by either the lame, or the blind, or the exquisitely sensitive in their olfactory nerves."

By 1830, omnibuses, each elaborately decorated and drawn by four matched horses, were added to the traffic of private coaches and handcarts. The clatter of the animals' iron-shod hooves contributed as greatly to the din as their droppings did to the mess on the streets. Traffic was equally hectic along New York's expanding waterfront. Port activity increased dramatically as the city edged out New England as the center of shipbuilding.

Shipyards first appeared in South Street and soon took up the waterfront from South Ferry to Twelfth Street. Breathing in the exotic fragrance of pungent spices from the foreign packet ships, visitors marveled at the enormous sail lofts where the sails were sewn, and the open stalls where ironworkers, gilders, and coppersmiths worked in noisy concentration. Most intriguing of all were the woodcarvers, who skillfully fashioned great mythological heads to adorn the ships' prows.

When night fell, the crowds — made up of curious New Yorkers, foreign sailors, and visiting merchants dressed in native costume — did not disperse. The mélange of tongues provided a musical background for the nighttime waterfront, which blazed with the light of torches, whale-oil flames, and charcoal fires. Samuel, who often walked to the shipyards after supper, felt stirred by the infinite promise of this port. He knew that it would make his beloved city the most important in the world.

It was the same feeling that guided Samuel Ruggles to participate in the opening of the Erie Canal in 1825. De Witt Clinton, who had first proposed the canal, was then governor of New York and a close friend of Sam's. The idea of linking the Hudson River with the Great Lakes excited Sam from the minute he heard it, and he defended it persuasively to the citizens and members of the legislature who first mocked the project they called Clinton's Ditch.

Samuel Ruggles fervently believed that the 1820s and thirties were crucial years in the shaping of New York's history. The Erie Canal would make the rich upstate land and its agricultural products accessible to the city and, through the city's port, to the entire world. It would also link New York and its markets to the states around the Great Lakes. Sam was simultaneously formulating plans for the development of the Erie Railroad, for he was convinced that the easier the access to New York from all points, the greater the city would become.

He was certainly right about the impact of the Erie Canal. Commerce boomed as shipping time and costs dramatically lessened. Within only one year after its opening, some five hundred new mercantile houses, twelve banks, and ten marine companies were established, and twenty-seven additional banks applied for a charter. Over three thousand new residential and commercial buildings were erected, and there was hardly an empty dwelling in or around the city.

Landlords took full advantage of this short supply, often refusing to grant long-term leases, on the correct assumption that they would be able to get higher rent from newly prosperous New Yorkers the following season. It was not uncommon in the twenties, thirties, and forties for families to move every year.

On February 1, landlords would visit their tenants and announce the rent for the coming year. If the occupants objected, a TO LET sign was slapped on the wall. By the end of the day, a third of the city's houses and stores might bear these announcements. On the first of May, the traditional moving day for New Yorkers, families and tradesmen would leave old quarters for new, their furniture-laden carts followed by porters, servants, and children hand-carrying such valuable possessions as candelabra, velvet cloaks, and clay fish kettles. Such an abundance of traffic and furnishings so filled the streets on May 1 that the city seemed to overflow. Indeed, the city jail routinely cleaned and minimally decorated some cells to accommodate citizens who had to vacate old quarters before their new ones were ready.

Many residential buildings were well beyond the city's early boundaries. The devastating cholera epidemics of the early 1820s had encouraged migration by families who believed that the dense population in the central sections of the city contributed to contagion. As a result, the once-bucolic Greenwich section of Manhattan quickly became the elegant residential community of Greenwich Village. The continued expansion of the city's downtown business district added to the lure of such quiet neighborhoods.

Much of the uptown land people moved to belonged to Sam Ruggles. By 1831, he had done well enough in real estate investments to retire from his law practice, except in an advisory capacity. It was estimated that during the decade between 1830 and 1840 he was worth a quarter of a million dollars. That sum lent him a status that brought him into social contact with people like John Jacob Astor and families like the Schermerhorns, Stuyvesants, and Brevoorts. Yet Sam remained engagingly unimpressed by his own achievements. As

Philip Hone, a prominent business leader and mayor of New York from 1826 to 1827, described him, "Unlike many who become suddenly rich, Mr. Ruggles is modest and unassuming, a gentleman of good sense and information without pretension."

Hone was so impressed with Samuel that he invited him to join the prestigious club that bore his name. Club life during the mid nineteenth century was almost as established in New York as in London. The Bread and Cheese Club was formed for the city's literati; James Fenimore Cooper, William Cullen Bryant, Samuel Morse, and Washington Irving were members. The Union Club, which Sam joined as a charter member in 1837, was intended for "gentlemen of social distinction," and its only tenet was "ease and comfort within the limits of courtesy." He also belonged to the more intimate and intellectual Kent Club, formed by the distinguished chancellor of the New York Court of Chancery, James Kent. Nonetheless, Sam accepted Hone's invitation to join a group, very "circumscribed in numbers," that would meet every two weeks over dinners of the "highest order of gustatory enjoyment" to exchange a similarly high order of conversation. There is reason to believe that, with such members as Daniel Webster and John Quincy Adams, these dinners were indeed stimulating.

Some evenings, Sam would invite one or two of his club friends to accompany him to the theater after supper. It was not unusual for men to leave their wives at home when they went to the theater in order to shelter them from the often rowdy behavior of visiting tradesmen out for a night's amusement.

Touring European actors like Charles and Frances Kemble, Edmund Kean, and William Charles Macready had to make considerable adjustment to some of these audiences. Fanny Kemble was fond of recalling the first time she looked out at the dress circle and boxes in a New York theater and saw only men, sitting with their hats on, loudly chewing on apples and pastry, some spitting tobacco on the crimson-carpeted floor.

Even more established, patrician New Yorkers had their cultural limitations. Samuel himself was a devout admirer of Italian opera, but it was slow to gain popularity in the city. The first performance in America of a full-fledged opera was in November 1825, at the Park Theater, with tickets going for the unheard-of price of $2.00 each. Although New York's social elite turned out in force, it was soon clear that they found the imported offering too exotic. To Sam's amused surprise, his guest, the normally reserved Chancellor Kent, leaped to his feet during one of the more impassioned moments in *The Barber of Seville* and fled the theater, shouting that the opera was "an insult to human nature!"

Several years later, when opera had become a more accepted part of the city's cultural life, Sam Ruggles and his family were living in a home that clearly reflected their high esthetics. Even more graceful than the house on Bond Street, the four-story building stood on one of several lots that Sam had developed on Union Place, a previously neglected and unsightly parcel of land just above Fourteenth Street. Under Sam's guidance and with his financial investment, the property became Union Square, a cultivated, invitingly open space surrounded by three- and four-story town houses as stately as his own. Some years later, he would persuade other homeowners, who also held property in the vicinity of Madison Square, to join him in making that area, too, an attractive public space.

These were not random efforts by Sam. As he watched New York City grow, his concern about the quality of life there kept pace with his excitement over the rich possibilities of its commercial expansion. In his opinion, early city planning had been sorely inadequate in its estimation of the value of open space. A report released in 1811 made the naïve assumption that New York received so much fresh and pure air from the "large arms of the sea which embrace Manhattan Island" that parks and squares, while desirable, were not vital for the well-being of its citizens. Consequently, as the century wore on, even land originally intended for public use was often sold off to commercial interests.

Sam was convinced that this pattern was foolhardy, that no amount of overall prosperity could compensate those who lived in neighborhoods that left no breathing space for body or soul. This fervent belief did not diminish as Sam acquired property farther and farther north of the rising city. His largest tract of land fell north and south, east and west, between Nineteenth and Twenty-fourth streets. It was traversed by roving woodcocks and rabbits, punctuated by deep swamps, and landscaped by massive, irregular hills. Sam estimated that it would take three million loads of earth to level this land into housing tracts. But Manhattan's expansion was worthy of investment, he explained to skeptical lenders. He predicted that, within five years, "the real estate upon this rocky island will be taxed at 250 millions of dollars," for the city was "marching onward and cannot stop."

There are those who feel that creating the neighborhood of Gramercy Park with his capital remains Samuel Ruggles's most notable accomplishment and the most graphic example of his visionary city planning. Although he had not yet visited London, it was a London square that shaped his dream. He paid countless visits downtown to St. John's Park, which had been modeled after an eighteenth-century London square. Gradually, he developed a picture in his mind of how his neighborhood should look, from the size and design of its brick and brownstone homes to the landscaping of the park in its center. He petitioned the city for tax-exempt status for his park; providing such space for the enjoyment of neighborhood residents, he argued, would attract homeowners, who would build far more valuable homes than if the park did not exist, and thereby give greater income to the city.

But the decision to put aside forty-two lots in the center of his property for use as a private park was more than pragmatic. Eager as he was to increase the value of the land for himself and for New York, Sam remained steadfast in his dedication to enriching urban life by providing gentle places of escape.

The deed for the parcel of land that would become the park is dated December 17, 1831. It established that, from then on, the property belonged to the people who purchased surrounding lots. To ensure that his gift would not be lost through neglect, Sam placed the park in the hands of five trustees, who were to be replaced as necessary by neighborhood election. The original trustees were given the task of following Sam's precise specifications for the park's design and maintaining the interior grounds.

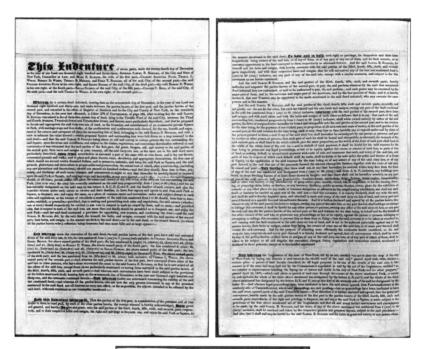

The original deed for Gramercy Park, presented by Samuel Ruggles to the park's first trustees

Even more important to Sam was ensuring "the free circulation of air," no matter how dense became the city around this area. He was therefore highly specific on what constituted acceptable construction in the neighborhood called Gramercy Park. His deed states that no one would ever be allowed to "erect within 40 feet of the front of any . . . of the said lots . . . any other buildings save brick or stone dwelling houses" and then proceeds to list all the establishments that would be out of keeping with the residential grace of the area. They include "any livery stable, slaughter house, smith shop . . . brewery, distillery, public museum . . . circus" or "any other trade or business dangerous or offensive to the neighboring inhabitants."

Since the early city fathers had assumed that traffic would run primarily east and west, from river to river, more New York streets ran crosstown than uptown. Believing that the city's upward progression was inevitable, Sam cut out a wide street, as he developed Gramercy Park, "parallel to and between the Third and Fourth Avenue." He petitioned the city to name it Lexington Avenue, after the famous Revolutionary battle. A piece of land that fell below Twentieth Street and his park he named Irving Place, "in respect and gratitude" to his friend Washington Irving.

Although Peter Cooper and other friends entreated him to lend his own name to one of these streets, Sam had no desire for fame. Nor did it bother him that many New Yorkers were still calling the park "Sam Ruggles's vacant lot." Let them laugh; it would be only a matter of time before more New Yorkers moved uptown.

On bad days, however, Sam grudgingly admitted that his dream was not being realized as quickly as he had hoped. There were not many people adventurous enough to move beyond the existing city limits. By 1845, only two houses had been completed in Gramercy Park, although seven more were under construction. Still, as one walked around the now richly planted park — shaded by willow, maple, and chestnut trees, its walks trimmed with flowering shrubs, lilacs, snowballs, and red Indian currant — one had an almost palpable sense of tranquillity that was lacking downtown. A stroll up to Ruggles's outpost at dusk became a pleasant activity for many New Yorkers. When they returned to their own crowded and noisy streets, they must have felt that his vision had once again anticipated their own needs.

On a June evening in 1845, one stroller from downtown was a young man who would soon become among the most important people in Samuel Ruggles's life. His name was George Templeton Strong, and his parents were friends of Sam and Mary's.

George had already met the Ruggles's daughter, Ellen, at a family soirée, yet it was not the idea of the young woman that attracted him to living in Gramercy Park. Greenwich Street, where he lived with his parents, was no longer gracious; it had become "a street of emigrant boarding houses and dirty drinking shops." As the sky deepened around Gramercy Park, casting cool shadows on the broad iron gates, he breathed deeply of the delicious silence. That night, June 16, 1845, he wrote in his diary of his interest in building a home in Gramercy Park. The diary, which he had begun at the age of fifteen, remains perhaps the most extraordinary portrait of nineteenth-century cultural life in America.

George Templeton Strong was one potential resident who did not have to be convinced of Sam Ruggles's acumen. He had always felt an extraordinary sympathy with and attraction to the older man, despite the difference in their ages. At forty-five, Samuel Ruggles was at the height of his financial success and public prestige. At twenty-five, George Templeton Strong was already embarked on a brilliant law career, his astonishing intellect fed by as many interests as Sam Ruggles continued to embrace. As it was Samuel's vision that created the tranquil setting in which George Templeton Strong's remarkable adult life began to take shape, it is only fitting that the two men went on to play important roles in each other's lives.

2

A
NEW FAMILY
IN THE PARK

———————✦———————

IT WAS nearly a year and a half after they were married that George
Templeton Strong and his beloved bride, Ellen, moved into their
new home in Gramercy Park. He never passed the Fourth Avenue
house that had been their first residence "without thinking how much
every commonplace abode in this city has to tell of the tragedy and
comedy of life that has passed within it. How serious a thing is any
row of monotonous twenty-five-foot brick fronts, if one considers
that each of them has witnessed . . . births and deaths and marriages
and all the events of social life, pleasant meetings, nice visits, sor-
rowful partings, household troubles escaped or endured. A new
house . . . has had not time to be the theater of human action and
sorrow and joy, and has no past to be remembered or imagined by
those who sojourn in it. [It] is like a western prairie, or an unex-
plored tropical forest."

That reflections like these were common to George Templeton
Strong is amply illustrated in his diary. In its original form, this
remarkable document runs close to twenty-five hundred pages, written in precise, minute script in small notebooks fortunately preserved

by his family. It took the historians Allan Nevins and Milton Halsey Thomas ten years to prepare the historically significant portions of the diary for publication. Reading through this thoughtful man's observations, recorded almost daily, about what was happening in the city and the world, the people he met, the important events of his time, gives one an intimate picture of life in the nineteenth century.

Before George Templeton Strong fell in love with Ellen Ruggles, he had often wondered whether he was a budding misogynist. Although he was both sensual and romantic, he frequently found himself judging harshly even the most attractive female. One of the city's most eligible bachelors, darkly handsome in his formal white waistcoat and embroidered vest, he was invited to a continuous round of parties. They only depressed him, however, as he noted after yet another disappointing evening: "Strongly tempted I am to pull back the one foot I've ventured in this treacherous bog of Fashionable Womankind, and peremptorily to cease from being one of the soirée-suffering aristocracy; to bore myself with neither call or party . . . and to resume my strong position as an implacable . . . woman hater."

That evening, he had positioned himself in a corner, staring critically at the extravagant plumage the women wore. In the style of the day, the natural female figure was completely obscured by yards and yards of cloth and "corsetboards," made of steel or whalebone. Broad belts with elaborate buckles, and huge leg-of-mutton sleeves puffed above the elbow, made the rigidly compressed waist seem even smaller. Flowing muslin collars, elaborately embroidered, and massive gold chains with long pendants that were often slipped inside the belt completed costumes that irritated George with their obvious conformity to fashion. Nor was he amused by the shallow social twitterings of the ladies. They all flirted with him, trying to tease him out of his sulks, but to no avail. He knew he was being impolite, but he simply could not respond to any of their giggling overtures.

George Templeton Strong was a privileged young man in every way. Born in 1820, he was the son of George Washington Strong, a leading lawyer in the city, and his gentle, loving wife, Elizabeth.

*George Templeton Strong, pungent, brilliant, vivid
guide to a journey back through time*

George's father doted on him, so delighting in the boy's exceptional
intelligence that nearly every evening he spent four hours studying
with him. At Columbia College, George was an outstanding student,
and at the age of eighteen he began practicing law in his father's
office. There he quickly distinguished himself in realty and probate
law. He was also a gifted pianist and organist, and had been reading
Greek literature in the original since he was ten. Clearly, his professional success was augmented by cultural and esthetic rewards.

Yet more and more George found himself unaccountably depressed. All the promise of his precocious youth had come true, but as the 1840s unfolded he felt "wretched . . . uncontrollably dreary and miserable," which made him angry with himself. After all, he was not so naïve as to look for some sort of absolute happiness, or to believe that such a feeling was even possible, no matter how privileged one's life. Why then, he asked himself, did he drag himself down so? "This dreary succession of listless, unsatisfying days, varied now and then by fits of intense and bitter disgust at myself and everything about me, deadness to all that's good, paralysis of every right feeling and impulse, I protest against most stoutly."

There were, to be sure, avenues of comfort. He could still lose himself in the glorious pleasures found in books. Years later, his book collection would be considered one of the most important in the city. George Templeton Strong never spent money more freely or gladly than when he acquired a rare manuscript or purchased something as valuable as Benjamin Franklin's edition of Cicero's *Cato Major* or several volumes from the library of Charles Lamb.

On a lighter note, he shared his fellow New Yorkers' obsessive delight with the work of Charles Dickens, affectionately known as "Boz." After reading *Nicholas Nickleby*, George declared, "I never enjoyed a work of fiction as I have enjoyed that. It has been drop by drop and each drop glorious. It is Boz's masterpiece. . . . To read the book seems to enlarge one's circle of acquaintance most wonderfully."

Early in 1842, George found himself caught up in the excitement over Dickens's approaching visit to America. George thought the feverish pitch of anticipation was a bit silly, but he had to take the planned events seriously when men like Samuel Ruggles, Philip Hone, and Washington Irving were in charge of so many of them.

People were so determined to see the great Boz that invitations to the ball being planned in his honor rose to three thousand from the sixteen hundred original guests. The Park Theater had been completely redecorated for the evening, with frescoes and huge shields painted with scenes from Dickens's stories. The theater's enormous dome was draped with British flags, and the stage and orchestra pit were floored over to increase space.

Thirty-year-old Dickens and, as George described her, his "little, fat wife" seemed to enjoy all the attention, although the writer actually shared George's amusement at the excess. The good-natured Dickens allowed himself to be whisked from event to event, but was particularly amused when one newspaper smugly declared that he "was never in such society in England as he has seen in New York. . . . Its high and striking tone cannot fail to make an indelible impression on his mind." It struck George, however, that Dickens's experiences were likely to result in some less than flattering portraits of his American hosts "when he gets home and takes up his pen again."*

When he was in a dark mood, his passion for music also sustained George Templeton Strong. He helped start the Philharmonic Society in 1842 and was repeatedly elected its president. Later, he formed the respected Church Music Association, which presented concerts of ecclesiastical music to a general audience. And he refused to be daunted by the general lack of interest in opera. He did everything he could to persuade friends to share his love of this particular musical form, and by the mid 1840s enthusiasm for it did seem to be growing.

Some of George's most perceptive musings on the fluctuating melodies in his life were inspired by an evening of music. One night, for example, after listening to a performance of Beethoven's Symphony in C Minor, he lit the candle on his desk and wrote in his diary, "If I were asked for an explanation of the symphony, and to tell the exact train of thought that produced it, I should be at a loss. The first general purport of its story would seem to be, for the first movement, weariness, sorrow, and perplexity . . . the disheartening sense that earnest minds feel at a certain stage of their development of the worthlessness of all that they're doing and living for, and their need of something that may wake them up to real and energetic existence. Then, in the second, is the glorious birth of the new principle of love, ambition, or some yet higher element and its exulting

---

*Dickens indeed did find much to criticize about New York and did so in *American Notes for General Circulation*, published on his return to England.

and triumphant progress in freshness and vigor, on to the victory and full function of the end."

For George, meeting Ellen Ruggles would mean passing into the second movement, with all its promise of joy and completion. The first time he met Ellen was nearly a year earlier, at a party Sam gave on Union Square, but George had apparently been too melancholy to acknowledge to himself the feelings she may have stirred in him. True, George was moved to note in his diary the following day that "there's a beautiful sunshiny face making itself visible to me every five minutes . . . in all sorts of inappropriate places. It's been a novel kind of hallucination." But then he retreated: "I must reform it altogether."

It was almost as if he were unable to let himself be happy; as if, despite his protestations of wanting to feel differently, he had accepted it as inevitable that he would go through life wearing the mantle of the "unspeakable disease of nervous dejection and instability." At one point, his life seemed so grim that he had actually taken up the habit of a surprising number of nineteenth-century young men about town, that of "dissipating on chloroform." Yet he was too honest with himself not to know that the insight and euphoria induced by the drug seemed far more profound than they actually were, and that there was no physical solution to staying his demons.

In this dark mood as the new year approached, George dreaded the established city routine of the New Year's Day call. Since the time of the earliest Knickerbocker settlers, the first of the year had been set aside to greet old friends and wish them prosperity and health during the next twelve months. Gentlemen were expected to pay their respects to the ladies of the house, many of whom began to prepare for the occasion well before Christmas.

Dressmakers worked night and day to finish magnificent gowns; hairdressers traveled from boudoir to boudoir across the city, arranging ladies' coiffures. Since this ritual began at midnight on December 31, those women who had their hair done during the night would not go to bed, out of fear of disarranging the elaborate curls and chignons. When New Year's Day arrived, mahogany dining room tables had been polished to a mirror finish and spread with opulent platters of meats and cheeses, sparkling cut-glass dishes of

New York's roving celebration, the dizzying ritual of the New Year's Day calls

shortcake and biscuits, and countless crystal tumblers filled with port and claret. The more guests a lady received, the more prestigious her social position, so New York's fashionable women sent large numbers of invitation cards to prospective callers for the auspicious afternoon.

One New Year's Day Philip Hone paid calls for five hours. Within those same five hours, his own daughters received 169 callers. One journalist commented wryly on the physical wear and tear of this ritual. By the end of the afternoon, he wrote, "the ladies are worn out with fatigue, and bored to death by the stupidity of their visitors. Carriages rattle up furiously; young men in various stages of booziness are ushered in. Some are dreamy and melancholy and hold on firmly to a chair or the corner of the table while endeavoring to get out their set speeches; others are merry and boisterous; others still are disposed to be a little too friendly with the ladies. It may be that the ladies themselves have had too much punch," he added, concluding, "Such things do happen." Many of these scenes were rehashed with gossipy delight on Ladies' Day, January 2, when the women of New York society paid calls on one another.

Perhaps because he was dreading New Year's Day so intensely, George was more amenable to Ellen Ruggles's charms when they met a second time just before the holiday. This time, he admitted to himself that he wanted to see her again, and even allowed himself to tell her so. He was filled with joy by her positive response, and that feeling dominated all others as they met again and again over the next few months. On March 11, 1848, he proposed marriage, and Ellen accepted. Unable to contain his happiness, he dashed around the city, sharing the good news with the friends who had stood by him so patiently during his gloomy moods, like his law associate, Henry Cram, and his Columbia classmate George Jones (who would later father Edith Wharton). He would have liked to shout the news from the top of Trinity Church, to celebrate his "perfect, entire happiness . . . happiness that I can dwell upon and luxuriate in freely and unrestrained, because it includes the anticipation of a life no longer cold and selfish and objectless and indolent . . . happiness that it bewilders me to look upon — that I do not even yet fully realize and appreciate."

The only real worry George had now was money. Successful as he was, he had not saved a great deal, and although the Ruggles family was not pretentious, Ellen had grown up in great comfort. George's father planned to build the couple a home on Gramercy Park as a wedding present, but it would be up to George to furnish and maintain it. George secretly worried that the burden would overwhelm him. In the social circles in which the Ruggles family moved, homes were routinely furnished with imported carpets, marble, and inlaid tables.

These doubts and anxieties were held in check on May 15, when George and Ellen were married in Grace Church, which, next to Trinity Church, was the most fashionable in the city. The recently built white marble cathedral on Tenth Street and Broadway was the creation of James Renwick, another of George's classmates at Columbia.

Renwick, who won the coveted contract when he was only twenty-three years old, would go on to design Vassar College, the Smithsonian Institution, and St. Patrick's Cathedral, among other extraordinary buildings. In truth, Jimmy Renwick was one of George's least favorite people; he found the architect vain, pretentious, and less devoted to his art than to "fat jobs and profitable contracts."

Be that as it may, the soaring, subtly ornamental Gothic church was the perfect background for Ellen Ruggles as she walked down the aisle on her father's arm. In the style of the day, her heavy satin gown was undoubtedly tinted yellow to give it greater richness, and it grazed the instep of her laced white satin boots. A generous veil of blond lace would have fallen to her shoulders from a crown of orange blossoms fashioned from fine silk. As he waited at the altar to meet her, George was certainly equally resplendent in a blue coat with brass buttons, high white satin stock, ruffled shirt, blue-and-white-figured vest, and silk stockings and pumps.

Following the service, there was a luncheon and a *soirée dansante*. Throughout it all, the bride and groom beamed at each other. As they raised their glasses, they basked in the delights of a day that was, according to George, "preeminently . . . jolly and brilliant and successful."

Along with two cases of Madeira wine, circa 1806, "to be drunk from time to time hereafter by you and yours in commemoration of the happy event of today," Samuel Ruggles gave the new husband and wife a contribution to the home that George Washington Strong was building for them. Sam would pay for the construction of a stone front to the house as well as the bay window for Ellen's "boudoir or snuggery" on the west side of the building. Furthermore, when they returned from their brief honeymoon trip to Long Island, they did not have to live with their parents or move into a hotel until the Gramercy Park house was ready; Samuel gave them the use of a house he owned on Union Square.

It was a two-hour trip to Rockaway on Long Island — traveling by ferry, railroad, and six-horse omnibus — much less time than the journey had taken when George was a child. Accessibility to the area had resulted in the construction of elegant boarding houses and hotels whose rooms looked out on a grand panorama of sea, sand dunes, and wild beach grass. Guests were often called to their sumptuous meals by the fanfare of hotel musicians.

Back in New York, even in temporary quarters, married life was wonderful; the success of this union so amazed George that even his money worries were more wry than despairing. Still, if there was anything dampening his spirits, it was the persistent concern that he had made a commitment way over his head. George would often stop by the construction site of his new home on the way to or from his office. He was proud that this graceful, appealing home was going to be his, but he would look into the half-finished rooms and think, "In the name of the Sphinx, what will I do with this when it's finished? Carpets and mirrors and Louis Quatorze chairs . . . unless I happen to pick up a large roll of $100 bank notes in the street, or find myself unexpectedly remembered with a bounding legacy in the will of one of my clients . . . or commit a brilliant and successful bank robbery . . . I don't see but that I'm likely to find the question of ways and means complicated and embarrassing. . . . I wish the house was finished. I wish the furniture was bought. I wish the furniture was paid for."

At least some of the furnishings in the new house would be familiar, for both Ellie and George had transported favorite possessions to the basement of their borrowed home on Union Square until they could be moved to what George now often called their "palazzo." He found it disquieting to revisit the site of his bachelor days to pick up these objects. There, he sat at the old work table in his library, a room that now seemed very small in comparison with the library taking shape in Gramercy Park. Time seemed to be playing another of its fascinating tricks. In the familiar space, the amazing six months that had elapsed since George had given his heart to Ellen might almost never have happened. George had no difficulty comparing how wretched he was then with how blissful he was now. "But it's strange how the thought that it's gone and over and never can come back makes one feel toward any period of past life; what beautiful melancholy light it sheds over times and things . . . seen from far off . . . becoming exquisite in form and glorious in coloring."

He had a similar wave of nostalgia when he packed up the books from his Greenwich Street library. The February day was bitterly cold, and even in his heavy woolen coat and pantaloons, George was chilled to the bone as he piled his books into boxes. To pull the books from their perch was "mournful work," for he remembered how happy it had always made him to add a newly acquired book to the others on the shelf, "where I've watched them accumulating and multiplying so long."

The books continued to multiply, although George knew it was imprudent to buy more when he had so many other expenses. He could not bear falling behind in his reading, though, and sought in each new work reflections that would help him in his constant quest for understanding and perspective.

One of his enthusiasms was Thackeray's *Vanity Fair*, which everyone in New York was calling a "work of genius." George considered that an exaggeration but was intrigued by the "new principle" it was based on, which he believed was a harbinger of artistic change. This principle, a lack of idealism in both character and plot, seemed to George appropriate for a city and a country that were becoming increasingly democratic: "People will naturally feel best satisfied and most at home with a class of fiction that has no characters or features or notions in its structure that rise much above their own experience of the world. . . . The elements of what we call Romance are but a cheap substitute, after all, for the awful interest of everyday realities."

Happily, Ellen shared her husband's delight in books. Although she may have been more inclined than he to the trappings of elegance, she understood fully why he would prefer buying a rare edition to a rosewood cabinet or red satin drapery. And on their first Christmas together, it bothered her far less than it did George that he could not buy her a lavish gift.

It was George who had insisted on going into Tiffany's one wintry afternoon. Once inside, the relatively impoverished bridegroom ruefully but proudly recalled that Ellen resolutely "turned away her eyes from beholding vanity and calmly defied the insinuating attacks of a whole bevy of the most eloquent and argumentative salesmen, con-

Ellen Strong, a gentle, devoted, lively companion

ceded that various gimcracks were beautiful . . . and *would* suit her exactly, but concluded with the avowal that she should not buy them or let me buy them was delightful to behold. It reminded me of the superhuman firmness of some Christian matron of the times of Diocletian . . . heroically holding fast her faith and refusing to burn incense on any terms before any heathen deity whatever."

Ellen shared her husband's devotion to music, too, and during the first year of their marriage frequently accompanied him to concerts and the opera. George invariably found her "resplendent in opera hat, pink satin, and bouquet, looking prettier than any six women in the house." Ellen also accompanied George to theatrical productions at several of the splendid new theaters around town. More women were attending the theater these days, but the custom of men going to the theater together continued. George's father-in-law served as his playgoing companion far more often than did his wife. These evenings frequently began or ended with a reception at Sam's house for the production's stars.

There was still a steady flow of European talent to New York, and Sam had become friendly with several of the actors who came season after season. One of his closest friends from the theater was the British actor William Macready, known for his fine interpretations of Shakespeare's plays, particularly *Macbeth*. For some time, there had been a fierce rivalry between Macready and the American tragedian Edwin Forrest. To Sam's consternation, the tension between the two men and their followers was exacerbated each time the actors came in contact with each other. It seemed absurd to Sam that such pettiness should interfere with the public's enjoyment of these two fine performers.

Fed by the press and some especially xenophobic New Yorkers, tension about an approaching appearance by Macready, in May 1849, spiraled upward. His temper heightened by some lurid marital problems, Forrest was in no mood to step aside for the renowned actor from England and did little to quiet his fans, including the young men known as the Bowery Boys, who were devoted to making trouble.

Forrest even wrote letters to the newspapers, accusing Macready of hissing him when he had played on the London stage. Now, both Forrest and Macready were playing Macbeth in New York, Forrest at the Bowery Theater, Macready at the Astor Place Opera House, and the announcements of these simultaneous performances sounded like a declaration of war.

Forrest's fans took over the opera house on the night of May 7 and pelted Macready with rotten eggs, potatoes, apples, and even chairs. They hissed and shouted so loudly that not even his resonant Shakespearean tones could be heard beyond the footlights. Furious, the actor stalked off the stage and announced to the theater manager that he was terminating his engagement, to return to the more civilized atmosphere of his own country.

The news disturbed many New Yorkers, who hoped to see their city become the cultural center of the New World. There would be little cultural or social progress if performances of such high order were allowed to degenerate into chaos, and distinguished actors could not expect the respect they deserved. Such feelings motivated forty-seven prominent New Yorkers, including Samuel Ruggles and Washington Irving, to write to Macready, urging him to reconsider his decision. They assured the actor that "the good sense and respect for order prevailing in this community will sustain you on the subsequent nights of your performance."

Almost as soon as the actor consented to finish his run, signs were posted all over the city by Forrest's followers, claiming that the crew of a visiting British ship would attack anyone who protested Macready's appearance. Other placards bore the question "Shall Americans or English rule the city?" and the atmosphere grew even more tense.

Well before curtain time on May 10, the night of the second performance, crowds began gathering outside the theater. Although the show was sold out, they stormed the entrances, demanding to be

The dreadful climax to theater history's most notorious feud:
the Astor Place Riot, 1849

admitted. At first, the three hundred policemen stationed outside the theater were able to hold back the hostile mob, and additional police in the boxes and balcony believed that they could deter any demonstrations of violence inside. As soon as Macready appeared on stage, however, the hissing and shouting began. When the noise reached an ominous pitch, the police began to remove people from the audience. At one point, a policeman stationed outside stuck a hose through the window and sprayed some of the demonstrators. All the while, the play continued.

The noise from outside grew deafening. Macready recalled that "stones came in through the windows, and one struck the chandelier." The police were unable to control the mob outside the theater any longer, and the militia was called in. Orders were given to fire over the heads of the crowd, but the sound of the rifles incited the rioters to such a degree that the militia began to shoot in earnest. Within minutes, there were twenty-two people dead and at least thirty-six people seriously wounded, making the Astor Place Riot the most violent in theatrical history.

With the help of Sam Ruggles, Chancellor Kent, and a few other close friends who had stationed themselves in his dressing room, Macready managed to escape from the theater. He exchanged clothes with another actor and was smuggled into a carriage that took him to New Rochelle, where he boarded a train to Boston. Keeping his presence there a secret, he waited for the first boat that could take him back to England. Ironically, Edwin Forrest's career was enhanced by the tragedy, because both New Yorkers and visitors were more than willing to pay the price of a theater ticket to see the man who had played so important a role in the Astor Place Riot.

For Samuel, the tragedy was sobering. Like George, he had little time for regret, however, because a far greater danger threatened New York very shortly afterward. The city was hit by another epidemic of cholera, which many felt was a result of the unsanitary conditions that still prevailed in the city's streets and daily life. Ellen, who was recovering from a nearly fatal bout of puerperal fever contracted when she gave birth to a stillborn child, was very vulnerable to the disease. Both George and Sam were desperate to safeguard her fragile health, and as soon as she was strong enough to travel, George bundled her onto a steamer to West Point. There, they took rooms overlooking the river, and in the calm, clean retreat George looked forward to spending time with the friends he had made on previous visits to the academy.

At the time, it was not understood that cholera was contagious, so George had few qualms about going back and forth to the city on business and possibly bringing back germs that could infect his wife. It was typical of him that he found the disease intellectually interesting and that even when he experienced some symptoms, he remained detached. "I cannot get up much anxiety about myself in reference to the disease," he wrote in his diary after an uncomfortable day. "I took a cigar and a stroll . . . with a feeling of interest and curiosity about the possible . . . consequences of the phenomenon, but certainly with no feeling of fear or personal uneasiness."

During the several weeks that the epidemic raged, nearly five thousand people died, and George thanked God that Ellie had been spared. By September 1849, her recovery was almost complete and she was once again excited about the approaching move to Gramercy Park. The house, perhaps, would help protect the Strong family from future health hazards, for it had the most up-to-date sanitation available, with running water and fully equipped bathrooms. It also had gaslight and central heating.

These modern comforts were real harbingers of the city's cultural growth. From a crowded town, provincial in its behavior and tastes, New York City had developed into a modern urban center. Marble and stone had replaced simple wooden structures, not to mention the new cast-iron buildings of five and six stories, to be described by Walt Whitman as "high-growths of iron, slender, strong . . . splendidly uprising towards clear skies." Lavish stores and hotels were springing up along what would soon be labeled the Ladies' Mile, the strip of land along Broadway that would eventually extend all the way up to Twenty-third Street. New Yorkers were developing ever more sophisticated tastes, and the homes they were building and furnishing were perhaps the best illustration of their newly elevated standards. As *Putnam's Magazine* commented, a nation's concept of itself is much more visible in its homes than in its public structures, for "here every man is a monarch in his own right . . . and palaces are built by the people for their own enjoyment."

And to be sure, at the end of September, when the Strongs finally moved to their new home, George was delighted. His books, arranged in graceful cabinets, looked as if they had found a comfortable resting place. There was a frieze circling the central hall, and though it was grand, the overall effect of the interior design was, to George's relief, tastefully simple, "quite free, I think, from the epidemic of humbug and sham finery and gin-palace decoration." The three parlors were warmly carpeted, though the middle one was still "as sparsely settled as the great West." No matter; the music and dining rooms were amply furnished, and Ellen and George would spend much of their time together in those lovely and congenial chambers.

The house had cost the senior George Strong well over $30,000, a sum that would be deducted from his son's share of his estate. George had not yet added up what the furnishings had come to, but outside the bow window, autumn bade him a glorious welcome as brilliant leaves fluttered around the black gates of the little park that now partly belonged to him.

Suddenly, he couldn't wait to show off the house and its furnishings to his friends, and what better time than on New Year's Eve? After all, this was the beginning not only of a new year, but of a new decade, and the Strongs had just settled in the house in which they planned to spend the rest of their lives.

As the evening deepened on December 31, George waited in his library for Ellie to come downstairs. Carriages rolled by the front windows, making a cold, muffled noise. Dressed to receive his guests, in formal coat and state breeches, he recorded in his diary, "not as of old . . . that I've got to go to a party, but to certify to incredulous generations yet to come that I'm going to have one!"

He was unaccountably nervous, anxious that all should go well. Soon the door chimes would sound, and his guests would appear, and he wanted them to enjoy themselves as much as he wanted Ellie to feel proud of her home and their hospitality. There was to be boned turkey and ice cream and champagne, and he wanted everything to look and taste appealing. Did everyone fret so when he gave a party?

Probably so, he decided, and then smiled to think how he "never used to appreciate or realize the awful state of mind in which people have been who received me . . . notwithstanding their beaming countenances and nonchalant demeanor."

When he heard the bell, he rose from his chair, straightened his waistcoat and tie, and went out to greet the first of his guests. At the door were George Anthon, a young professor of Greek, and another classmate from Columbia, John (Jack) Ehniger, along with George's cousin and law partner, Charles Strong, and his fiancée.

As he ushered in each guest, George looked past them to the horizon beyond the park and the new buildings that indicated the city's amazing development. Impossible as it was to believe, the population of New York was already half a million, all living together far more easily than the city fathers could ever have imagined. He was thirty years old, and the thought that his own life would necessarily become more complicated only lifted George Templeton Strong's spirits that night, as the 1850s, and his life in Gramercy Park, began.

George Templeton Strong's "palazzo" in Gramercy Park

3

ENTREPRENEURS
IN THE
PARK

———————◆◆———————

THE NEIGHBORHOOD around Gramercy Park was expanding. In 1852, Samuel Ruggles's good friend Peter Cooper moved into a handsome red brick house on the corner of Lexington Avenue and Twenty-second Street. Wide and square, with a high stoop and a cupola in the middle of the roof, the house had an elaborate garden designed by Mr. Cooper. He had also instructed that his study and bedroom be adjacent to the front door, for, although he had an imposing fortune, he preferred to answer the doorbell himself.

As Frank Leslie's *Sunday Magazine* would eulogize Peter Cooper after his death in 1883, "No sentinel has ever stood at that man's door, and there has not been a time in the last forty years that the plainest man . . . could not ring his doorbell and go in and shake hands with Peter Cooper."

Cooper was a gentle yet commanding figure as he strolled through the neighborhood, greeting children as they walked to the park, tipping his soft black hat to their parents, or nodding cheerfully to their nursemaids. His white hair fell almost to his shoulders, and he was nearly always dressed in a black frock coat in the style of his youth.

Peter Cooper, inventor, philanthropist, and New York's most beloved citizen.
When he died, the whole city mourned.

His severely nearsighted eyes were framed by gold-rimmed spectacles with rectangular lenses, and he peered through the thick glass with an engagingly benign expression.

Cooper's physique was bony, so he designed a special air-filled pillow to sit on. He used this ingenious device not just in the old black buggy in which he rode around the city, but at formal parties or dinners, where the chairs tended to be uncomfortably hard. The pillow was quickly named a "Peter Cooper," and its inventor talked his friend Charles Goodyear into producing it for public sale. Cooper had discovered his genius for invention early on, and created more new products and product improvements "than I have time to remember," but he never dreamed that such discoveries would make his fortune. Instead, he turned his imagination to the shrewd analysis of current and future business opportunities, and to making sure that he was ready to seize them.

Peter Cooper returned to his native New York City from Newburgh, in upstate New York, in 1808, when he was seventeen, and began to try his hand at a variety of ventures. First he was a coachmaker; then he made machines for shearing cloth; later he built furniture and ran a successful grocery business. Yet no matter what he did professionally, the urge to invent persisted, often enriching his personal life. Cooper invented the first lawnmower, and, after becoming a father, designed a musical self-rocking cradle "to sing the child to sleep," with a cloth attached to "keep the flies from the little one" as the cradle rocked. He impulsively bartered the rights to this invention for a peddler's horse and wagon, for among the wagon's contents was a hurdy-gurdy. "I had heard one played before on a steamboat trip," he shyly explained, "and I thought it the sweetest music . . ."

In 1821, Peter Cooper took over a glue factory in an area far from the main part of the city. The factory stood on the south edge of the village of Kips Bay, between Thirty-first and Thirty-fourth streets, next to a small lake called Sunfish Pond. Under Cooper's ownership, the factory began to manufacture ink, household cement, isinglass, and, to the delight of many housewives, gelatin. Packaged for the first time in America, the gelatin was sold with recipes, written by Mrs. Cooper, printed on each little packet.

It was with ownership of the glue factory that Peter Cooper began to amass his fortune. In the nineteenth century, manufacturing was one of the few ways for men of little capital or education to make enormous amounts of money. The self-made man was an American phenomenon, and a combination of innate skills and hard work allowed poor boys like Andrew Carnegie, Henry Frick, and John D. Rockefeller — the sons of humble working men — to accumulate savings and invest them in their own businesses. These enterprises, like John Jacob Astor's fur-trading business, grew steadily larger and became more complex, and the ethic of self-reliance kept the businesses free of outside control.

Peter Cooper soon became so prosperous that he was able to invest substantial amounts of money in real estate: "As fast as I obtained money I purchased houses that would bring me in some revenue." As early as 1828, Peter Cooper claimed to own twelve houses on Third Avenue and the Bowery. He also owned stables, commercial buildings, and parcels of land throughout the city and beyond.

One of his largest investments was far outside New York City; in fact, it was in another state, in the city of Baltimore. The scheduled building of the Baltimore and Ohio Railroad was expected to result in a substantial increase in the existing populations, so the Maryland city was experiencing a land boom. In 1828, with two partners, Peter purchased three thousand acres of land in the Baltimore area. His partners turned out to be swindlers, but there were even greater problems with the railroad itself.

In the autumn of 1829, word reached Baltimore of a newly invented British steam engine that the Delaware and Hudson Railroad was bringing to America. The B&O's "brigade" of open, horse-drawn cars clearly did not represent the wave of the future in railroad transportation, but the English steam engine could not run along the sharp curves of the recently laid B&O tracks.

This was alarming news to Peter Cooper. Since much of his Baltimore land had turned out to be impossible to develop, he had tried to recoup his investment by mining the iron ore he discovered on the site. Obviously, the success of even this venture greatly depended on the construction of the railroad. He made an appointment with the president of the B&O and offered to design a steam engine that could negotiate the railroad's sharply twisting tracks. And so, said Peter Cooper, "I got up a little locomotive."

He named his steam engine the Tom Thumb, because of its size; hardly larger than a contemporary handcar, still it negotiated the railroad curves with ease. On a clear August morning in 1830, Peter Cooper drove the engine at the amazing speed of eighteen miles per hour, with the officers of the B&O sitting behind him in an open car. The railroad men were giddy with relief and excitement, and a few of them actually took out paper from their pockets to "write their names and some connected sentences to prove that even at great ve-

locity it was possible to do so." This triumph helped establish con-
clusively that steam railroads were superior to horse-drawn transport,
and that investing in railroad bonds made good business sense.

In fact, the railroads were responsible for Peter Cooper's move to
Gramercy Park. For many years, he had lived near his glue factory
in the open country of Twenty-eighth Street and Fourth Avenue,
amidst clover fields and buttonwood trees. By the 1850s the New
York and Harlem Railroad ran right past his house, even though the
area was relatively rural. Locomotives and long lines of horse-drawn
cars regularly passed the Cooper home, and cars filled with cattle on
their way to slaughter often parked for the night in front of his door.
Peter, who was carefully following the progress of Sam Ruggles's
dream, decided to move to Gramercy Park once it became a reality.
With its quiet elegance and active intellectual life, Gramercy Park
would make a more tranquil home for the Cooper family, who were
unsuited to the gilded mansions that other fashionable and prosperous
New Yorkers were building along Fifth Avenue.

Their family was, unfortunately, much smaller than Peter and
Sarah Cooper had hoped it would be. Only two of their children had
survived into adulthood. Peter's description of one daughter's suffering stands as graphic testimony to the primitive medical care available at the time. No amount of money or prestige could ameliorate a
person's helplessness when serious illness struck: "Sarah Amanda
when born was a beautiful child, one of the prettiest we ever had,"
wrote her anguished father. When her nurse put the newborn infant
near the fire to keep warm, the brilliant flames that shone on her
face caused cataracts to form in both eyes, and the child became
blind. A leading surgeon, Dr. Valentine Mott (who would later reorganize Bellevue Hospital and become a resident of Gramercy
Park), was brought in to operate.

During the early nineteenth century, even so delicate a procedure
as eye surgery was performed at home, and the doctor, as was also
customary, brought several medical students to observe. To Peter and
Sarah Cooper's horror, the doctor "found he had forgotten the instrument to do it with, so he made a temporary instrument to hold
the eye, and when he attempted [to use this] it was too large and it

went right over the eye. Then he tried to bend it some more, trying three times before he could hold the eye, and ruined the eye entirely and caused the child intense suffering. . . . I was so overcome with the screams of the child that it made me almost frantic." Maimed and blind, Sarah Amanda survived for four years before she died of a throat infection.

After so tragic an event, it was not surprising that the Coopers were reluctant to allow their remaining children to leave Gramercy Park. Both Edward and Sarah Amelia were in their twenties and unmarried when the family moved to the new home. When Edward did marry, his father bought him property across the street, on Lexington Avenue. And when Sarah Amelia married Abram B. Hewitt from New Jersey (who became mayor of New York after Peter's death), the couple first spent all their winters with the Coopers in Gramercy Park and later moved back there permanently.

Abram S. Hewitt. His motto was "Be just and fear not."

Although Hewitt was like a second son to Peter Cooper, he occasionally struggled against his father-in-law's patriarchal attitude and personal frugality. For a long time the Cooper household had only one servant and one man to do both the heavy work and to look after the horses. When Mrs. Cooper bought a carriage, Peter found her choice too "fashionable" and insisted that she exchange it for a much more modest one, willingly paying the dealer's substantial penalty for the switch. And though the proportions of the Gramercy Park home were lavish, the décor and design were relatively spare. When Peter Cooper died years later (an event that placed the entire city in mourning), his son-in-law wasted no time in commissioning their Gramercy Park neighbor Stanford White to redo the house completely; thereafter it took fourteen servants to keep the house functioning to Hewitt's taste.

Although their home was comparatively simple, living in Gramercy Park was a major step up the social ladder for Peter and Sarah Cooper. Cyrus Field, whom Peter liked instantly, lived next door, and Cyrus's brother David Dudley Field was one door down. David, a brilliant jurist, contributed much to Jacksonian legal theory before ending his professional career as official counsel to Jay Gould, Jim Fisk, and the notorious William Tweed. Other neighbors in Gramercy Park were John Bigelow, co-owner and editor with William Cullen Bryant of the *New York Evening Post;* the distinguished politician Samuel Tilden, a future governor and presidential candidate; and the publisher James Harper.

Through these men, Peter's social circle continued to expand. At their dinner tables, he would find William Cullen Bryant, Samuel Morse, Charles Scribner, George Putnam, and such important visitors to the city as the presidents of Yale and Dartmouth and even Harriet Beecher Stowe. While the conversation at these dinners usually centered on business, Peter Cooper often spoke about his dream of creating a free arts and science institution for young men and women. He knew what it was like not to have enough money to get an education, and the idea had become almost an obsession. The city was filled with young people with good, possibly even great minds — full of imagination and innovative thought — whose families did not have the means to open the doors of Columbia, Harvard, or Yale.

Through his work with the New York Public School Society, Peter Cooper had done his best to educate all the city's children, regardless of their parents' income. Until the legislature established public education in 1841, the society was the only source of such learning; it maintained seventeen schools and provided most of the necessary funds. Now, Cooper was determined to extend the privilege of education to older youths and even to mature adults, offering evening classes to those with jobs that prevented them from attending school during the day even if they had the money.

If there was free education at convenient times, as well as reading rooms for study, Cooper maintained, students could expand their personal and professional horizons. As a result, New York would be richer, for with their new knowledge and skills, these men and women would find and fill those places "where their capacity and talents can be usefully employed with the greatest advantage to themselves and the community in which they live." The more Peter dreamed of this college, the greater his determination grew, even if its founding meant that "I was compelled to live on bread and water for the remainder of my life."

Of course, he didn't really have to worry about going hungry. Every year, through a mixture of invention, shrewd investment, and farsightedness, Peter Cooper saw his fortune increase. The income from the glue factory alone made him a very wealthy man, and he was constantly taking out new patents for improvements on his gelatin and glue, and shipping his products as far away as London. His investments in real estate all over the city continued to grow. In addition, he poured great sums of money into the country's new industries as heavy manufacturing and efficient transportation systems became part of American life.

Peter Cooper's plans for his school were elaborate and quickly exceeded the $300,000 he had set aside to pay for the project. When the vast brick-and-stone building with its iron pillars was finally completed, the cost was more than double that sum. During his lifetime, Cooper, who was so frugal, would spend close to $1 million on Cooper Union, motivated by the deeply held belief that his for-

Cooper Union, devoted to the working people of New York City,
"irrespective of age, sex, or financial means"

tune carried with it a moral obligation to others. "I do not recognize myself as owner . . . of one dollar of the wealth which has come into my hands," he said. "I am simply responsible for the management of an estate which belongs to humanity."

There was no doubt that Mr. Cooper could be as casual in giving away money as he was deliberate in not spending it on himself. When times were hard, he routinely dispensed fifty cents or a dollar to anyone who asked for it. To the affectionate chagrin of some of his neighbors in Gramercy Park, there were often long lines of men and women in front of his house waiting their turn for these donations. He made a habit of buying the creations of struggling inventors, once paying someone $10,000 for plans for which he had no use. And, on the day of his golden wedding anniversary to the woman he never sat next to without holding her hand, he gave $10,000 to the city to provide entertainment and clothing for needy children.

Still, no money he spent ever pleased Peter Cooper more than what he paid for the intellectual and structural designs for the Cooper Union for the Advancement of Science and Art. With his remarkable ability to foresee change, he left an oval space from the top to the bottom of the building for an elevator. Although a successful model of an elevator had not yet been made, Cooper was certain there would be one eventually, and he planned to be ready for it. Recalling the terrible fires that had swept the city earlier in its history, he designed a complex system of water pipes and tanks. Set off by a warning bell, these could supply water to any corner of the union in under a minute.

The top floor of the union was designed as an observatory "with choice astronomical and microscopic apparatus"; the lecture halls would be open to the public for celebrations and conferences; students would run their own government; and — a radical move — women would be allowed to attend the regular night school as well as to enroll in the all-female School of Design.

Cooper's explanation for this last stipulation was simple: allowing women the same educational opportunities as men would save them from possibly having "to resort for a livelihood to occupations which must be peculiarly revolting to the purity and sensitiveness which naturally characterize the feminine mind," or, he would add, from being forced to marry abusive men just so that they could be supported. Cooper's liberalism existed alongside a traditionally paternalistic view of family life, and he routinely gave an annual reward of $250 to the female student who exhibited the greatest "efforts and sacrifices in the performance of duty to parents."

Astor Place, the neighborhood around Cooper Union, was becoming a major cultural center. When the school opened its doors, in 1858, it was surrounded by several prestigious institutions. One, the Astor Library, had been funded by a $400,000 bequest from the late John Jacob Astor. Astor, himself barely literate, was not known for his generosity, but the impulse to fund the library was one he shared with Peter Cooper and other self-made men. They believed in "self-improvement," and a library was an important steppingstone on this path.

Housed in a massive yet elegant brick-and-brownstone building, the Astor Library had a collection of over 100,000 books, from European classics and works of science and history to rare first editions and original manuscripts. But though the library was intended for the use of working people, they were rarely able to take advantage of it, for it was open only during the day.

Near the Astor Library was the New York Society Library, and, where the Astor Place Opera House once stood, was the serene and popular Mercantile Library. The Mercantile Library circulated a large collection of books in order to make information and literature accessible to those who could not afford to study with fine teachers or buy books on their own. The particular group served by the Mercantile Library were "clerks," the nineteenth-century term used to describe people who lived on a salary.

INTERIOR VIEW OF THE ASTOR LIBRARY, NEW YORK.

The Astor Library, a place for self-improvement, where the
talented and ambitious poor could begin their upward climb

All the wonderful reading rooms around Astor Place, however, were diminished in scope by those at Cooper Union. Three thousand people a week, both day and night students, working men and women, began to use the Cooper Union library every week, and the figure climbed steadily over the years. Many of Peter Cooper's advisers thought his libraries more trouble than they were worth, because unemployed New Yorkers often went in to keep warm, and some stole valuable books to sell for supper money. Nevertheless, Peter would not allow restrictions on access to the library, and when he gave $100,000 to the school on his eightieth birthday, he directed that the interest on the money be used for a new lending library for workers and mechanics.

It had always been Peter Cooper's intention, from the conception of his school through its construction and expansion, to give art and science equal respect. The art school, therefore, taught students the principles as well as the practices of art, and the science curriculum stressed theory as much as technology. In this, he had the complete support of his old friend Sam Ruggles, who had known Peter Cooper since the days of the Erie Canal. The two men often discussed the need for education to unify art and science. It was at Yale, Sam explained, that he became convinced that "there are in this world but three things which a man needs to know. First, What he is. Second, Where he is. And Three, Where he is going." It was, Sam continued, the duty of a college to make its curriculum address these questions.

Some years later, Samuel Ruggles addressed Yale alumni, including the surviving members of his class of 1814. He stressed this theme again, applauding his alma mater for maintaining a "harmonious equilibrium" between the contending claims of science and the classics, "for using the strength of the one to invigorate the elegance of the other, and, in its turn, adorning the vigor of science with the grace and polish of classic culture."

Another value Peter Cooper shared with Sam Ruggles and George Templeton Strong was a belief in the sanctity of free speech. In the Great Hall of Cooper Union (he had built the auditorium below street level to minimize noise), controversial figures aired their often inflammatory views, with Peter Cooper's blessing. Here, the notorious feminist Victoria Woodhull spoke of free love and women's rights, and when Peter was criticized for allowing such talk inside his school, he invited Woodhull to lecture again. Another time, when the outspoken agnostic Robert Ingersoll was threatened with violence if he aired his "blasphemous" views, Cooper personally escorted him to the speaker's platform.

Every day of his life, barring illness or travel, Peter Cooper would appear at his school — first to supervise its construction, later to roam the halls and see whether the students needed anything. He always enjoyed the company of young people, acting not just as a mentor, but as a friend. Age was no barrier to appreciating good company, he claimed, and his own intellect and zest for life were certainly not diminished by his increasing years. On his ninety-first birthday he bragged that he had never felt better and definitely didn't feel "old." His many enthusiasms remained high, he said, adding gleefully that he had fewer aches and pains than when he carried grocery baskets through the streets as a boy.

When Cyrus Field and Peter Cooper became neighbors, the fact that the former was in his thirties and the latter in his sixties did not matter at all to Peter, who quickly developed affection and respect for the younger man. Much of Cyrus Field's life mirrored Peter's own history. Like him, Cyrus had started on his own at a young age, with little money to support his dreams of success. Like Peter, he did succeed, going from one job to another, building skills and embracing new ambitions. Eventually he settled into the ownership of a paper-manufacturing company. His business thrived, yet he remained eager for new ideas and ventures. He seemed to be in constant motion, restlessly moving from one task or idea to another. As one of his brothers commented, "I never saw Cyrus so uneasy as when he was trying to keep still."

One major difference between the two men, though, was in their attitude toward luxury. Although the Field home was no more elaborate on the outside than Peter Cooper's, it was decorated inside with an opulence unknown to the Cooper family. Cyrus had hired an interior decorator from France, allegedly the first time a private homeowner had done so. The designer's tastes ran to heavy Italian curtains, Greek statues, marble, and frescoed ceilings. George Templeton Strong often mocked the finished product, but many who heard him suspected some envy over the unlimited budget called for by such elaborate décor.

There was also an English butler in the carefully run household, and when guests sat down to dinner, they were served on delicate, blue-and-white Minton china, taken from the 262 pieces displayed on the walls of the dining room. Mrs. Field had the first private greenhouse in the city, and she loved it as much as her husband loved his second-story library.

Behind the house were the family stables, where, along with their horses, the family kept a cow that grazed happily in the still-rural neighborhood. Cyrus Field would watch the pastoral scene as he ate his breakfast, first making a list of what he would do that day, then putting the list inside the hat he kept on while eating. The idea of wasting time horrified him, and he was fond of reminding people that one could lose much potential accomplishment in unplanned hours.

Sometimes Cyrus's brother David Dudley would join him at the breakfast table. Members of both families visited back and forth so frequently that the two men connected their Gramercy Park homes. Unfortunately, a younger brother, Henry, of whom Cyrus was equally fond, was not allowed inside his home because of his friendship with, and eventual marriage to, a woman Cyrus's wife persisted in calling "that murderess." A fourth brother, Stephen J. Field, born in Connecticut like Cyrus, David Dudley, and Henry, lived in New York City for a while with David Dudley, but then moved to California. In time, he became an associate justice of the United States Supreme Court.

The woman whom Mrs. Cyrus Field barred from her home was Henrietta Desportes, and she had once been employed as a governess by a duke and duchess in her native city of Paris. When the duchess was murdered, the duke was charged with the crime, and in the lurid trial that followed, evidence suggested that Henrietta Desportes was not only the duke's mistress, but his accomplice, too. The scandal and possible consequences of the trial were too much for the duke; he took his own life, which led to Henrietta's acquittal. Legally, but not morally, absolved by her countrymen, the beautiful Henrietta thought it prudent to leave France. She had little trouble in persuading a visiting American clergyman, Henry Field, into securing her a teaching position that would ease her way to America.

Although her future sister-in-law banished Henrietta from the Fields's Gramercy Park home, the school she taught in was, ironically, in Gramercy Park. It was Miss Desportes's duty to take the thirteen little girls in her care for their daily constitutional. Mrs. Field might turn away when she saw the comely Frenchwoman briskly leading her charges — in their bonnets, muffs, and buttoned gloves — six times around the park and then up to Lexington Avenue and back again, but Peter Cooper, George Templeton Strong, and other male residents of Gramercy Park would go out of their way to begin their own day with this quite lovely scene. And, with his blithe disregard for social form, Peter Cooper hired Henrietta to supervise the work on the School of Design at Cooper Union.

Many, many years later, in 1938, the novelist Rachel Field, Henrietta's grandniece, described the pretty Gramercy Park parade in the novel she wrote about her aunt's life, *All This and Heaven Too*. Ludwig Bemelmans's illustrations for the story *Madeline* show similar jaunts around Paris led by a teacher named Miss Clavel. Bemelmans also lived in Gramercy Park, and it is said that he based his drawings on this bit of neighborhood folklore.

Soon after Henry Field and Henrietta Desportes were married, they left Gramercy Park for Massachusetts. Perhaps the Reverend Mr. Field felt that his brothers would be better off if they were free of even this once-removed scandal. Certainly, both Cyrus and David were sufficiently prominent citizens to be prime targets for gossip.

Cyrus Field, still in his early thirties, had made so much money in the paper business that he had retired from its operation, and was now eagerly searching for another challenge. In January 1854, he was introduced to a man named Frederick Gisborne, who had recently returned from an unsuccessful attempt to build telegraph lines across Newfoundland. The concept immediately excited Cyrus, who had often spoken with his Gramercy Park neighbor Samuel Morse about the possibility of linking the continents by underground cable. He believed, as Morse did, that the idea was ultimately feasible.

As early as 1844, Samuel F. B. Morse had told members of Congress that the future must surely hold such progress in communications. That Cyrus Field was not a scientist did not limit his contribution to helping Morse's prediction come true. History would record that although the idea of interoceanic telegraphy was not his, it was Cyrus Field who must be credited with its achievement. For, as one account later assessed it, "It was he who first made up his

Cyrus Field, tireless, undaunted dreamer of a daring scheme:
communication under the sea

mind that it could be done and showed the world how to do it and did it in the end."

Not surprisingly, the first person Cyrus tried to interest in the project was his next-door neighbor, Peter Cooper. Cooper had money to invest and, more important, the scientific and engineering background to understand that the dream could be realized. True to form, Mr. Cooper was immediately enthusiastic.

As Cooper later explained, the idea seemed to him "the consummation of that great prophecy, that knowledge shall cover the earth as waters cover the deep." He admitted that many of his friends thought anyone who could believe in such a fantastic project ought to be summarily settled "in an asylum where they might be taken care of as little short of lunatics. But believing as I did, that it offered the possibility of a mighty power for the good of the world, I embarked on it."

So one day early in March 1854, Cyrus Field, Peter Cooper,

Samuel F. B. Morse,
gifted artist and inventor of the "talking spark"

and three other major investors met at the Clarendon Hotel on Fourth Avenue and Eighteenth Street to discuss the financing of Gisborne's work in Newfoundland. By the end of the meeting, $40,000 had been committed to the project, and in a series of subsequent meetings, plans were made to form a company to charter the rights for laying cables on the island.

Early that May, Peter Cooper walked the short distance to the home of his neighbor David Dudley Field. As "the first rays of the morning sun streamed into the windows," he and his associates assembled to sign legal documents establishing the New York, Newfoundland, and London Telegraph Company, with Peter Cooper as president. With an operating budget of nearly $1.5 million, the company was to begin wiring Newfoundland for telegraph lines, and its founders already planned a connection of Newfoundland and Nova Scotia.

Almost every night after that, the men assembled in Cyrus Field's library, where they would study reports sent back from Newfoundland and compare the information with the painted landscapes on the huge globes flanking the handsome room. The results were not always encouraging. No globe could convey how truly desolate and impassable much of the interior terrain of Newfoundland was, how severe were its rocks and mountains, and how dense the forests filled with roving wolves and bears. An eight-foot-wide road had to be cut through this unwelcoming land, and there were times when the task seemed beyond the ingenuity and effort of any man.

Six hundred men at a time were working with equipment that had been carried by ship from Nova Scotia and hauled by mules to the work site. But the land was often so rocky that even this massive strength was unequal to the task of digging hills for telegraph poles, and the men would have to waste precious time trying to secure the poles in stone embankments. By December 1854, however, enough progress had been made for the men in New York to anticipate laying cable across the Gulf of St. Lawrence.

For the first of what would eventually be forty times, Cyrus Field went to England to purchase a cable to ship to Cape Ray in Newfoundland. His partners were eager to participate in the historic sinking of the cable, and they decided to charter a boat to carry them to the ceremony, sharing the cost of $750 a day. By this time, Samuel Morse had joined the investors, and he went on the trip, often passing the time with Peter Cooper by demonstrating the miraculous accomplishments of his telegraph machine.

Unfortunately, the trip was the high point of the adventure, for a series of mishaps kept the cable from being successfully submerged. In fact, it would take two more years for the telegraph line to be laid and the Canadian shore connected to Newfoundland by cable. The partners remained undaunted and were determined to fulfill their even more ambitious dream, the laying of an Atlantic cable.

Throughout the early part of 1857, Peter and Cyrus lobbied for money, supplies, and commitments from the government, traveling many times to Washington, D.C. On August 7, two steamships set out to sea, one from Liverpool, England, and one from Newfoundland, spooling out cable and planning to connect in midocean. Long before they reached that point, the cable on the American boat broke and sank, and with it went a million-dollar investment.

Amazingly, neither Cyrus nor Peter was seriously discouraged. Indeed, in 1858, after repeated false starts involving broken cables, fierce storms, and near collisions, two ships met in midocean. This time they spliced their cables together and moved past each other — one toward Ireland, the other toward Newfoundland — laying 1950 miles of wire on the ocean floor as they steamed along. Cyrus Field and Peter Cooper were vindicated in their stubborn certainty that the "rat hole," as the project was often called, was actually a door to shared experience for a once-separated world.

Previously skeptical New Yorkers went crazy with excitement. No one could dismiss the importance of the event, although George Templeton Strong showed some of his characteristic irritation with the resulting hyperbole. "Newspapers vie with each other in gas and grandiloquence," he wrote in his diary. "Yesterday's *Herald* said that the cable (or perhaps Cyrus W. Field, uncertain which) is undoubtedly the Angel in the Book of Revelation with one foot on land, proclaiming that Time shall be no longer. Moderate people merely say that this is the greatest human achievement in history."

Strong thought the city was overreacting, but the initial response was calm compared with the two weeks of excitement following August 16, 1858, when Queen Victoria and President James Buchanan actually greeted each other across the seas. Long after the sun set, the streets of New York, lined with flags from all nations, were blazing with light from indoor gas lamps and enormous outdoor calcium lights on the tops of buildings. Torchlight processions began at Battery Park and headed for the gorgeous Crystal Palace, New York's new exhibition hall on Forty-second Street.

Made of cast iron and glass, the Crystal Palace had the largest dome of any building in America. City officials waiting there greeted the cable celebrants with speeches about how the "Whisper of the Kremlin" and "The Song of the Persian Dancing Girl" would soon be heard all over America. The city band even paid a late-night visit to

While all the city cheers, the firemen light their torches in Union Square to celebrate the laying of the Atlantic Cable.

The Crystal Palace, the country's first iron-and-glass exhibition hall and a triumph of American design

Gramercy Park to serenade Peter Cooper with foreign songs and thank him for his role in helping to span the continents.

Unfortunately, only a few weeks after its initial success, the cable went "obstinately silent." As George Templeton Strong described it, the cable reminded him of "a slowly dying person whose breathing is scarcely perceptible, whose lips at times move faintly but form no intelligible words." While the unhappy news was spreading through the city, the autumn sky suddenly danced with flame and a "majestic column of smoke." Despite the attempts to fireproof the building, wood and other combustible interior materials of the great Crystal Palace had caught fire. It burned uncontrollably, and within fifteen minutes the site held nothing but a mountain of ashes, full of fragments of iron and glass; the building's collapsed dome lay amid the debris.

New York recoiled from these bitter conclusions to its dreams of grand design. The destruction of the Crystal Palace seemed to illustrate vividly the city's disappointment over the now-certain failure of the Atlantic cable. It had become clear that the casing of the copper conductor was malfunctioning, and that the conductor itself was not large enough for its task. The press, which had celebrated the historic achievement, now excoriated the company for poor preparation and sloppy procedures. Cyrus Field, once a hero, was considered by many to be a swindler and fraud. Outside Gramercy Park, where his neighbors remained loyal, citizens literally turned their backs when they saw him approaching. Peter Cooper, still venerated, remained unwavering in his vocal support of Field and thereby kept public feeling from running dangerously high. "We will go on," the older man said when Cyrus could no longer contain his pain and wept bitterly in Cooper's library one day.

Raising money from his reluctant friends, and contributing a substantial amount of his own, Peter financed another trip for Cyrus to raise capital in England for yet one more try. English investors were as suspicious and disillusioned as Americans, however, and it was to be many years after the bitter intrusion of the Civil War before the Atlantic cable was attempted again.

In the summer of 1865, after several more fruitless attempts at submerging the newly designed cables, the dream finally became a reality, and the cable was successfully laid. Restored to grace once again because of his now-unarguable success, Cyrus Field was honored at a banquet by New York's Chamber of Commerce. No guest was more moved or gratified than Peter Cooper, who toasted his embattled neighbor and friend with an understatement that must have pleased even George Templeton Strong: "God rewards patient industry."

4

PURVEYORS
OF
CULTURE

————————◆◆————————

BOTH PETER COOPER and Cyrus Field had clearly felt the need
to complement their commercial ambition with esthetic interests. Like Samuel Ruggles and George Templeton Strong, they
shared a passion for ideas, and found extraordinary pleasure in learning and in hearing fine language in the service of thought and truth.
No room in Cooper Union was more important to Peter Cooper than
the Great Hall, the site of many absorbing lectures and fevered
debates.

During the mid nineteenth century, the lecture reached its zenith
as popular entertainment. Prominent citizens, accomplished in many
different fields, would travel the country, presenting their views. At
"lyceums" all over America, speakers exposed their audiences to aspects of culture they could not experience elsewhere. It was a source
of pride to many farmers and small-town tradesmen that the lectures
they heard had also been given to the worldly wise audiences of
Cooper Union, the Mercantile Library, and the New-York Historical Society.

Even such famous citizens as William Cullen Bryant, Horace

Greeley, and Ralph Waldo Emerson supplemented their incomes by traveling the lecture circuit, covering as much of the country as possible with the same speech. Some lectures were, of course, less meaningful than others, and the irreverent George Templeton Strong often mocked the "instant experts" who made much ado, at a price, of unimportant knowledge. Once, during the unhappy period before he met and married Ellen, he mused, "What shall I do to find some agreeable novelty? Take to drinking? or to politics? or to amateur woodsawing? . . . I don't know but I'll turn popular lecturer — deliver a series of lectures before the Sixth Ward Library Association or the Comminpaw Lyceum on the life and times of Sir John Snooks, the History of the Steam Engine during the fourteenth century or the peculiar features of the farthingales of the Elizabethan era."

Despite his sarcasm, some of George's most enjoyable evenings were spent at lectures, and one of the many delights of his relationship with Ellen was that she, unlike many of his friends' wives, greatly enjoyed such diversions. One of George's favorite series of lectures was given in 1852, when William Thackeray, whose work he admired so much, came to New York. These six separate talks on important English writers were given at the edge of Gramercy Park, in the huge Byzantine First Unitarian Society, on Twentieth Street and Fourth Avenue. The church rector, who lived in the parsonage on Fourth Avenue, was the much revered, highly influential Henry Whitney Bellows.

Tickets to Thackeray's lecture series were at a premium, and New York's most notable citizens filled the enormous church chamber. Their enthusiasm ran high. As William Cullen Bryant described their response, everyone was "perfectly united in the opinion that they never remembered to have spent an hour more delightfully in their lives." George found the writer "spirited and original," as well as engagingly "plain-spoken." As always, it irritated George when serious events were corrupted by fashion, and there were many people in the audience who were there to be seen rather than to listen. It amused him greatly, therefore, that Thackeray unknowingly offered an antidote to the "vanity of human greatness" when he asked an American colleague who the Mr. Astor was who had left a card for

William Makepeace Thackeray, a welcome visitor to New York's lecture circuit, who embraced the city's "rush of life"

him. The author was, of course, referring to William Astor, who, in 1852, was the wealthiest man in America.

Actually, some members of New York society were worried about Thackeray's visit, although they entertained him extravagantly. Would he allow himself to be lionized and fêted, only to go home and "abuse us, like that unmitigated snob, Dickens?" In fact, no one resented the $12,000 Thackeray quickly earned from his lectures in America, for he had nothing but admiration for the "bustle" and "rush of life" that he found in New York.

"The luxury of the city is prodigious," Thackeray wrote. "I never saw such luxury and extravagance, such tearing polkas, such stupendous suppers and fine clothes. I watched one young lady at 4 balls in as many new dresses, and each dress of the most 'stunning' description." His delight was endearing, and the press, like George, found Thackeray unaffected and "sweet," free of malice and clearly full of integrity. Those who had not yet read his novels were eager to do so, which was a happy set of circumstances for the writer and for his American publishers, Harper & Brothers.

It was no accident that Thackeray's visit to New York coincided with the publication of his newest novel, *Henry Esmond*. James Harper, a Gramercy Park resident, was a founding partner of Thackeray's American publishing house and had built the firm on a foundation of judicious literary taste and merchandising acumen.

James Harper had first left his father's farm in Newtown, Long Island, on a bitterly cold December day in 1810, when he was fifteen. He had read the autobiography of Benjamin Franklin and wanted to apprentice himself to a printer in New York City so that he could follow in Franklin's footsteps. "Don't forget your home or your religious duties," his mother warned as she and her three other sons waved James and his father away on their horse-drawn sleigh. The senior Mr. Harper was taking his oldest son to the home of the man who would take him on as a printing apprentice and, as was customary, give him lodging. Bundled in heavy jackets and scarves against the fierce wind, father and son rode on desolate country roads to the foot of Brooklyn Heights, where they climbed aboard a dilapidated scow that ferried them across the icy East River. When his father finally bade him goodbye, James had one shilling in his pocket and a scanty collection of homespun shirts and trousers.

At the same time, William Astor, whose name William Thackeray did not recognize, was beginning his trade in the city. Standing at the river's edge that cold day, James would have found it difficult to imagine a time when the Harper name would be as prominent in its own way as the Astor name had already become. William Astor's extraordinary real estate empire would earn him the nickname "the Landlord of New York," but, unlike James, he did not start from scratch. William's father, John Jacob Astor, had accumulated a vast fortune from trading in furs. Although James boarded and worked only a few streets from William's magnificent home at 223 Broadway, there was no possibility of their meeting socially, nor did it seem there ever would be.

An Astor would have known very little about the sort of work this farmer's son was engaged in with Paul and Thomas, Printers. The work was brutally hard and had progressed very little since the days of Benjamin Franklin. Printing presses were hand-operated by two men known as "partners." One of them applied the ink with large hand balls, and the other laid on the sheet, "pulling out" the printed impression.

*James Harper elevated the country's reading taste
and drove the pigs from New York's streets.*

The home of James Harper in Gramercy Park, marked by the "mayor's lamps"

It didn't take very long for James to realize that what he really wanted was to be a book publisher rather than a printer. When his brother John came to the city in 1812 to work as a printing apprentice, James's ambition and its course grew clearer. In 1817, James, then twenty-two, and twenty-year-old John started their own printing business. They had two old hand presses and rented factory space, financed by a loan from their father and $500 they had managed to save from their meager wages. They took on an assortment of printing jobs for other businessmen, yet managed to publish their first book — an English translation of Seneca's *Morals* — during their first year of operation.

As their business grew, the printing process itself made progress. From hand power, the brothers moved to horse power. They kept a young horse in the cellar of a house that adjoined their factory and, at seven each morning, harnessed him to a beam attached to the shaft that operated the presses. The horse would walk around and around, generating the power that kept the presses moving. At lunchtime, he was unharnessed and taken back to his stable and generously fed; then he went back to work for the rest of the long afternoon. When the horse grew too old to work, he was retired to the Harper family farm, where, legend goes, he spent his remaining days walking around and around a tree until the twelve and six o'clock whistles blew.

As the publishing house grew older and more prosperous, it truly became a family firm. The remaining two Harper brothers, Wesley and Fletcher, had joined the business, and in 1833 its name was officially changed to Harper & Brothers. All the brothers achieved great stature, but James, who was the first to arrive in the city and realize his dreams there, achieved particular prominence.

In 1844, James was elected mayor of New York. Among other distinctions, Harper & Brothers had become the established leader in publishing reprints of British books. It was common practice for publishers to greet packet ships from England, when they pulled into pier, and try to make the first claim on bundles of printing proofs from English authors. Prized copy in hand, the victorious publisher would run back to his plant to print and distribute the book as quickly as possible to American readers. As an old man, Fletcher Harper reminisced about the excitement of this competition, boasting about printing and binding a book called *Peveril of the Peak* only twenty-one hours after the copy was off the ship. Harper & Brothers was also publishing a growing number of works by American authors, including William Cullen Bryant, Herman Melville, and Richard Henry Dana, Jr., author of the very popular *Two Years Before the Mast*.

In the 1830s, there was a tendency to publish books anonymously. It became a kind of intellectual game for readers to guess who had written a particular novel or adventure story. In this manner, the Harpers published the early novels of Walter Scott; and even Edgar Allan Poe wrote a mock autobiography, *The Narrative of Arthur Gordon Pym, of Nantucket*.

As the book business became more sophisticated, Harper & Brothers startled the publishing and reading community by hiring the first person to serve as an editor, then called a "reader." One of many authors who objected to this practice was James Kirke Paulding, who complained that the reader's guiding principle was profit for the firm rather than "any intrinsic merit of the work or its author." And in his book *A Glance at New York,* published in 1837, Asa Green explained the new vocation: "As certain Kings and great men . . . used, in former times, to keep a tester, whose business it was to see that the food was not poisoned: so do Harper & Brothers employ a reader."

In fact, the Harpers had already employed a series of advisers who examined the accuracy of scientific books and other special material. To the Harpers, employing a reader was simply another way of ensuring "high literary acquirements and correct taste" for their publishing list, and the public certainly appeared to admire the brothers' dedication and integrity. There seems little doubt that James Harper won his mayoral race because the city was seriously in need of reform, and his own moral strength was unquestioned.

Understanding that he would not be able to give much of his attention to his business, James was ambivalent about becoming mayor, up to the moment of triumph. On election night, he stood on the balcony of his home on Rose Street and told the cheering crowds, "I feel like the boy who had made a kite, the pride of his life, and set out to fly it. Higher and higher it went till it caught in the limb of a tree. He climbed up to release it. He passed branch after branch, and then began to creep along the one on which his kite was hanging. On he went till further advance was dangerous. He resolved to go back, but found he could not. In fact, he was stuck. And that is just what I am now, fellow-citizens."

Nonetheless, he was proud of the office and was diligent about cleaning up the city, literally and symbolically. He banished the pigs from the streets, and forbade citizens to drive cattle below Fourteenth Street during the daytime. He hired 350 men to sweep the streets and established an ordinance that made garbage collecting a regular city routine. Perhaps his most significant reform was dividing the city into police districts, each with its central headquarters. He ordered the policemen to wear uniforms, made of blue cloth, that bore the letters M.P., for Municipal Police, on their high collars.

James Harper also cracked down on the disorderly drinking that had become an unpleasant part of New York life. From the seamy "bucket shops" to the "gin mills" and "grog shops," rum and malt liquors were sold in vast quantities, often to men who were using their family's food money for drink. Drinking was by no means confined to the lower classes, however, and the respectable hotel bars in the Wall Street area served a good deal of whiskey and champagne to brokers and bankers.

The visiting British writer Charles Mackay reported that inside the hotel bar "gin-sling, brandy-smash, whisky-skin, streak of lightning, cock-tail, and rum-salad . . . are consumed morning, noon and night, by persons who in similar rank of life in England would no more think of going into a gin-shop than of robbing the Bank." Even women were beginning to enjoy liquor in public when they were escorted to fashionable restaurants. (Absinthe was a popular choice among New York's females.)

James Harper, a temperate man himself, ordered his new police force to arrest people for public intoxication, a practice that continued through future administrations. Harper also ruled that bars had to be closed on Sundays, and that no liquor could be sold on July 4, to prevent the national holiday from being turned into another excuse for drunken brawls.

Although he was proud of his office, James Harper declined to run again. Among the memorabilia he kept from his experience were the two "mayoralty" lamps that had stood outside his Rose Street home. In the days before official mansions, these lamps told citizens where the mayor lived, should they require his counsel or protection during the night. The lamps, which he took to his new home, provided further embellishment to what was, in 1847, one of the loveliest homes in Gramercy Park. A graceful Greek Revival building decorated with iron grillwork in a range of elaborate motifs — rosettes, flowers, and vines — the house stood at 4 Gramercy Park. Visitors from the South were often astonished to see it there, because it was so reminiscent of the houses found in their native cities, particularly New Orleans.

Fletcher Harper soon moved to nearby Twenty-second Street, just across the street from Samuel Morse. ("Twenty-second Street" became the nickname for the regular Monday evening dinners that Fletcher gave for authors and business associates.) John Harper's house was on Fifth Avenue, where he turned neighboring lots along Twenty-seventh Street into gardens, a carriage house, and stables. Only Wesley lived outside the Gramercy Park area, in Brooklyn Heights, but the physical distance did not indicate a lack of emotional or intellectual connection. The four Harper brothers worked easily together, each complementing and respecting the special strengths of the others.

A favorite illustration of the brothers' excellent relationship had to do with a pompous visiting clergyman who paid an uninvited visit to James Harper in Gramercy Park. James tried to be polite, but his patience began wearing thin as the cleric questioned him ceaselessly about the publishing industry in general and Harper & Brothers in particular. "You say that your brother John sees to the accounts, that your brother Wesley looks after the correspondence, and that your brother Fletcher receives authors and supervises the publication of new books. . . . But you, Mr. Mayor, I have never been able to discover what you do." "Oh, they leave me an enormous amount of work," James answered. "I have more to do than all of them put together." "Indeed! That is very curious. Allow me to ask what it is." "I'll tell you," said James, "but you must never tell a soul. I entertain the bores."

It was often acknowledged that Harper & Brothers had become a major arbiter of America's literary taste. Some even said that it had done more than any university to heighten the intellect of the country. As the 1850s began, the firm was doing so well that it expanded its headquarters on Cliff Street and built two spacious new buildings on Pearl Street. The brothers' happiness in their new quarters was relatively short-lived. In December of 1853, the entire plant was destroyed by fire when an employee accidentally tossed a roll of burning paper into a pan of camphene, a solution used to clean the printing rollers.

The flames leaped so high that they were visible in Gramercy Park, where George Templeton Strong "saw the smoke swelling out in great masses against the clear sky at two o'clock, and put for the scene. . . . Fire on both sides, sometimes arching the street. . . . Walls thundering down at intervals, each fall followed by a rush upwards of tawny, ropy, blinding smoke and a rain of powdered mortar. Across Pearl Street there stood in beautiful contrast with the lurid masses of flame and smoke, an arch of rainbow, brightening and fading as the northwest wind fell, formed on the spray of the engines. . . . The loss to the Harpers must be immense."

And indeed it was. Fifty thousand New Yorkers gathered to watch the disaster as the brothers struggled to save lives and then to rescue valuables. As many important papers as they could collect were put into a large safe that they dragged out onto the sidewalk; then, along with the other spectators, the Harpers watched the horrifying collapse of their lifework. The newspapers made much of the literary contents of particular flames. One journalist claimed that it seemed as if one could tell "when poetry went sparkling skyward, when romances cast a lurid glare around, or when smoke . . . came from the tomes of orthodox divinity."

·   ·   ·

The loss to the firm was estimated at $1,115,000, an extraordinary sum for the time. Yet when the brothers met in Gramercy Park on the night of the fire, they agreed without hesitation to go on with the business. The next day, Cyrus Field offered to lend James $10,000, and when the Harpers decided that they had to build a new plant right away, it was Peter Cooper whose sacrifice helped make the plan possible.

After long and costly study and experimentation, Peter had begun to manufacture wrought-iron beams in his New Jersey plant, and Cooper Union was to be the first building in the country constructed with them. Only two tiers of beams had been laid when the Harper disaster struck, and Peter offered to suspend work on his college so that the material could be used by the Harpers. If he felt some regret over the delay, he was surely pleased by the knowledge that nearly 750 male and female New Yorkers would be employed by the new Harpers' publishing plant. What's more, even before the fire, the firm had begun to venture into magazine publishing, making good reading material readily accessible to the general public, and Peter was eager for this to continue.

A magnificent new plant rose from the ashes in 1855. The two main buildings on Franklin Square were completely fireproof, for the Harpers knew full well how uncertain the city's firefighting system was. Charles Mackay, the British journalist, was amazed by this system and the people who served as firefighters.

According to the description of a parade of the city's fire companies he sent to his London newspaper, each company dragged its favorite engine through the New York streets. The companies were as fond of their engines, wrote Mackay, "as a captain is of his ship, gaily ornamented with ribbons, flags, streamers and flowers preceded by a band of music." The firemen, young men who usually worked at other jobs during the day, wore "dark pantaloons, with leather belt around the waist, large boots, a thick red shirt, with no coat or vest," to complement the more traditional helmet. The firemen actually felt a chosen lot, for each had to be voted into the department "like a member of the London Clubs"; nor were they paid a salary, Mr. Mackay reported incredulously.

In fact, these men invariably spent substantial amounts of their own money, not only on their uniforms, but on decorating both their engines and the firehouse rooms where unmarried members of the force stayed at night. While the sleeping rooms tended to be rather spare, many firehouse parlors were startlingly lavish, "fitted up with a degree of luxury equal to that of the public rooms of the most celebrated hotels. At one of the central stations which I visited, the walls were hung with portraits of Washington, Franklin, Jefferson, and other founders of the Republic; the floor was covered with velvet pile carpeting, a noble chandelier hung from the center, the crimson curtains were rich and heavy, while the sideboard was spread with silver claret-jugs and pieces of plate."

Firemen answering a night alarm in a race to be the first wagon on the scene

The camaraderie of the firehouse was often forgotten when several companies arrived on the scene of a fire, as they did for the Harper blaze. By unwritten rule, the director of the first engine to arrive became "director general" of the evening. So eager were the young firemen to arrive first that they often carried their uniforms with them as they pulled their engines through the streets with heavy ropes, hastily dressing when they approached the flames. Many a New Yorker was run down by this racing army of firefighters, and if one of the men fell, his company rarely stopped to aid him. If two companies reached a site at the same time, it was not unusual for the firefighters to engage in territorial fistfights and ignore the fire altogether.

In general, British visitors were more amused than amazed by the foibles and habits of New Yorkers, but other visitors found this rapidly rising metropolis astonishing. When members of the first Japanese mission arrived in New York in the spring of 1860, one of the many things that surprised them was how brilliantly illuminated the city was. The streets of Gramercy Park, like those of several other neighborhoods, were lined with gaslights that threw the buildings into brilliant relief against the sky. And as the men strolled around the park at dusk, the lights inside the lovely libraries and parlors moved one Japanese visitor to rhapsodize, "The light in the rooms of the houses shining through the glass windows at night is so wonderful and is such a surprise . . . that I cannot describe it!"

New Yorkers were hospitable to the people Walt Whitman called "from Niphon come," but they always were most attentive to British visitors. The 1850s came to an end. As 1860 began and the approaching calamity of Civil War seemed unavoidable, New York was in a frenzy of excitement over the visit of the young Albert Edward, Prince of Wales.

On the day of the prince's arrival in the city, October 11, 1860, crowds began to gather at dawn. Shops were closed and very few brokers could be seen on Wall Street. George Templeton Strong had been appointed to the reception committee, as had Cyrus Field, and both men tried to adopt the proper attitude toward their guest. In truth, neither man was particularly awed by royalty, but they decided to bow to the prince rather than shake hands, even though he was much their junior. To their surprise, the prince extended his hand in greeting when they were introduced, and it seemed "ungracious" not to return the gesture. After all, George wrote, it would hardly do to say "Sir, I am so well bred as to know my place, and I am unworthy to shake hands with a descendant of James I and George III and a probable King of England hereafter."

Peter Cooper was not impressed by royalty either, but he reluctantly agreed to become chairman of the gala planned to celebrate the prince's arrival. At the age of sixty-nine, Peter purchased his first dress suit in honor of this post, but he was persuaded to do so only because colleagues told him that it would be an insult to the Queen of England if he didn't wear one. "Very well," the elderly man grumbled, "I won't do anything to displease a lady," but he never wore the suit again after the ball.

For a democratic country, most Americans did make quite a fuss over visiting nobility. George Templeton Strong tried to sum up this apparent contradiction. He believed that in part there was an underlying "feeling of respect and regard for Great Britain and for Her Britannic Majesty." But, he added, one must also note that "no community worships hereditary rank and station like a democracy."

Whatever their flirtations with the ruling class, New Yorkers had glimpsed the spirit of true democracy when Abraham Lincoln visited New York in 1860. On February 27, he gave a speech in Cooper Union's "Great Underground Hall" that, he would later claim, secured his election.

William Cullen Bryant had invited Lincoln to the city to give New Yorkers a personal impression of the only man he believed could unite the country's many diverse groups. The weather was terrible on the night of Lincoln's speech, and the residents of Gramercy Park wrapped themselves in lap robes as they headed downtown to Peter Cooper's "other home." Peter, who declined to sit on stage with Bryant and David Dudley Field, sat with the audience in the packed auditorium. As he nodded to citizen after citizen, he thought what a glorious night it was, for his dream of bringing important issues and ideas to ordinary men and women had been realized.

That evening, of course, ordinary citizens were mixed with distinguished figures from politics and society, and all were united in their efforts to understand this gangly giant who stood before them. He seemed unable to control his large, awkward hands as he tried to accommodate his voice to the dimensions of the large hall. Passion soon overcame his discomfort, and his voice rang out, silencing the titters and mutterings that had accompanied his opening remarks. It was as if, one by one, those in the audience had come to understand that this was no ordinary man, but a person previously unknown to politics — a man who was able to speak simply of great truths. Reason, compassion, and fairness seemed to give him eloquence.

The weather was still cold and wet when Lincoln's speech ended, but the people who assembled outside ignored the elements. There was among them an overriding understanding that they would do anything they could to elect this man President. There were, of course, others who wished just as fervently to prevent this strange-looking country lawyer from becoming their leader. Few would have argued, however, that the nation, under Lincoln's presidency or not, was soon to be torn apart by civil war.

II

Behold the
Empire City

———✦———

1860-1900

5

WAR AND THE CITY

---◆---

O N APRIL 13, 1861, George Templeton Strong wrote in his diary, "Here begins a new chapter of my journal, entitled WAR — EXSURGAT DEUS. . . . This morning's papers confirmed last night's news . . . that the rebels opened fire at Sumter yesterday morning. . . . In substance, the despatches say that firing ceased at six P.M. yesterday, but shells continued to be thrown into the fort all night at intervals of twenty minutes. . . . So Civil War is inaugurated at last. God defend the Right."

Along with his father-in-law, George had long decried the tendency of New Yorkers to play down the possibility of conflict between North and South. Now, all of a sudden, prosperous northern businessmen who dealt extensively in southern commerce were looking on the South as a serious threat to the Union. They began to raise money to supply the northern soldiers, who, they believed, would keep the nation from splitting permanently in two.

Just after the first shots were fired, the city was draped with flags that symbolized the rising patriotism in every New Yorker's heart. As one merchant passionately declared, "There is but one feeling here now, and that is to sustain our flag and the government at all hazards."

When Samuel Ruggles took his place at the Chamber of Commerce meeting on April 19, the large room was packed. He felt as if he were taking part in an extraordinary drama as the members rose to pledge their allegiance to the country and to the Lincoln administration. The next day masses of people assembled in Union Square in a display of patriotism the *New York Times* described as "the greatest popular demonstration ever known in America." George Templeton Strong estimated the crowd at 250,000 people, and four separate platforms had been set up for different sets of speakers. From one, the voice of Peter Cooper rang out, "Let us . . . unite to sustain the Government by every means in our power, to arm and equip, in the shortest possible time, an army of the best men that can be found in the country."

Throughout the early months of war, these mass gatherings continued. Hundreds of thousands of men, women, and children sang and waved flags in time to such rousing patriotic songs as "Hail, Columbia," "Yankee Doodle," and "The Star Spangled Banner," serenading the hastily outfitted, ill-equipped soldiers as they marched to battle. Although New York's quota of soldiers for 1861 was seventeen regiments, the number was close to five times that by the end of the year. New Yorkers also cheered troops from other states as they marched through their city on the way to Washington. These scenes brought tears to everyone's eyes. "I was half choked with sympathy," recalled George Templeton Strong. "God be praised for the unity of feeling here."

George was past the age of enlistment, but several days after war was declared he called a meeting at his house to form a regiment called the New York Rifles. Money was quickly raised to supply recruits with equipment, and a drill officer was appointed to train the men in rented space downtown and to march them up and down the Washington Square Parade Grounds. It was not the intention of this group to leave New York for battle; rather, it saw its duty as defending the city if the fighting ever reached home ground.

Recruitment for the front did become a fevered part of daily life in the city, however. City Hall Park was lined with enlistment tents, flanked by huge placards decorated with pictures of victorious soldiers and messages challenging the allegiance of young New Yorkers. ATTENTION! YOUNG MEN WHO WISH TO AVENGE THEIR COUNTRY! a sign might say, and follow with a listing of the benefits the volunteer would receive: good money every month, lots of healthful food — bread, meat, vegetables, and even wine and beer — and, when battle was over, a tract of land on which to take up civilian life once again.

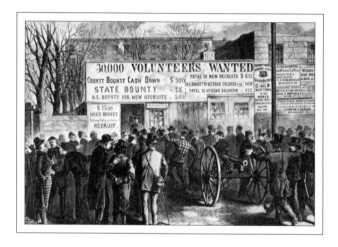

Patriotism and promises of bounty lure the prospective soldier.
Civil War recruiting in City Hall Park.

It quickly became evident that the reality of war was very different from the blandishments of recruiters. The trains the new soldiers boarded for Washington were often inadequate to accommodate them, so they were forced to travel in filthy, foul-smelling cattle cars. There was little to eat or drink on the trip, and the conditions in the capital were not much of an improvement. The soldiers frequently had to stand for hours in heavy rain or brutal sun before room could be made for them in the existing camps, and the beds finally assigned to them were made of rotting bundles of straw covered with threadbare blankets. Seasoned military men gloomily predicted that many of these young volunteers would not have to fear death on the battle-field, for half of them would probably be felled by the appallingly unsanitary conditions in their training camps.

When they visited Washington, Gramercy Park neighbors Samuel Ruggles, George Templeton Strong, and the Reverend Henry Bellows saw for themselves how grim life was for the corps of northern soldiers. The Harvard-educated Bellows was a sagacious and eloquent man, as evident both in his Unitarian sermons and in the many essays he wrote for Christian and secular publications. Indeed, the city's literary elite respected him as much as the religious community did. There were some who criticized his egotism, but he was defended by his friends as possessing qualities that were far more important than occasional displays of conceit. George Templeton Strong called his neighbor's foibles "a trifling drawback" in a man who was so committed to the public good and was invariably "farsighted and wise."

At the end of April, Bellows, along with one of the city's leading physicians, Dr. Elisha Harris, began to work on solutions to the growing problem of military health care. Peter Cooper gave over his Great Hall for a mass meeting on medical relief for the military, with David Dudley Field presiding. By the time the meeting was over, almost a hundred of New York's most prestigious women, including Ellen Ruggles Strong, had formed the Women's Central Association of Relief, and physicians and surgeons from different New York hospitals started a similar group.

As spring progressed, maintaining the health of northern soldiers became an ever more pressing issue for these concerned New Yorkers, and a committee headed by the Reverend Bellows traveled to Washington to confer with military authorities. What they found was disheartening. The medical branch of the War Department was embroiled in bureaucracy and ignorance. Bellows and his committee knew what had to be done: make drastic improvements in camp sanitation, increase the number of ambulances and the supply of medicine, employ hospital boats, attract more surgeons to the military, and, in general, provide a higher level of medical care in every area. Yet all this, it seemed, the army was unable to do.

The only solution was to create a broad-scale organization of ci-
vilians who could step in and fill the shocking gaps in military health
care. George Templeton Strong was quickly chosen as the newly
formed Sanitary Commission's treasurer. He wrote to his friend
Francis Lieber, professor of history and political economy at Columbia and a brilliant political theorist, that "the old Medical Bureau
was, by the universal consent of all but its own members, the most
narrow, hidebound, fossilized, red-tape-y of all the departments in
Washington. It was without influence or weight with Government.
Lincoln actually did not know who the Surgeon-General was. He
said so in my presence. Government is responsible for the most
abominable neglect."*

By June of 1861, the Sanitary Commission was officially appointed, blessed by Lincoln himself. On Friday evening, June 21,
the new group met in Dr. Bellows's home in Gramercy Park. Bellows was the commission's president, and Alexander Bache, a physi-
cist and the great-grandson of Benjamin Franklin, was appointed
vice-president. Frederick Law Olmsted agreed to leave his work on
Central Park to become general secretary and act as liaison between
the commission and government leaders. He was in charge of hiring
personnel, supervising operations, and coordinating all of the commission's diversified activities.

Some thought Olmsted an odd choice, since he was not known for
his patience or tact, but those who worked with him quickly understood the reason for his selection. As Strong later acknowledged, "He
is an extraordinary fellow, decidedly the most remarkable specimen
of human nature with whom I have ever been brought into close
relations. Talent and energy most rare: absolute purity and
disinterestedness."

Other charter members of the commission were Cornelius Agnew,
surgeon general of New York, and Wolcott Gibbs, a brilliant chem-

---

*Francis Lieber would make a profound contribution to the war effort. He was con-
sulted by the Union government on formulating official rules of war, and his ideas were
implemented in a treatise called "Instructions for the Government of Armies in the
Field." It was the first such publication in any language and was adopted by other
countries, becoming the foundation of an international code of military conduct during
wartime.

ist. George and his father-in-law had fought unsuccessfully with Columbia College — both were members of the college's board of trustees — to appoint Gibbs to the chair, previously held by James Renwick, Sr., in natural and experimental philosophy and chemistry. The battle over the appointment of Gibbs, a Unitarian, almost tore apart the Episcopal college.

Within days of the Sanitary Commission's creation, George Templeton Strong was at work in his Gramercy Park library, writing letters to the city's wealthiest men to raise funds. He enlisted Cyrus Field as an associate member to help with this campaign, explaining passionately that "if the merchants and capitalists of New York are prudent enough to sustain the Commission, it will . . . save the nation, thousands of men and millions of money within the next three months. If they do not sustain it, the loss is theirs and will be felt in the depression of New York property for ten years to come. An epidemic of camp fever or dysentery or cholera among our volunteer regiments is inevitable within sixty days unless . . . a sanitary system be created for them."

Persuasive as George and his assistants were, the going was slow. After one late-night meeting of the commission in Gramercy Park, George bade good night to the group and then went back to his desk to work. He noted in his diary, "Have corrected and re-corrected proofs of a begging letter, a mendicatory whine some twenty pages long. Unless we . . . [are] soon reinforced with money, we must begin to wind up." He went on to describe what was, in reality, a much greater obstacle to the success of the commission: "Battle with the Surgeon-General is upon us at last. The *World* of a week ago published an attack upon his inefficiency. The *Times* . . . defends him by assuming that the attack came from the Commission (which it didn't . . .), and charges the Commission with presumption and ambition in assailing government officials and trying to supersede them. . . . Other shots will follow."

Indeed, the incompetence of the United States surgeon general proved to be the most awesome obstacle facing the commission. To George, Dr. Clement Finley was "utterly ossified and useless," responsible in large part for the "rigor mortis" of the Medical Bureau. He was not evil; he was simply unable to cope with the urgent demands of so many men suddenly at war. He was also enamored of bureaucratic routine, and deeply resented the intrusion of the commission into his carefully established regimen.

Moving back and forth between Washington and Gramercy Park, George was grateful for his ability to function without much sleep, and for his wife's acceptance of the strain on their marriage. Together in New York, they watched the momentous year come to a close. "Poor old 1861. . . ." wrote George. "[A] gloomy year of trouble and disaster. I should be glad of its departure, were it not that 1862 is likely to be no better. But we must take what is coming. Only through much tribulation can a young people attain healthy, vigorous national life."

Strong and Bellows never let up in their efforts to reorganize the Medical Bureau. On January 27, 1862, members of the commission had a hearing before a House committee on the issue of medical care, and Bellows and Strong also had a private meeting with Lincoln. They asked the President to speak to the commission before choosing a surgeon general if a bill was passed that gave the President power to appoint one instead of accepting the person who rose to the post through seniority.

"It was a cool thing," George reported. "Lincoln looked rather puzzled and confounded by our impudence, but finally said, 'Well, gentlemen, I guess there's nothing wrong in promising that anybody shall be heered before anything's done.'" Using "heered" instead of "heard" was not the President's only slip in the hour the two men spent with him. The "Chief Magistrate" was in fine humor, and kept his visitors amused by telling them anecdotes he had "heered" in Illinois. His lack of presidential polish was surprisingly endearing, recalled George. "His evident integrity and simplicity of purpose would compensate for worse grammar than his, and for even more intense . . . rusticity." Both Bellows and George agreed that the man who was leading the country through its grimmest hours was "the best President we have had since old Jackson's time at least."

Finally, in April 1862, a year after the war began, the bill the

commission had worked so diligently for became law: An Act to Reorganize and Increase the Efficiency of the Medical Department of
the Army. Although it contained some compromises, it was vital to
the changes the commission was desperate to make. The surgeon general and other high-ranking officers would be appointed, and there
would be a group of eight medical inspectors empowered to institute
reforms; improvements would be made in hospital administration;
and the transportation of sick and wounded soldiers would become
more efficient.

For these plans to succeed, it was crucial that the next surgeon
general be someone of genuine ability. George and the Reverend
Bellows were immensely anxious about the appointment and believed
that the post should be given to Dr. William A. Hammond, a relatively young man with an impressive medical background. Doctors
from all over the country were sending petitions to Washington on
his behalf, but Strong and Bellows heard that the President was being
pressured by the military to give the office to someone from inside
their ranks. One day, while the President was getting shaved, Bellows was able to present a passionate appeal for the commission's
choice, and the next evening, when Bellows managed to meet the
President again, Lincoln immediately reassured him, "Shouldn't
wonder if he was Surgeon-General already." The two men then shook
hands. In his diary, George recalled, the President said to Bellows,
"I hain't been caught lying yet, and I don't mean to be."

Under Hammond's leadership, the work of the Sanitary Commission grew more efficient and ranged more widely. It distributed vast
amounts of food, clothing, medicine, and supplies, and recruited
legions of doctors and nurses. There were sometimes as many as five
hundred inspectors keeping tabs on medical care in all the camps and
collecting vital data for future operations. The inspectors also provided information to citizens hungry for news about the condition of
sick or wounded loved ones. In addition, private hospitals were successfully entreated by the commission to admit suffering soldiers
when military medical facilities couldn't meet their needs; and hospital boats were enlarged and staffed with both medical professionals
and carefully trained volunteer nurses. The seal that the commission

had designed to reflect its mission seemed totally appropriate: a winged figure of Mercy emerging from the clouds over a bloody battlefield, wearing a cross on her bosom and offering a cup of consolation to the wounded soldiers.

George continued to work tirelessly to raise money, holding musical, theatrical, and social fund raisers regularly in New York and other cities. He also sponsored Sanitary Fairs, where games of chance and exciting merchandise tempted visitors to part with their money. The small city of Poughkeepsie, Samuel Ruggles's boyhood home, raised $16,000, amounting to a dollar per citizen.

The most memorable of these fairs was held in New York City, with Ellie Strong in the role of treasurer. Many, many months in the planning, the Metropolitan Fair was held in the spring of 1864. Every trade, artistic, professional, and labor group in the city cooperated in filling two buildings, on Fourteenth Street and on Union Square, that had been erected for the occasion. The Fourteenth Street building had shops that sold clothing, elegant fabrics and furnishings, as well as books and original art. There was also a restaurant, dining hall, and library. The building on Union Square sold toys, clothes, and books for children, and articles of art and decoration that had been contributed by sympathetic European nations.

At a cattle show on Seventh Avenue and Fifteenth Street, even animals were sold, from a Shetland pony to a white ox that weighed thirty-five hundred pounds. Fenimore Cooper donated an original, unpublished manuscript; James Bowie, the hero of the Alamo, gave his famous knife. At the formal opening of the fair on April 4, the New York City chorus performed "The Star Spangled Banner" and sang a special soldier's hymn written by Oliver Wendell Holmes. By the time the fair was over, it had netted $1 million for the commission, far surpassing the $72,000 raised by a Sanitary Commission fair in Chicago and the $225,000 from Cincinnati. The triumph was duly and gratefully celebrated in the Strong and Bellows homes in Gramercy Park.

Ellie was justifiably proud of the fair's success, but George had long had other reasons to admire her spirit and tenacity. Her frail constitution did not prevent her from rising courageously to face the harsh realities of war; engaged in many of New York's activities to help the war effort, she was straining to do more.

In the spring of 1862, she persuaded George to allow her to serve on one of the commission's hospital ships as a nurse. In 1861, a precedent had been set when Dorothea Dix, known for her benevolence and her compassion for the ill, offered her nursing services to the government. Throughout the war, Dix went from battlefield to battlefield, hospital to hospital, camp to camp, organizing nursing care. Now multitudes of women were following her lead, leaving their protected lives to help heal the victims of the war's dreadful carnage.

Although George had serious misgivings, he felt that he could not deprive his wife of this opportunity to serve her beliefs and her country. In any event, marital decisions were seldom left entirely up to George, tempting as that arrangement may have sometimes appeared to him. So he armed Ellie with medicines to ward off infections, and saw her off one May evening on what was the first of her many trips into the heart of battle. The Reverend Bellows was along on her initial voyage, serving as chief pastor for the *Knickerbocker*, the spacious steamboat that had been converted to a surgical ship.

"What a plucky little thing she is," George thought proudly when he read her first letter, delivered a few days later by Mrs. Bellows. Ellie was clearly "enjoying her Bohemian life, works hard, sleeps profoundly, finds coarse fare appetizing, and has a good time generally." What's more, George told his father-in-law, who needed reassurance of his daughter's well-being, "I have brilliant reports of her energy and efficiency . . . of her cordial acquiescence in drudgery. God bless her for her vigorous devotion to this work."

Not everyone in New York was as dedicated to the war effort as Ellie Strong. Although the war had initially brought financial distress to the city, in a relatively short time commerce was booming again. The city's already legendary dry-goods store, A. T. Stewart, had bought up almost all the blankets and material for uniforms manufactured in the country, which meant that the United States government had to go to Stewart's for nearly all of these supplies. Other stores, and even restaurants, were so crowded that the *Times* ran repeated admonitions against spending frivolously money that should be used to aid the country's cause.

Hotels, filled with visitors, turned away as many guests again as they were able to accommodate. Rents were extravagantly high. Brownstones along Fifth and Madison avenues that had rented for $2000 to $3000 a year before the war now commanded double those amounts. And even the city's underground economy was flourishing. Prostitution had always existed in New York. In 1850 there had been ten thousand women working as prostitutes; by the 1860s there were at least twelve thousand. New and luxurious brothels became immediate neighbors to the city's most important families and institutions. Julia Brown, a madam, ran a stylish operation on University Place and Twelfth Street, and her colleague Miss Ida Thompson operated out of a house that the magazine *Gentleman's Companion* described as "elegant . . . furnished in the most elaborate and magnificent style. The carpets, mirrors, furniture and paintings are of the latest and most costly designs. This is truly a splendid establishment of the first class." No doubt the young women who serviced customers in these establishments were a far cry from the streetwalkers a working man might turn to for sexual release.

Wartime prosperity widened the division between rich and poor, but many foreign visitors continued to be struck by the mingling of the classes in the city's commercial life. "Ladies and washerwomen, gentlemen and labourers . . . hustled together in omnibuses without the slightest mutual sense of incongruity . . . all clothed in almost the same manner and style; the coachman, the street-porter, the merchant, the artisan, the banker, the lawyer," a Scotsman reported to his countrymen about New York City during the war.

One issue that did cause class lines to be sharply drawn in the city, however, was the Conscription Act of 1863. As Allan Nevins explains in his commentary to George Templeton Strong's diary, New York's response to the draft was divided when names of the first draftees were published in the newspapers. "The foreign-born population of the city . . . felt it had powerful reasons for discontent.

For one, most of the foreign-born were Democrats, and they had been assured by Democratic newspapers and politicians that the acts of the Lincoln Administration were highhanded, oppressive, and even unconstitutional. For another, the provision by which well-to-do men could hire substitutes for $300 seemed unjust to the poor. For a third, the Irish and other day-laborers had felt keenly the competition of Negro freedmen now flocking up from the South, and many of them were filled with hatred of the blacks."

It was perhaps inevitable, then, that a huge crowd gathered in front of draft headquarters at Third Avenue and Forty-sixth Street on July 13, 1863, following the publication of the conscripts' names. By noon, a riot was raging that would spread throughout the entire city before it was quelled. When he first heard the news, George Templeton Strong left his Wall Street office early, but he was able to get only as far as Thirteenth Street on the omnibus, because stalled passenger cars and crowds of pedestrians blocked the streets. Walking the rest of the way, he could see that the local merchants had all closed their shops to protect themselves from attack. Fires were being set everywhere one turned, and a particularly tragic blaze destroyed the Colored Orphan Asylum on Fifth Avenue and Forty-third Street.

During the Civil War draft riots, more than twelve hundred New Yorkers were killed.

There were reports that Gramercy Park would be struck, and when George came home from work on July 16 he found "Gramercy Park in military occupation." Twentieth and Twenty-first streets were lined with troops ready to defend the neighborhood against the marauders assembling around First and Second avenues. "They are in full possession of the western and eastern sides of the city," George recorded in his diary. "I could not walk four blocks eastward from this house this minute without peril."

It took four days of "tumult and terror" for the riots to end, and then only because vast numbers of soldiers had been dispatched to defend the city. Some two thousand policemen were also organized to keep order, and brave citizens and battle veterans supplemented their efforts. The final battle was fought in Gramercy Park on the night of July 16, when the militia had to keep back rioters who were beginning to break into and loot homes. Thirteen men were killed in the neighborhood before the confrontation ended.

The moral and physical casualties of the conscription riots were agonizingly high. Nearly a thousand people were killed during the four-day period, and $1.5 million worth of private property was completely destroyed.

It was a sad time for the residents of Gramercy Park, but everyone was busy trying to maintain a semblance of prewar order in his or her life, so there was little time to brood over the threat to the neighborhood. Even Sam Ruggles — who had the most to lose from the destruction of the environment he had so carefully created — had little time for backward reflection; he was nearly as busy as his son-in-law.

Serving on various war-related committees, Sam was a frequent visitor to official Washington. In addition, he was often summoned to the capital to consult with William H. Seward, then secretary of state. Seward was a lifelong friend who had always relied on Samuel's political guidance.

In 1863 Seward made a formal acknowledgment of Sam's role in government by asking him to represent the United States at an international conference in Berlin. Attending countries would discuss

An older Samuel Ruggles, inspired public servant,
distinguished citizen, genial mentor and friend

their resources and how they could assist each other. Because he was busy developing the Pacific Railroad, Samuel was reluctant to go, but, he told his family, "Seward won't take no for an answer." Once he agreed to the assignment, Sam was excited by the idea of convincing Europe that a united America could provide the rest of the world with all the food and gold it needed, and that the other nations should therefore support the country's war efforts.

As his son-in-law noted admiringly, Mr. Ruggles boarded the steamer for Hamburg "full of concentrated essence of America; railroads, grain, gold, production, transportation, continental nationality; he is charged with large, sound propositions on all these matters in a highly condensed, concrete form, and I think he will show his Old World colleagues that the gas of American brag can be solidified and made palatable and is Real Matter after all."

As 1864 approached, the re-election of President Lincoln was a major priority for Samuel Ruggles, George Templeton Strong, and most of their neighbors in Gramercy Park. Although the President was extremely popular in the North, a certain amount of war-weariness had set in that could easily turn the tide, so his re-election was by no means certain. Many party leaders felt that a major rally of support in the country's principal city was necessary to infuse new energy into the campaign. A representative from a Unionist group was sent to ask Peter Cooper for letters of introduction to the city's influential War Democrats, who could help round up people for such a meeting.

"There's no time for letters or palavers. . . . Just get into my buggy," Peter responded as he ushered the emissary out of the house and into the street, where the old black carriage waited. And away the two men went, into the heart of the business district at high noon, with Peter driving at his usual reckless rate. "From door to door to door we drove," the politician reported incredulously, climbing down into the crowded streets time and time again to demand an individual's presence and cooperation at the upcoming rally. The *New York Herald* called the Cooper style of invitation a "trumpet call" that brought out all the major Jacksonians, or War Democrats, and acknowledged that their impassioned platform speeches "must have done much to decide the waverers in the dense throng."

With the start of 1865, victory for the North seemed certain. New York's prosperity continued, and, with George Templeton Strong still acting as treasurer, the Sanitary Commission had been able effectively to tap into its resources. It spent more than $250,000 every month, supervised more than five hundred workers across the country, and maintained a large number of convalescent homes for wounded soldiers. It had its own hospital facilities on land and sea, and its own wagon trains for transporting people and supplies wherever necessary.

The assurance of Lincoln's continued leadership was a source of great comfort to commission members, as it was to most of the New Yorkers who came out in force on March 6, 1865, to celebrate his second inauguration. Cheering crowds lined the streets, and other people hung out of windows and climbed to the rooftops to watch the three-hour victory procession. At night, there were endless rounds of red, white, and blue fireworks lighting the sky in brilliant strokes of national color. But with a startlingly accurate premonition, George Templeton Strong noted in his diary, "All this extravagant, exuberant rejoicing frightens me. It seems a manifest omen of mishap." Only a month later, George's fears were confirmed. On April 14, 1865, Lincoln was shot at Ford's Theater in Washington, D.C., and died the following morning.

The citizens who had recently celebrated the President's victory mourned en masse. Anyone who spoke lightly of the assassination put his own life in danger. A group of waiters at a hotel in Gramercy Park were fired on the spot for making snide comments about Lincoln's politics and death. Town house and tenement, shop and office alike, were swathed in black muslin. Families pinned black rosettes to their curtains, and all flags were lowered to half mast and tied with bands of black crêpe.

April 16 was Easter Sunday, and every church in the city was packed to the doors with mourners. At Trinity Church, where the Strong family attended services, "the crowd packed the aisles tight and even occupied the choir steps and the choir itself nearly to the chancel rails," George wrote. "What a place this man . . . will fill in history."

The fact that the assassin was a brother of a Gramercy Park neighbor, Edwin Booth, was yet another bitter blow. Edwin Booth had long known that his brother John Wilkes Booth was capable of irrational behavior, and when his theatrical dresser told him the name of the rumored assassin, he believed the story immediately. The owner of the Boston Theater, where he was performing, hastily delivered a note to the stricken star, explaining apologetically that he felt it best to close the theater, and urging Booth's cooperation. Booth immediately replied, "With deepest sorrow and in great agitation, I thank you for relieving me from my engagement with yourself and with the public. While mourning, in common with all loyal hearts, the death of the President, I am oppressed by a private woe not to be expressed in words."

It took enormous courage for Edwin Booth, the country's preeminent actor, to make his way back to New York and confront its judgment. His face, which had mirrored a million expressions, now seemed set in stone. The house on Nineteenth Street where he lived with his mother and daughter was dark when his carriage drove up, but he had to push past crowds of curious onlookers to enter it.

Those neighbors who attempted to pay calls of sympathy in the ensuing days found the actor "in the deepest affliction and humiliation over his brother's crime." To some, he even vowed never to appear on stage again, since he could not imagine facing the public after this terrible family shame. The Reverend Bellows was summoned by Edwin to act as a "spiritual adviser," but it was almost impossible to find words to comfort the tormented man. Still, Bellows and other friends always believed that this extraordinary artist would somehow survive his despair and go on with his career. Other New Yorkers, who knew him only as a figure on the stage, were suddenly consumed with questions about who this man named Booth really was.

6

DRAMA IN GRAMERCY PARK

---✦---

ON NOVEMBER 25, 1864, less than six months before John Wilkes Booth murdered Abraham Lincoln, the fashionable Winter Garden Theater on lower Broadway was the site of a historical theatrical event. For the first and only time, three sons of the theater's illustrious Booth family were appearing together on stage. The occasion was a benefit performance of *Julius Caesar* to raise money for a statue of Shakespeare in Central Park to commemorate the Bard's three-hundredth birthday. Their father's namesake, Junius Booth, played Cassius; Edwin, the most famous brother, was cast as Brutus; and John Wilkes took the role of Marc Antony. Since there was to be only a single-night performance, the theater raised the price of orchestra seats to an unprecedented $5.00, but they quickly sold out.

The very next night, Edwin began what turned out to be a hundred-night run of *Hamlet*, a performance record that had never been matched. Booth, already considered the primary interpreter of Hamlet, had worked on this new production for several months. The character he brought on stage this time was a wistful, lonely man. George Templeton Strong was struck by how Booth played Hamlet

Edwin Booth as Hamlet, a role in which he had "no living equal"

always with the "bearing . . . of a gentleman, even in his difficult, ambiguous dealings with poor dear Ophelia."

The critics were immediately certain that Edwin Booth had surpassed even his own work, as well as that of any other actor who had ever taken on this complex role. In the *Tribune*, the celebrated critic William Winter wrote that this interpretation was an "absolute realization of Shakespeare's haunted Prince . . . a dark, mysterious, afflicted, melancholic vision of dignity and of grace."

As a boy, Edwin Booth could not have envisioned such celebrity for himself, though he had always been drawn to the stage. Edwin's special relationship with his gifted and erratic father, Junius Booth, made the world of the theater his total environment. By the time he was in his early teens, this fourth son of ten children was his father's constant companion and guardian. It was Edwin's job on the road to prevent his father from drinking himself into a stupor and to check the untamed nature that threatened to ruin his career.

After a performance, Junius Booth would remove the grand Shakespearean tunic of purple velvet and the ermine-trimmed cloak, and quickly change into one of his favorite pepper-and-salt suits. "I want to walk," he'd announce to his son in the same resonant, musical tones that held his audiences spellbound, and he would take off for a wild journey into the darkened streets and rowdy taverns of whatever town he was playing in.

Edwin would then search for him through the night, along the docks where his father wove drunkenly beside an icy waterfront, or in the meanest drinking parlors. When Edwin finally caught up with him, Junius often shouted obscenities or threatened to beat him. But eventually the father grew quiet, and allowed himself to be led back to the hotel.

Each night, Edwin prayed that his father could work off enough of his dissipation to go on stage the following evening or travel to the next city on their tour. If the night's demons prevented the actor from falling asleep, his son stayed awake too, no matter how much he longed for rest. Often Edwin sat on the edge of his father's bed, playing his banjo and singing softly, as one might to a child.

The actor Joseph Jefferson always remembered his first glimpse of the teenage Edwin escorting his father to the theater. The boy looked weary, "strained and anxious," he recalled, as if no one had cared for his needs in a very long time. But Jefferson, who was also an artist, remembered as well the youth's striking looks, "with his dark hair and deep eyes, like one of Murillo's Italian peasant boys."

To be the son of "crazy Booth, the mad tragedian," as Junius was known, had always been painful, but as time went on this extravagant, mysterious man moved closer and closer to insanity. His lack of self-control was making him into a theatrical legend during his own lifetime. One evening, while playing Richard III at the Park Theater, Junius chased the actor playing Richmond off the stage and

Junius Booth with his appreciative but apprehensive protector, Edwin

onto the street. Another time, while playing Othello, he nearly choked Desdemona to death before the other actors pulled him away. Occasionally, he decided to abandon a performance in the middle of a play, and would later publicly apologize to his stranded audience.

It was such bouts of lunacy that led Junius to recruit his son as caretaker. Although the scenes continued despite Edwin's relentless attention, the son, like the audiences, remained loyal. Edwin understood that the intensity of his father's acting was not only fueled by his untamed spirit, but could also blur the line between reality and illusion for him off stage. As Walt Whitman assessed it, Junius Booth's acting "illustrated Plato's rule that to the forming of an artist of the very highest rank, a dash of insanity (or what the world calls insanity) is indispensable."

Such praise did not make Junius less ambivalent about his dreams for Edwin and his other children. As they traveled across the country, Junius would instruct Edwin to find a more stable profession, one that was exact and clearly bounded, like law. If being a lawyer did not attract him, he should look for "anything that was true, rather than . . . that unreal world where nothing is but what is not." Just how Edwin was supposed to pursue an education while acting as his father's guardian, Junius did not bother to explore.

As Edwin stood in the wings watching his father night after night, he was equally unsure of what sort of life he should make for himself. Awe and excitement did battle with the loneliness and anxiety he knew were part of this all-consuming profession. He also knew that actors were generally considered vagabonds and ruffians, in spite of his father's acclaim, and he hated the thought that he would never be considered a gentleman, no matter how cultivated his diction or dress. Yet when Edwin was recruited by his father into performing a minor part, as he was from time to time, he felt an ambition and a passion that were hard to ignore.

Whether he performed well on these occasions, he never knew, for Junius barely acknowledged his son's attempts at acting. However, one evening in the spring of 1851, while playing Richard III at the National Theater in New York, Junius decided that he didn't feel well enough to go on stage. Outside their rooms a rented carriage waited, a wicker basket filled with Shakespearean costumes strapped to its side. When Edwin pointed this out and anxiously asked, "But what will they do without you, Father?" Booth answered calmly, "Go act it yourself."

Edwin had memorized the role of Richard — listening so often to his father perform, he'd learned his entire repertoire — but the thought of playing a starring role was overwhelming. Only the desire to protect Junius's declining reputation, to prevent his testing again the tolerance of managers and audiences by missing a performance, brought him to the stage that evening, dressed in Junius's outsize tunic and cloak.

At first, the audience did not realize there had been a substitution, for the manager had chosen not to announce it. Soon, however, a hum of whispered confusion filled the theater, turning, as the play progressed, into pleasure: the young actor's performance was indeed impressive. When Edwin took his bows, the applause was tremendous, and, in the wings, the other actors saluted his debut.

It was a night of both triumph and destiny. To Edwin, the sound of such applause was intoxicating. As he bowed and watched the admiring smiles, he sensed that he was making a commitment to the theater as inviolable as an oath of love or honor.

Edwin couldn't share his excitement with his father, however, when he raced back to the hotel and found Junius in the same position as he had left him hours earlier. It was clear that Junius wanted only the most succinct response to his question "Well, how did it go?" Yet something in his manner made Edwin suspect that his father had planned this evening to test him, and that he had surreptitiously gone to the theater to watch Edwin's performance.

Afterward, Edwin sought several independent acting jobs, but roles were scarce for an inexperienced performer, even one with the distinguished Booth name. So when Junius Jr., who had gone to San Francisco to manage a theater, offered his father a job, Edwin once again accepted the role of chaperon. He would see his father safely across the country and perhaps find encouragement in the booming new environment of the West for his own fledgling acting career.

After an arduous journey that involved riding on muleback through the jungles across the Isthmus of Panama before they could take a steamer from Panama to California, Junius and his eighteen-year-old son were greeted by nearly every actor playing in San Francisco and by a brass band playing Stephen Foster's "Oh, Susanna!" After such a welcome, Booth's optimism ran as high as the hills that loomed above the city, but though Junius at first played to packed houses, the critical response was troubling. The drama critic of the *Alta California* called him a "splendid ruin, aged and crumbling," but "majestic and magnificent even in decay."

In Sacramento, the response was even more disheartening. The miners, who came down from the mountains in covered wagons and arrived at the theater in clay- and sweat-covered work clothes, were too tired to pay attention to Junius's performance. After opening night, attendance dropped drastically, and Junius angrily cut short his run. California was not for him, he declared. He would return home, making appearances in various cities along the way to make up some of the money this venture had failed to earn.

Summoning up his courage, Edwin told his father that he did not want to accompany him back east. He found California fascinating and the prospect of trying to act away from Junius's overpowering presence immensely attractive. Still, it was difficult to say goodbye. Junius did his best to ease the tension, waving his sons off casually when they escorted him to the dock. Jauntily swinging his carpetbag, he seemed eager to be off, undaunted by both his failure in California and Edwin's desertion. Without someone to watch over him, however, he took no care of his health while traveling home, and after drinking some murky river water to quench an alcoholic thirst, he succumbed to a virulent infection. For days he lay in his bunk, racked by vomiting and burning with fever. He died alone on shipboard.

Edwin was overcome with grief and persistent guilt over his father's death, but he blossomed as an independent personality in the ensuing months. His brother Junius hired him to join the company of a new theater he was managing. Presentations at the San Francisco Hall covered a wide range, from comedies of manners like *She Stoops to Conquer* to operettas and even burlesque. Whether they were watching Shakespeare or the broadest farce, these audiences of miners were raucous and unsophisticated. A play's villain was always shouted down, and favorite stars had to duck buckskin purses full of gold nuggets that were thrown to them as signs of appreciation.

Although he aspired to more elegant theatrical surroundings, Edwin's spirit was emboldened by the freewheeling atmosphere in San Francisco. He moved outside town to an actors' colony and rode to rehearsals every morning on a white horse. He dressed in a bright red shirt with a black serape thrown over his shoulders, Hessian boots, and a slouchy hat. By contrast, his face, framed by shoulder-length, jet-black hair, seemed to be fashioned from fine alabaster, and his manner was good-humoredly aristocratic. When colony companions asked him to help with the chores, he refused with a smile, saying, "It's a poor company that can't support one gentleman."

As recognition of Edwin's talents grew, so did his self-assurance as an actor. Undoubtedly influenced by his father's acting technique, still he began to develop his own interpretations of even Junius's most celebrated roles. Unfortunately, he did not work nearly as hard at avoiding some of his father's habits. Edwin's drinking was rapidly becoming as much of a problem as Junius's had been, frequently bringing him to the edge of real danger. Once, he fell into the Sacramento River, dead drunk, and was saved only because another actor saw him and pulled him out. Even when he began to work his way back east in the fall of 1856, determined to conquer Boston, Philadelphia, and, ultimately, New York, he continued to drink heavily.

Nonetheless, the eastern states welcomed "Edwin Booth, Son of the Great Tragedian." Edwin was thrilled by the enthusiastic response he received during both a triumphant southern tour and a lengthy run in Boston, but he hated this form of billing. He vowed to perfect his own technique and remove every trace of resemblance to Junius Booth.

On May 4, 1857, Edwin Booth opened at New York's Metropolitan Theater (later renamed the Winter Garden) in *Richard III*, though he had begged the theater manager to allow him to play something less closely associated with Junius. While his performances elicited standing ovations from audiences night after night, his acting was, predictably, compared with his father's by the critics. Nonetheless, two of the more discerning reviewers recognized that Edwin Booth's interpretations of Shakespeare were startlingly innovative. The reviewers were William Winter, who was soon to begin his remarkable career at Horace Greeley's *Tribune* and would later praise the actor's Hamlet, and a free-lance writer named Adam Badeau, who would become General Grant's military secretary.

Badeau and Winter saw that the twenty-four-year-old Edwin Booth was full of unfocused energy and undisciplined power. If these characteristics made him seem awkward, they were also signs of an extraordinary dramatic style. On stage, Booth discarded traditional postures, like standing in place to recite the great Shakespearean soliloquies, and, instead, prowled across the stage, acting by intonation, gesture, and movement, in addition to declamation. The famous actor Lawrence Barrett described his young colleague as a "rapidly moving, nervous embodiment of all the passions."

The run in New York was the turning point in Edwin Booth's career; indeed, the theater itself was undergoing significant change. In the early 1850s, as they made more money and had more leisure time to enjoy it, many of New York's half-million people looked to the theater for entertainment. In an 1857 editorial, the *New York Times* proclaimed, "It is impossible that men should go through the wear and tear of business day after day and week after week . . . without recreation and relaxation of some sort. . . . Those who work with the brain need it most, but those who labor with their hands need it also, and ought to have the means and opportunity for it much more abundantly than they have at present."

The *Times* was eager to see New York become the country's theatrical center. Philadelphia had always been able to make that claim, because it treated actors seriously and gave legitimate criticism of their work. Boston, though an enthusiastic city for actors to play in, could not compete for leadership because of its resolute moral attitudes toward entertainment. No performances were allowed on Saturday evening in anticipation of the Sabbath, and theaters had to be billed as "museums" or "athenaeums" to attract respectable audiences.

Traditionally, the theater had experienced difficulty in separating serious productions from frivolous fare. To many people, dramatic actors were no different from variety-show performers who satisfied the public's apparently voracious appetite for novelty entertainment. In 1853, Franconi's Hippodrome opened near Madison Square, and for two seasons (it was demolished in 1855 for the construction of the Fifth Avenue Hotel) ten thousand people at a time could watch ostrich and chariot races, dancing horses, and hundreds of actors playing dueling knights. Minstrel shows and burlesque were also very popular. The enormously successful Christy Minstrels sang and danced in groups of as many as forty people at the Fifth Avenue Opera House, and touring burlesque shows had evolved from spoofs of leading political figures to concentration on the figure itself, usually a voluptuous blonde.

It was not until after the war, in 1869, that New York got its first full-fledged burlesque show, *Lydia Thompson and Her British Blondes*, but scantily clad women had been seen on stage as far back as the 1840s, when "artist-model" shows enjoyed a flurry of prurient popularity. At Palmo's Opera House on Chambers Street, audiences first viewed "living men and women in almost the same state in which Gabriel saw them in the Garden of Eden on the first morning of creation." The enormous success of this offering led to many more "artistic" renditions of a nearly naked Neptune rising from the sea and of Esther in the Persian bath. One theater charged the huge sum of $1.00 for a look at nude women posing behind a gauze-draped doorway. At another, naked men and women danced the polka and minuet. The era of artist-model shows came to an abrupt end when a theater was attacked by a gang of rowdy young men who threatened the audience and chased the naked actors and actresses out of the building and down the Bowery. Soon afterward, in 1848, such shows were outlawed.

More sophisticated "girl-show" extravaganzas came to the city during the war years. They were not quite as blatant as burlesque, but audiences found them no less enticing. In the late sixties, Mark Twain wonderingly described one of these shows as "nothing but a wilderness of girls — stacked up, pile on pile, away aloft to the dome of the theatre." He went on to advise Edwin Booth that if he wanted to continue being successful, he would best "make a little change and peel some women."

Nonetheless, as the Civil War raged on, theatrical tastes began to change. People wanted more than just entertainment. There was a strong desire for relevance and realism in dramatic theme. Consequently, audiences had little patience for broad, unrealistically extravagant performances. This made Edwin Booth's style of "vigorous truthfulness" especially welcome. Whatever the role, audiences were astounded by his realistic power, and their wild enthusiasm regularly brought them to their feet in thunderous rounds of applause.

As his reputation grew, Edwin Booth found it difficult to keep his head, and he relied more and more on Adam Badeau, who had become an intimate friend, to provide some stability in his life. Badeau told Edwin that his acting would be richer and his career more sustained if his intellectual horizons were broadened, and Edwin immediately became an eager pupil. During his free time before evening performances, Edwin visited libraries and art galleries with Badeau, listening intently to his friend's explanation of paintings, or poring over books that Adam recommended. When Edwin wanted someone to drink with, he looked to others, but it was Adam who sympathized with his remorse and discomfort the morning after. When Edwin went on the road, he missed Adam's calming presence and companionship, and wrote his friend long letters that were at once amusing and sad. The depression that "Ad" too often witnessed in his friend pervaded Edwin's spirit even more deeply when he was traveling. The sense of rootlessness and fragility that he had felt as a child took hold of him in lonely hotel rooms, and intensified "the feeling that evil is hanging over me, that I can't come to good."

There were, of course, as many opportunities for consolation on the road as there were in the city. Many women were only too eager to walk on the arm, or be in the bed, of a man so obviously on his way to stardom, especially a man so broodingly handsome. Edwin was well aware of his own charm, and flirted with the actresses in every stock company he joined as a guest star. What's more, now that women were regularly attending the theater, he was besieged with signs of their admiration. When he returned to his dressing room after a performance, there were always piles of gifts waiting for him — jewelry, expensive scarves, great bouquets of flowers — all accompanied by perfumed notes on expensive paper.

A typical note might say, "Though you do not know me, dear Mr. Booth, I have admired you so long and so warmly, I can scarcely feel myself to be a stranger to you." Edwin barely skimmed most of these missives, though he often did accept one invitation or another. His companions of the evening were invariably mature women who were able to slip away from a stuffy husband. When young girls knocked on his dressing or hotel room door, he sent them away. It was fairly common, remembered Adam Badeau, for Booth to save "some foolish child from what might have been disgrace" by sending her home to her family.

But the adulation that Edwin received from women paled in comparison with the attention given his younger brother, John Wilkes Booth. His mother's favorite, John Wilkes had learned early to manipulate women, and with his extraordinary good looks, he was virtually irresistible.

.   .   .

John Wilkes Booth. "Between the acting of a dreadful thing and the first motion, all the interim is like a . . . hideous dream" (Julius Caesar).

John Wilkes Booth was a figure of striking elegance, often clothed in a claret-colored coat with velvet lapels, a pale buff waistcoat, and dove-gray trousers that he strapped under his boots so that they fitted tightly and provocatively over his hips and legs. Whatever the season, he sported a wide-brimmed straw hat. Waitresses literally fought with one another to serve him, and hotel maids changed his bed linen daily (not then the usual routine) for the vicariously intimate contact. Still in his teens when Edwin was first reaching stardom, John Wilkes was already known for debauchery; society matrons and actresses alike regularly succumbed to his charms.

Although he was more successful with women than Edwin was, John Wilkes was envious of his brother's theatrical success. He was eager for fame of his own, but he took full advantage of his brother's reputation in order to win acting roles. As for Edwin, he had many misgivings about his younger brother's career. After getting him the role of Horatio while he played Hamlet in Richmond, Virginia, Edwin reported to Junius Jr., "I don't think he will startle the world . . . but he is improving fast, and looks beautiful on the platform."

John Wilkes continued to improve as an actor, often demonstrating real talent, but he lacked the discipline necessary to achieve the fame he so desperately craved. His bombastic acting style was very much like his father's, which did not go unobserved. John Wilkes, commented one theater owner, had the same "fire . . . dash . . . touch of strangeness" as his father.

This "strangeness" had troubled Edwin from the time John Wilkes was a small boy. While Edwin displayed the Booth tendency toward melancholy, John Wilkes had Junius Booth's wildness, a kind of warped brilliance that blurred the boundaries of reality.

Much as Edwin wanted to help his brother, and much as he tried to avoid conflict, relations between the two were constantly strained. A major source of controversy was John Wilkes's intense sympathy for the South. Having been raised in Baltimore, Maryland, the Booth children were divided in their allegiance between North and South. Junius and Edwin were solidly for the North, but their brother Joseph served as a doctor with the Confederates. John Wilkes's sympathies for the South were, like all his responses, feverishly intense. The reasons for his hatred of Lincoln and his violent anti-abolitionist sentiments were largely obscure, though his reactions were fed in part by the fact that his greatest popularity as an actor was with southern audiences. A southern stage was practically the only place where John Wilkes Booth didn't feel eclipsed by his brother Edwin.

Despite their differences, John Wilkes came up to New York for Edwin's marriage to the young actress Mary Devlin on July 7, 1860, and after the service he threw his arms around his brother and gave him and then his bride a hearty kiss. The soft-spoken, gentle Mary Devlin Booth later confided to a startled acquaintance that such displays of affection had never altered her feeling that John Wilkes Booth was "the most false, malignant, wicked man" she had ever known.

Mary retired from the stage after she married; her husband was convinced that he could not be married to someone in the theater.

She dedicated herself happily to his career, believing, as she had since the first moment she saw him perform, that he was the finest actor who had ever lived. "A mission has been given to me to fulfill. . . . My ambition is to see you surrounded by greatness," she told him.

The Booths' first home was the Fifth Avenue Hotel, and Edwin found it difficult to leave his bride when he had to go on the road. He found her love enormously healing. To this son of the tumultuous, wandering Booth clan, family unity was taking on a serene new meaning, and he was thrilled when Mary told him that she was pregnant. Unwilling to be away from her then for any extended period of time, Edwin insisted that Mary accompany him on an English tour. On December 9, 1861, their daughter, Edwina, was born near London, in a bed her father draped with an American flag to compensate for a foreign birth. "Our child was, literally, born under the Stars and Stripes," he proudly proclaimed, easing, to some extent, the anguish of returning to a war-torn America.

Although he was very happy with Mary, Edwin had not yet "got the control of my devil," and his drinking was often a serious problem. Indeed, Edwin Booth had apparently reached the point where he could not keep alcohol from affecting a performance, but he managed to adapt his drunkenness to whatever role he was playing — "melancholy drunk for Hamlet, sentimentally drunk for Othello, savagely drunk for Richard III." However, he was now entering his thirties, and even this level of discipline was weakening. Like his father, Edwin abandoned all remaining restraints when the curtain fell.

In February 1863, Edwin left an ailing Mary and their baby in Dorchester, Massachusetts, where they were currently living, to play a run in New York. Mary had made light of her illness to Edwin, but she suddenly took a sharp downward turn. The doctors tried to summon Edwin to her bedside, but he was too drunk to pay attention to the telegram when it arrived at his dressing room before an evening performance. It was only after the theater manager hurried to him with a fourth wire, which he had opened himself while Edwin was on stage, that the news of Mary's condition got through to the actor, and by that time the last train for Boston had left for the evening.

Edwin Booth's adored wife and too brief love, Mary Devlin Booth

The next train was not until seven in the morning. After a sleepless, tormented night, Booth cabled his wife MARY, I'M COMING, but when he arrived, he learned that she was dead. During the funeral services, he followed Mary's casket, in which she lay surrounded by flowers, dressed in white silk, and wearing a miniature of Edwin on her breast. He was wrapped in a long cloak; above it, his beautiful face was filled with despair. More than one mourner noted his resemblance to the grief-stricken Hamlet when Ophelia was put to rest.

When friends expressed their hope that his acting would help to console him, Edwin answered, "The beauty of my art is gone. It is hateful to me. . . . It has become a trade." He was severely depressed and almost paralyzed with remorse. Because of his abandonment, Mary, like his father, had died alone, but for his daughter's sake he tried to pull his life together. His mother agreed to help take care of Edwina and to move with him to a house he had rented from George Putnam, the publisher, on East Seventeenth Street. A few months later, they moved again, to the house he bought on Nineteenth Street.

His daughter, by then nearly two, was, according to Booth, "the light of my darkened life." The most dramatic sign of Edwin's devotion to his daughter was that he stopped drinking. Now, instead of adapting his drunkenness to a role, he took his sorrow onto the stage, filling his performances with a breathtaking new level of tragic authority.

Although much original drama was being written and performed in the mid nineteenth century, Shakespeare's plays still formed the heart of serious theater. It was not uncommon for people to attend competing productions of the same play to compare one actor's interpretation of Hamlet or Richard with another's. Catering to this taste, actors often switched major roles in their own productions, as when Edwin and Edmund Kean took turns playing Othello.

One of the peripheral benefits of the excitement over theater was an apparent softening of the prejudice against actors. The more conservative press might continue to attack the profession, insisting that "a large number of those connected with the stage are libertines or courtesans," but it seemed likely that an actor of Edwin Booth's stature could win genuine public respect and social approval.

John Wilkes Booth, who frequently visited Edwin and their mother on Nineteenth Street, did not take any aspect of his brother's reputation in good humor. His own career was floundering, mainly because his voice, which had never been properly trained, had become alarmingly hoarse and was often too weak to sustain a performance. His dreams of stardom turned bitter, and his behavior became more and more outrageous. When he was with Edwin, whose loyalty to Lincoln and the northern cause was absolute, his political diatribes were taunting and ugly. Finally, Edwin declared that there would be no discussion in his home about the President, slavery, or the war, a dictum that made John Wilkes furious with frustration when he came to visit his mother.

At the same time as John Wilkes's distorted plans to achieve immortality by ridding the country of Lincoln's "tyranny" were taking shape, Edwin was having a very different experience with the Lincoln family. In March of 1865, while Edwin was waiting for a train in Jersey City, a tall young man fell off the platform just as a train was approaching. Moving with the swift grace he showed on stage, Edwin reached over and pulled the young man to safety. Robert Todd Lincoln, the President's son, immediately recognized his benefactor and introduced himself.

Less than a month later, on April 14, 1865, John Wilkes Booth shot Abraham Lincoln and, after a desperate attempt to escape apprehension, was himself caught and killed. Edwin's unrelenting grief for his tortured brother was matched only by the shame he felt for himself, his family, and for the acting profession. Whatever social gains that profession had begun to make had been destroyed by this terrible act. Theaters were closed while the country mourned the President, not just out of respect for Lincoln, but because they were perceived once again as places of evil.

Now Edwin could not bring himself to leave the seclusion of his Nineteenth Street house. As he told his neighbor the Reverend Henry W. Bellows, he felt he could never act again. Only financial necessity made him overcome his feelings; about nine months later he returned to the role of Hamlet at his favorite theater, the Winter Garden, in January 1866.

It took enormous energy and courage to force himself on stage for his opening scene. The *Herald* had published an open letter to the theater's manager, asking, "Can the sinking fortunes of this . . . manager be sustained in no other way than by such an indecent violation of propriety? The blood of our martyred President is not yet dry in the memory of our people . . . still a Booth is advertised to appear before a New York audience!"

Wanting to avoid confrontation, Edwin arrived at the theater early, but crowds were already massed outside, with police stationed nearby to calm especially unruly protestors. Not everyone was hostile, however, and when the curtain rose, Edwin saw many of his Gramercy Park neighbors in front rows. They were joined by the rest of the audience in nine rounds of applause when Edwin made his first appearance. Some people even left their seats to toss bunches of flowers onto the stage, and Edwin was so deeply moved that he could barely speak his lines. Yet William Winter reported in the *Tribune*, "He never acted better than he did on that memorable occasion."

Although he continued to act, Edwin Booth never again played in the city of Washington, and when he appeared in the familiar and nearby Baltimore, no flowers from Washington were accepted. The name of John Wilkes Booth was not to be spoken in his presence, nor did he ever say it himself. But his private mourning was clear to those who knew him well.

In 1867, the Winter Garden burned down, and Edwin, who was only thirty-four years old and at the peak of his career, decided to build his own theater. It was to fulfill all his theatrical dreams and associate the Booth name with glory rather than disgrace. Unequivocally dedicated to "high drama," the Booth Theater was built on the southeast corner of Twenty-third Street and Sixth Avenue, just above the boundary of the Ladies' Mile, New York's finest area for shopping and recreation. The Booth Theater took two years to complete and cost $2 million. It was, without a doubt, the most beautiful theater in the city. Made of New Hampshire granite and built in the Renaissance style, it was decorated with magnificent frescoes and bas-reliefs, deep carpeting, and a glorious crystal chandelier. It was also the most modern theater in the city, with each seat carefully placed for the best view of the stage.

The sunken orchestra pit, a new development in theater construction, kept the heads of the musicians from obscuring the stage. The enormous stage itself was designed to eliminate right angles in the wings, so stage sets seemed to extend to the sides as well as the rear of the proscenium. The scenery was moved by machinery instead of by hand, and with such comparative speed that it had the effect of "dissolving views."

Edwin hired fine artists to create scenery, described by one critic as gratifyingly different from the "rough daubs with which most playgoers are familiar." On February 13, 1869, when the theater opened, George Templeton Strong was in the audience, and he reported his admiring response to the Booth Theater in his diary: "Very handsome building, within and without. . . . It will be a humanizing and educating influence."

Edwin Booth eventually lost his theater in 1874 because of the financial drain of his lavish designs and production methods, but his response to bankruptcy was philosophical: "This is by no means the heaviest blow my life has felt. My disappointment is great, to be sure, but I have the consciousness of having tried to do what I deemed my duty. Since the talent that God has given me can be made available for no other purpose, I believe the object I devote it to be worthy of self-sacrifice."

As Edwin lengthened his work schedule in order to pay his debts, tragedy continued to dog him. Shortly after he opened his theater, Edwin Booth had married again, primarily to give Edwina a mother. But his new wife, Mary McVicker, became afflicted with mental illness after her baby boy died at birth. Her erratic, tormented behavior distressed friends, who could not bear to see more misfortune befall Edwin Booth.

As her condition worsened, Mary would not let Edwin out of her sight. Not only did she force him to spend every moment off the stage with her; she began to insist that he take her with him whenever he performed. The actor Otis Skinner remembered that the second Mrs. Booth would sit imperiously in her husband's dressing room through "all the robing and makeup, and in parts like Richelieu and King Richard, would gather up the trailing robes and, walking close behind, follow him to his entrance, never releasing him until his cue was spoken from the stage."

In 1881, Mary McVicker Booth died, releasing Edwin from the misery of his second attempt at married life. He and Edwina, who was then approaching twenty, spent a great deal of time together. Having left their Nineteenth Street home some time earlier, they took rooms at various hotels in the city between extended European and national tours.

Edwina's marriage in 1885 was a bittersweet experience for her father, for it put an end to this companionship, and made him feel homeless once again. Indeed, Edwina had barely left on her honeymoon when Edwin wrote to her, "Darling, I can't tell you how I feel — the separation has been a wrench to my nerves; but when in the midst of my selfishness the thought comes of your happiness and the good that will come to you, I cease to grieve." With Edwina gone, Edwin Booth returned to the road, but he always ended his tours with a triumphant performance in New York City, where, happily, Edwina had returned to live.

· · ·

It may have been the pain of renewed rootlessness that gave Booth the idea of creating a permanent and respectable setting for the congress of actors. The idea of establishing a club that would match any other gentlemen's club in the city in taste and refinement suddenly seemed a fitting project for the last years of Edwin Booth's life. "He wished," explained his friend William Winter, to have the Players' Club "represent all that is best in the dramatic profession, to foster the dramatic art, and to exalt the standard of personal worth among the actors of America."

It was equally important to Edwin Booth that actors work to deserve this kind of respect by making themselves into men of grace and learning. For that reason, he opened club membership to other professions as well. His regret at being poorly educated had never lessened, and he believed that actors might broaden their minds by socializing with men of diverse educational backgrounds.

Edwin Booth's club would be "a beacon to incite emulation in the 'poor player' to lift up himself to a higher social grade than the Bohemian level." This was a goal many doubted could be achieved. After acknowledging that "Mr. Booth's club is a very generous gift," one newspaper snapped, "Let's wait and see of what moral sort of use it's going to be to the profession. As for tiger-skin rugs and tiled fireplaces making a man's soul bigger or making a bum actor more a gentleman, go to! Thou talkest rot!"

Edwin Booth was undaunted by this type of response. In its way, his dream was as personal and clearly defined as Samuel Ruggles's had been when he planned Gramercy Park. No wonder, then, that Booth looked to Gramercy Park as the natural setting for the club. In April 1887, he purchased a four-story stone house at 16 Gramercy Park for $150,000, and hired Stanford White, now a neighbor, to remodel it into the Players' Club.

Although White waived his commission, the renovations almost doubled the original cost. The third floor was set aside as Edwin's personal quarters, with his bedroom in the front, facing the park. White supervised the interior decoration, but Edwin took an active role, even selecting the quotes from Shakespeare that would appear on the walls of various rooms (for the toilet, "Nature her custom holds, let shame say what it will"). Booth moved the costumes and

The Players' Club, realization of a life's dream and a living theatrical shrine

Edwin Booth's bedroom at the Players' Club,
where he often tossed with restless memories

memorabilia of a lifetime in the theater into the building, and persuaded many other actors to do the same, prompting Gramercy Park neighbors to wonder whether a museum rather than a club was taking shape in their streets.

But it was a club, and it followed Edwin Booth's design to the letter. Membership was mixed, as he had wanted it to be, with charter members including General William Tecumseh Sherman and Mark Twain, along with actors John Drew and Lawrence Barrett.

The Players' Club officially opened on midnight of New Year's Eve in 1888. Booth stood on a dais in the main hall, in front of a beautiful marble fireplace ornamented with carved masks of Comedy and Tragedy. The theater manager and playwright Augustin Daly had been elected vice-president of the club, and it was to him that Edwin handed over the deed, just as, fifty years earlier, Samuel Ruggles had handed over the deed of the park that could be seen outside the gracefully draped front windows.

Edwina had sent her father a laurel wreath with a card that began, "Hamlet, king, father . . ." and his friend Barrett read it aloud. When he reached the line "Tragedian, take the crown!" he passed the wreath to Booth, who was overcome with emotion. At the stroke of midnight, Edwin held a loving cup high in the air, poured wine into it from his father's flagon, took the first drink, and passed it on so that it went from hand to hand in the circle the men had formed, their faces glowing in the candlelight.

Edwin Booth did not go to bed until 5:00 A.M. on New Year's Day. When he came downstairs at one o'clock, he was thrilled to find the grill room already serving lunch to members while other members were settled in deep armchairs in the library, reading from the collection he had started with his own library of a thousand books. It was as if the Players' Club had always existed, he told Edwina later that day, his voice brimming with the pride of accomplishment. Some of New York's "best men" were already filling the rooms, and he happily predicted that his club would, from that day on, "no doubt, be the rendezvous of the choicest."

7

ART
AND
ARCHITECTURE

✦

STANFORD WHITE, who had generously donated his services to Edwin Booth in designing the Players' Club, was invited by Booth to become a charter member. Booth believed that White, whose architectural designs were already having an extraordinary impact on the changing image of Manhattan, would add luster to his new club.

Among the architect's early commissions were several renovations in Gramercy Park, where descendants of the men who had first followed Samuel Ruggles to the neighborhood were making changes that suited their own, often more elaborate tastes.

As a native New Yorker, Stanford White could well appreciate the special history and charm of Gramercy Park, and in the 1880s he lavishly renovated one of its houses for himself. Still later, the architectural firm of McKim, Mead, and White moved to the area, opening offices on Fifth Avenue and Twentieth Street.

White was born on Tenth Street on November 9, 1853. His father was the well-known drama and music critic Richard Grant White, and his mother, Alexina Black White, shared her husband's passion for music and literature. Their son showed a precocious interest in both art forms, but he dreamed of becoming a painter. He and his brother Richard visited their aunt in Newburgh every summer, and Stanford would spend hours by himself wandering along the Hudson River, sketching in a book he always carried with him.

Stanford White desperately wanted to study painting formally, but despite the richness of the family's cultural life, money was short, and he was forced to earn a living well before he could complete even a general education. Painting was too uncertain a profession, his parents agreed, so it was decided that he would learn architecture, a field that required no formal schooling at the time.

The profession was taught through apprenticeship, and thanks to the influence of his father's friend Frederick Law Olmsted, Stanford was taken on by the most important architect of the time, Henry Hobson Richardson. Whether the lusty tastes of the master architect influenced Stanford White's famous sensual appetites is not certain. There is no doubt, however, that Richardson — who was given to serving rich meals and magnums of champagne on a huge, black-oak table in a dining room with a blood-red ceiling — was a man who lived life on a grand scale and approached architecture in the same way.

Stanford White fell completely under Richardson's creative spell and was grateful for the older man's conviction that architecture was neither a trade nor a profession, but a fine art. Nevertheless, over the years, White still regretted not having become a painter. While traveling in Europe in 1878, he wrote to his mother, "To think that at Douai — a wretched little French town — there could be a portrait by Paul Veronese that nearly squeezed tears out of my eyes! To think that such a lovely thing could be done, and that I could not do it! And above all, Raphael's wax head at Lille — the loveliest face ever conceived by man. Architecture seems but poor stuff compared with things like these."

Yet there was no more exciting a time to be an architect in New York than during the late nineteenth century, when the city was reshaping itself for the new era just ahead. Manhattan had not only spread out over the years, its new streets stretching in all directions;

the city also moved dramatically upward. George Templeton Strong had viewed many of the city's first tall buildings as "hideous, top-heavy nightmares," but Manhattan's skyward climb was now a fact of life.

New York had always defined itself to a large extent by its buildings, and these new "skyscrapers" were apt symbols of the city's booming social and financial power. By 1870, the population of the city itself was close to a million, with nearly a million and a half more people living in what would later be called the greater New York area. Imports and exports passing through the city were up to nearly $600 million worth a year, and more goods were manufactured in Manhattan than in any other city in America.

This tremendous industrial and residential growth meant that more offices and more living space were needed, and, with the invention of a safe and reliable elevator, developers began to plan vertically as well as horizontally. The new six-, eight-, and ten-story structures dwarfed New York's older three- and four-story hotels and offices. To many amazed tourists, New Yorkers had, in effect, "added a new dimension" to space.

By the 1880s, with the development of a steel skeleton for structural support, the city climbed even higher. In 1888, construction began at 50 Broadway for the Tower Building, planned to be an amazing thirteen stories. Crowds gathered every day at the site, offering predictions of disaster. Indeed, the owner of an adjoining building was so terrified that the new structure would collapse under the first strong wind that he moved his offices to a safer corner. One Sunday morning in 1889, when construction had reached ten stories, a storm with eighty-mile-an-hour winds tore through the city. New Yorkers' curiosity was greater than their need to keep dry, and Broadway was packed with people waiting to see the new building topple to the ground. When the storm ended, the onlookers returned home, sodden and astonished, leaving the building standing firmly in place.

The actual need to build upward created another major change in New York life. In the 1870s, the first apartment houses began to appear around Manhattan. They were generally referred to as

"French flats," since the concept of multiple housing had begun in Europe, but once they were introduced in New York, the idea quickly caught on. Bachelors and small families saw that they could live well without going to the expense of building or buying large private homes, and this was an important consideration to middle-class New Yorkers.

A successful physician might not earn more than $10,000 annually, but by now it cost close to $2000 a year to rent even a modest house; an Irish cook was paid $18 a month, a chambermaid $12; a good nursemaid would not work for less than $15 a month. Butter cost fifty cents a pound; a dozen eggs were the same price; chicken at a decent market cost twenty-five cents a pound; good quality beef was never less than thirty-five cents a pound. Without the added income of successful investments, supporting a comfortable and fashionable life was a considerable challenge in late-nineteenth-century New York.

Apartment houses clearly met a need, and in 1875 alone, 112 apartment buildings went up in New York City, against the objections of traditionalists, who felt that these new living quarters were little better than the tenements of the immigrant class. To their minds, no lady or gentleman would ever "consent to live on mere shelves under a common roof!" As more apartment houses were built, however, they became increasingly elaborate and could be found in even the most fashionable parts of the city. In fact, the most popular locations for apartment houses in the 1870s and eighties were near the famous Ladies' Mile and near Central Park, which seemed a perfect background for the grand proportions of these new dwellings. Many apartment buildings soon took on the look and quality of luxurious hotels, often providing hotel services; and almost all of them designated space for servants' quarters, since it was obvious that such elegant living accommodations would require considerable staffing.

Walt Whitman found these "cloud-touching edifices" — hotels, offices, apartments — gloriously grand, a celebration of the city's achievements, but others shared George Templeton Strong's early distaste for what seemed symbolic of the city's rampant materialism. In the developers' rush to build new buildings, lower Manhattan had already lost many of its original landmarks. St. George's Chapel, which was built in 1749, at Beekman and Cliff streets, had been torn down, for the land on which it stood had increased in value from £500 to $500,000. The *World* commented scathingly on this example of urban progress: "At present the graves of Revolutionary heroes serve as a depository for ashes and rubbish. Vessels are emptied daily from the windows adjoining, on places where a hundred years ago, were carved the sacred words never to be effaced, '*Requiescat in pace.*'" The federal government had even sold the nearby Middle Dutch Church to the Mutual Life Insurance Company, which razed it for an office building, and Cyrus Field bought a pre-Revolutionary mansion at 1 Broadway and replaced it with a commercial building.

If the city landscape was infinitely taller and more crowded at the end of the century, it was not much cleaner than it had been in earlier days. With all the destruction and construction, even the finest shops or homes fronted streets that were covered with mud and debris. With uneven paving blocks, broken horse-car rails, and iron girders from the new elevated railways, even a brief walk through the city could be genuinely hazardous. Some years later, on a visit to New York, Rudyard Kipling found the city as appalling as it had been during the days of the scavenger pigs. Indeed, he called New York a "long, narrow, pig-trough, first cousin to a Zanzibar foreshore, or kin to the approaches of a Zulu kraal."

The telegraph, electric, and telephone wires that had begun to crisscross lower Manhattan also contributed to the dangers and delights of city life. Some poles on Broadway had as many as fifteen horizontal arms, each laced by a dozen wires, and telephone poles could hold as many as fifty crossarms. The esthetic effect was dreadful, according to a visitor from Australia; it was as if the whole city was "crossed with gigantic cobwebs." Even worse was the fragility of the wires, which could tear in bad weather, halting not only service but traffic, threatening the life of anyone who tried to make his way on foot.*

---

*In 1884, the city passed a law that all wires had to be laid underground.

Hazards aside, New York's social and industrial growth was drastically altered by the advent of phones and electricity. Fashionable New Yorkers were hanging messenger callboxes on the walls of their homes or offices. A mere turn of a crank of one of these little boxes brought a messenger boy from the nearest telegraph office to pick up and deliver your telegram. Alexander Graham Bell exhibited his "speaking telephone" in the city in 1877, and the Bell Company opened its first office on Nassau Street in 1879, charging subscribers $60 a year.

When Stanford White returned from Europe in 1879, the New York telephone directory was a card that listed the 252 people who had availed themselves of this amazing service. There were no telephone numbers; you simply gave the operator the name of the person you wanted to speak with and were connected with numbers up to thirty miles away! By the early 1890s, phone service could travel much farther; there were nine thousand subscribers, and between the hours of 8:00 A.M. and 6:00 P.M. around 120,000 calls were made by fast-paced businessmen.

To be sure, the pace of city life was astonishingly fast. New Yorkers were often described by Europeans as "nervous," "spasmodic," as if they were "bent on making amends for having come into the world half an hour too late." To Stanford White, with his bright red hair and flaming mustache, Manhattan's pace was wonderfully appealing, perfectly suited to his instincts and temperament. He seemed to be everywhere within the city's stretching boundaries, hurrying down the street, always talking, exulting in some new delight he'd just discovered. "You haven't seen it?" he'd ask about a painting or play or restaurant. "Why, it's the finest thing of its kind in America! It's bully! It's wonderful . . . gorgeous!"

Home from Europe, his imagination fueled by Old World style, Stanford White wanted to make New York "gorgeous," to transform it into a city as lavish, decorative, and brilliantly colored as the life that flowed on its streets every day. While working for Henry Hobson Richardson, White had met another young architect, Charles Follen McKim, and they had become fast friends. Now, on White's return to New York, he joined McKim and another architect, William Mead, in forming the new architectural firm of McKim, Mead, and White.

Their offices, located first at 57 Broadway overlooking New York Harbor, had the atmosphere of an artist's atelier rather than that of a business establishment. Often, fevered discussions about the changing shape of American art went on far into the night among the partners and such visitors as William Merritt Chase, Francis Millet, John Singer Sargent, and Stanford's dearest friend, the sculptor Augustus Saint-Gaudens.

Charles McKim, William Mead, and Stanford White, whose architectural partnership influenced taste throughout the country

The three partners were markedly different from one another in style and temperament. Mead was a restrained, moderate man, and McKim was scholarly and deliberate, although very charming. He was not, however, as charming as Stanford White, who approached his work with infectious festivity. White was as much an impresario as he was an architect; he produced dramatic settings for his clients' lives. In his eagerness to create, he never wasted time worrying about the rules of his profession. When one of his draftsmen reported in despair that the axis of their plans couldn't be achieved, White replied, "Then bend the axis!"

The principle that united the partners was H. H. Richardson's belief that architecture must be practiced as a fine art, and they did not hesitate to borrow from European influences to carry it through. White in particular believed that it was foolish for America to try to be completely original in its architectural designs.

Paul Goldberger, the present architectural critic of the *Times*, has explained that White's great later works, like the original Madison Square Garden, Madison Square Presbyterian Church, and the Metropolitan and Century clubs, show that "White did not so much want to imitate historical architecture as to exploit it, taking advantage of its cultural associations while working them into something new and very much his own."

Although Stanford White designed churches, libraries, and public buildings, his special delight was the transformation of American homes. In New York, this meant breaking away from the prevailing brownstone structures, those handsome buildings which suggested both British baronial elegance and New World democracy. (It was difficult to judge the relative wealth of the owner from the exterior design.) White challenged these sober façades, changing the colors of Manhattan and transforming it from, according to a journalist, "one of the dullest, brownest, most monotonous cities on earth to one of the most interesting and beautiful."

Stanford White's remodeled houses often featured blond brick, white marble, burnished terra cotta, and Missouri blue limestone. The exterior renovations opened into magnificently appointed rooms that displayed the homeowner's wealth. Furnishings were a cheerful mix of oriental rugs, Italian marble, and French antiques, always bright and light in comparison to tastes of the past. In fact, the firm was sometimes teasingly referred to as McKim, White, and Gold.

By the 1880s, conspicuous consumption had reached new heights, and Manhattan's growing affluent population unabashedly enjoyed what would later be called the Gilded Age. Stanford White's family had valued culture and intellectual accomplishment above money and material possessions. But the clients who hired him to build or renovate their homes were often people whose social station was determined primarily by their enormous wealth. Postwar prosperity and an absence of personal taxation had helped multiply many family fortunes to a dazzling degree.

Some of New York's more thoughtful citizens found this skyrocketing prosperity very discomforting and worried about the widening division between the city's classes. With typical foresight, Samuel Ruggles, friend of many of the city's elite, had cautioned in the 1850s that "the very exuberance of our commercial property, our rank and rapid growth in wealth and luxury, are scattering far and wide the seeds of a deadly disease." He and his son-in-law George Templeton Strong even urged their fellow trustees of Columbia College to divest the profits gained from large real estate holdings and use the money for the good of the community. In the 1880s, the journalist Jacob Riis shocked many New Yorkers with his book *How the Other Half Lives*, a grim picture of the appalling poverty in such areas of the city as the Lower East Side, where as many as 333,000 people were squeezed into every square mile.

Many of the city's millionaires did try to share some of their wealth by building libraries or funding hospitals. At the same time, they spent huge sums on luxuries. James McCabe, a southern journalist who wrote several guidebooks to the city he both loved and deplored, reported in 1882 that New York society was the most extravagant in the world. A rich woman's annual wardrobe might cost over $20,000, and when she went to Saratoga Springs for the summer, she might bring as many as sixty dresses and several trunks filled with lingerie.

Fashion itself had changed dramatically. In earlier times, a fashionable woman needed only a morning frock, a dress to go visiting in, a low-necked dress for dinner, and a ball gown. Now, she needed almost as many dresses as hours in the day, and women of means ardently avoided wearing the same dress twice. Dress was also more provocative. The crinoline and the bustle were on their way out, and in their place were close-fitting dresses and skirts draped in the back with intricate arrangements of ribbons and fringe. Daytime skirts now ended at the ankle, revealing pointed boots worn with black stockings. For a gala evening dress, the form-fitting skirt might end in a train, and black stockings were exchanged for white. Perhaps to compensate for the narrowed skirt, bodices were elaborately trimmed with lace, and sleeves were often enormous. Favored fabrics were silk, pongee, velours, and velvet, in such wild colors as crimson, heliotrope, and yellow. And all this glamour seemed only to reinforce the desire to live in conspicuous, glittering style.

These outfits were acquired along the astonishingly lavish shopping strip known as the Ladies' Mile, which began at Ninth Street and Broadway and ran up to Twenty-third Street, reaching its apex at the intersection of Broadway and Fifth Avenue. Macy's, Tiffany's, Arnold Constable, Lord & Taylor, and B. Altman were only a few of the department stores found along the Ladies' Mile. A new business phenomenon, these elaborate emporiums met the acquisitive needs of the emerging upper classes, and shopping became the major pastime of wealthy women. Indeed, the department store was a symbol of their station. What clearer sign of social status than for a lady to have nothing to do but shop?

The precedent for these "commercial palazzos" had really been set before the war by New York's first super merchant, A. T. Stewart. His original dry-goods store had been near City Hall Park, but in the 1860s Stewart took advantage of the public's desire for "things" and moved uptown. The cast-iron building he erected ran the full length of Broadway between Ninth and Tenth streets. The store was entered through a vast rotunda, and employed nearly a thousand people. (In this era of the shopgirl, eight hundred of these employees were women.) It carried everything from the finest fabrics and men's furnishings to Aubusson carpets. On the fourth floor, hundreds of sewing girls turned lace and velvet into gowns cut in expensive patterns of the customer's choice.

Stewart's determination to profit from the desire for consumption made him a stern taskmaster. Employees were fined for anything from being late for work to eating or sitting down on the job. It was not uncommon for an inexperienced worker to find that the first month's wages had been eaten up by these penalties.

A festive procession of fashion and beauty, the Easter Parade up Fifth Avenue past the Croton Reservoir

While husbands slaved, their pampered wives grew ever more bold. An artist depicted married life in New York.

THE HUSBAND   MARRIED LIFE IN NEW YORK   THE WIFE.

An exclusive and elegant gathering of high-fashion ladies in one of Delmonico's sumptuous dining rooms

Silk, satin, velvet, lace, fringes, and bows. Hundreds of sewing girls at A. T. Stewart's follow the patterns chosen by elegant customers.

A hundred and fifty thousand shoppers attended opening day of the bargain counter at Siegel-Cooper's department store, September 1896.

The splendor of Stewart's store was matched and often eclipsed by stores that opened farther along the Ladies' Mile, such as Stern's on Twenty-third Street near Fifth Avenue. Soon commerce so filled the formerly residential streets with traffic and noise, it is no wonder that the rich began to look even farther uptown for a place to build their new mansions.

The desire for spectacular living quarters that marked the Gilded Age was not completely without precedent. In 1859, a multimillionaire named Leonard Jerome had moved into what George Templeton Strong called an "elegant and commodious" red brick and white marble villa on East Twenty-sixth Street, very much out of

place among the surrounding brownstones. A white-and-gold ballroom held up to three hundred dancers, and seventy guests could fit
in the breakfast room alone. The Jerome house also had a private
theater that accommodated six hundred, and evening entertainments
were often furnished by several of Mr. Jerome's young female pro-
tégées. He adored beautiful women, and when his wife and three
daughters were traveling in Europe for extended periods, he was free
to enjoy the company of other, preferably complaisant ladies. (On
one of her visits abroad, Jerome's daughter Jennie met Lord Randolph Churchill in London. He proposed marriage almost immediately, and despite Mrs. Jerome's protests that Churchill wasn't rich
enough or good enough for her beautiful daughter, the young people
did marry. Their son Winston was born in 1874.)

Mr. Jerome was known for lavish parties, with champagne and
eau de cologne pouring from crystal fountains, but the parties thrown
by prominent New Yorkers in the eighties and nineties were no less
extravagant. Two thousand dollars' worth of champagne might be
consumed in a single evening, a dinner might cost more than
$5000, and it could take $15,000 to $20,000 to give a truly
grand ball.

McKim, Mead, and White's clients, who ranged from the merely
wealthy to the astonishingly rich, were quite familiar with such ex-
travagances, as evident in the grand designs they commissioned for
their new homes. In their retreat from commerce, they moved first
to Fifty-ninth Street and then beyond, on Fifth Avenue facing Central Park or one block east on Madison. In keeping with Stanford
White's philosophy, no single architectural style dominated, and the
eclectic results amazed European critics.

An English journalist reported that "each millionaire seems to
have commissioned his architect to build him a mansion of any ancient style from Byzantine to the last French empire, provided only
it was in contrast to the style of his neighbors."

One of the most controversial new houses in New York was
Charles Tiffany's, created for him by Stanford White in the sparsely
inhabited regions of upper Madison Avenue. Opinion varied greatly
on how successful White had been in blending Classical architecture
with New World novelty. In England, Sir Edmund Gosse, writing

his *Impressions of America,* said that "the Tiffany House on Madison Avenue is the one that pleased me most in America. . . . I think that it is the most beautiful domestic building that I have ever seen." The *Real Estate Record,* however, complained that the house seemed "not so much to make a picture out of a building, but to make a building out of a picture."

In fact, it was this very quality in American architecture that pleased observers like Sir Edmund most of all. "In America," he wrote, "I have seen a tendency to combine the arts, to make the sculptor and the architect work together, that seems to me to be the right thing. I was delighted to find men like John La Farge, Augustus St. Gaudens and Stanford White — painter, sculptor and architect — working together."

Augustus Saint-Gaudens, considered the leading American sculptor of his time, was five years older than White. Before they met, their careers ran parallel; both worked on Trinity Church in Boston — Saint-Gaudens for John La Farge, White for H. H. Richardson.

Their actual meeting was an event they liked to recall. One afternoon in 1875, Stanford White was in a downtown building where Saint-Gaudens had a studio. As he came down the stairs, White heard someone singing in a deep bass voice. He paused to listen, first to the andante from Beethoven's Fifth Symphony and then to an exuberant French rendition of an aria from Mozart's *Don Giovanni.* When the impromptu recital ended, White looked into the room, and at the sight of the other ebullient redhead felt an immediate kinship that continued for the rest of his life.

"Every time I see Saint-Gaudens, I hug him like a bear!" White would say. The hundreds of letters he wrote to his friend over the years began with salutations like "My beloved Snooks" or "My dear old fellow" or even, with unself-conscious affection, "Beloved." As for Saint-Gaudens, "Stanny's" opinion of his work was the only criticism he ever really cared about or that would make him question his own creative judgment. One time, when White was not pleased with a medallion head Saint-Gaudens was making of him, the sculptor immediately destroyed it.

Augustus Saint-Gaudens was born in Dublin, Ireland, on March

Augustus Saint-Gaudens at his easel. In his sculptures, he captured humanity's grandeur and its elusive yearnings.

1, 1848, but was brought to America as an infant. After a stay in Boston, the family moved to New York, and when Augustus was twelve, his father relocated to Gramercy Park, where he opened a shoemaker's shop on Twenty-first Street. Mr. Saint-Gaudens's designs were handsome and attracted a large number of loyal customers, including Horace Greeley and the Peter Cooper family. The nursemaids of Gramercy Park also brought the neighborhood children to Bernard Saint-Gaudens's shop, where Mrs. Saint-Gaudens would make them leggings to match their winter coats so that they could keep dry and warm while playing in the snowy park. It was strange to the young Augustus, when he walked around the neighborhood delivering shoes, to see the same children through the park gates and not be able to go in and talk with them, as he did so easily inside his father's store.

When Augustus was thirteen and still attending school on Twentieth Street, he and his father had a conversation similar to the one that took place a few years later in the White household. "My boy, you must go to work," Mr. Saint-Gaudens announced. "What would you like to do?" Without a moment's hesitation, Augustus, who had already been seized with a passion for drawing, answered, "I don't care, but I should like it if I could do something which would help me to be an artist."

The senior Saint-Gaudens was not surprised by this response. He had seen his son's drawings on school slates, drawing paper, and, after an occasional burst of creative enthusiasm, on whitewashed walls. In his memoirs, Augustus recalled an "ambitious painting, on the fence in the backyard, of a Negro boy with a hole in his trousers, through which the bare knee was seen." Many years later, he could still recall the overwhelming sense of creative pleasure at attempting this more complex portrait: "The joy derived from that knee!"

The Saint-Gaudens family apprenticed Augustus to a cameo cutter named Louis Atvet. "It was the fashion of the time," Augustus explained later, "for men to wear scarf-pins with heads of dogs, horses, and lions cut in amethyst, malachite, and other stones." Atvet, whose work was sold at Tiffany's and the shops of other fine jewelers, was a difficult, harsh man. "I can only describe my years with him as composing a miserable slavery," Augustus remembered.

Perhaps because he felt bad about the grueling conditions of his son's life, Bernard Saint-Gaudens took fourteen-year-old Augustus to Peter Cooper's institute the following year. Students had to be sixteen to enroll, so Saint-Gaudens carefully planned a strategy. He had Augustus bring along a large roll of brown paper, and while he spoke to Abram Hewitt, Cooper's son-in-law, who was fortuitously visiting the school that day, Augustus covered the paper with drawings. The age rule was waived for this impoverished but talented Gramercy Park neighbor.

Over the next two years, Augustus attended art classes at Cooper Union six nights a week. The classes, at which students worked from both casts and live models, ran from 7:45 to 8:45, but Augustus often worked at his drawing board until midnight. He was usually so exhausted that his mother had to pull him out of bed in the morning, but he knew that sleep was a small sacrifice for learning as much as he could about art.

It may have been Atvet's resentment over his apprentice's obvious absorption in art that caused him to explode one day and fire Augustus because he had not swept the floor after lunch. The boy quietly removed his overalls and went back to the Gramercy Park shop to tell his father what had happened. To the surprise of father and son, Atvet turned up shortly afterward, apologized for his outburst, and offered Augustus $5.00 more a week to come back. With a glance at his father, the sixteen-year-old boy refused. "This was no doubt the most heroic act of my existence," Saint-Gaudens would often say, "if not the only one having real style."

Augustus soon found a job with another cameo cutter who was far more congenial than Atvet. Ready to move on in other ways, too, he shifted his studies from Cooper Union to the National Academy of Design, then in its new, more convenient building. This elaborate replica of the Venetian Doge's Palace stood at the far end of the Ladies' Mile, right next to his father's shop in Gramercy Park, on Fourth Avenue and Twenty-third Street.

The National Academy of Design had been founded in 1826 by a group of thirty European-trained artists who were determined to offer American training to Americans. Indeed, they aimed to cultivate a uniquely American art. Samuel Morse, one of the founders and the academy's first president, like his friends Samuel Ruggles and Peter Cooper believed that art must be an accessible and appreciated part of a developing society.

Membership in the National Academy of Design was open to anyone. Women's classes, however, were held separately, and female students had to be at least twenty-one years old to attend the life class, where the male model could not be completely nude. There were also classes in painting, sculpture, architecture, and engraving, and, in the tradition of Cooper Union, tuition was free.

The flowering of the academy was connected to New York's development as a center of wealth and culture during this postwar period. Before the Civil War, Americans were relatively unsophisticated about and uninterested in art, and the galleries that tried to stimulate their interest or elevate their tastes with exhibits of primarily European art were unsuccessful. Then, in the last years of the nineteenth century, the climate began to change. As the country expanded, landscape art captured the attention of Americans, and the growing numbers of artists who studied abroad and came home to show the interesting foreign influences on their own work made such painting more acceptable to American viewers. In addition, the new materialism made many people eager to have portraits to hang in their parlors, and to develop art collections that demonstrated their affluence.

The National Academy of Design would have its critics, including Augustus Saint-Gaudens, who came to find it too conservative and unresponsive to new ideas. Nonetheless, it was through its training of artists, through generous endowments to sustain their work, and through regular exhibitions that the public came to know the work of those who were to become America's "Old Masters." Painters like Winslow Homer, John Singer Sargent, and William Merritt Chase, as well as sculptors and architects like Daniel Chester French and Charles McKim, were all members of the National Academy of Design.

Augustus Saint-Gaudens was quickly recognized at the academy for his talents. Although he was always grateful for the opportunity Cooper Union had given him to hone his artistic skills, he found the atmosphere of the academy far more advanced than that of the institute. At the academy, the emphasis was on art for the sake of excellence, rather than as a way of earning a living. As the gifted, passionately determined young man sat over his drawing table in a quiet studio, the silence "broken only by the shrill whistle of an ill-burning gas jet," dreams of honor and glory fired his mind and hands, making him once again indifferent to the fact that he would have little chance to sleep before the next morning's demands.

One other difference between the academy and Cooper Union was that many of the academy's students were wealthy, and as the year 1867 approached, many of them were making plans to visit the Paris International Exhibition, at which the best art from countries all over the world was to be displayed. To Augustus's surprise and delight, his father managed to arrange a trip for him. "I went over in steerage," Augustus recalled, "where I was sicker than a regiment of dogs." But the moment he walked out of the Gare du Havre, clutching his heavy carpetbag, he was overcome by the beauty of the glittering French city.

Augustus did not return home after seeing the exhibition. He had decided before he left New York to study sculpture at the École des Beaux-Arts. In spite of the relative hospitality toward artists in the United States, he wanted to study abroad, because few of the newly established leaders of American art were willing to spend their time teaching. At the Beaux-Arts, Saint-Gaudens would be able to study with the sculptor François Jouffroy — famous for his religious and military statues — whom he greatly admired. To support himself, the aspiring sculptor cut cameos in a studio near his little room in Montmartre.

Part of Jouffroy's attraction as an instructor was that many of his students won the coveted Prix de Rome, which enabled them to study in Italy. To his dismay, Augustus did not receive the award during the first two years he was at the Beaux-Arts, but "the steadiness of Jouffroy's compliments consoled me for my inevitable failures in direct competition," he said, recalling the arrogance of his youth. "These failures did not for a moment discourage me . . . or create any doubts in my mind as to my assured superiority."

Augustus rewarded himself by going to Rome on his own in his third year of study at the École des Beaux-Arts. The ancient Italian city immediately became more precious to him even than Paris. "It was as if a door had been thrown open to the eternal beauty of the classical," he wrote. There was no question that in this atmosphere Augustus Saint-Gaudens could create sculpture that would "astonish the world."

Saint-Gaudens's major creation during this period did not astonish the world, but it did establish him as a serious sculptor. Supporting himself once again by cutting cameos, he began work on a statue of Hiawatha. (He would later comment that trying to sculpt an Indian was an inevitable early "mistake of every American sculptor.") He was able to complete a plaster cast of the piece when he was subsidized by a visiting New York lawyer, Montgomery Gibbs, who planned to ship the cast to America for exhibition and eventual sale.

In a letter to Saint-Gaudens, in the early 1870s, Gibbs wrote, "I am sure the last thing of which I stand in need is a marble statue, particularly on the dimensions of your 'Hiawatha.' But for the fact that I sympathize very strongly with you in your struggles to maintain yourself here until your genius and labors shall have met the reward to which I feel they are entitled, I would not have thought of attempting any arrangement by which you might be enabled to complete your large work and make yourself known."*

After finishing a clay model of Hiawatha, Augustus came home, his money for passage advanced by Mr. Gibbs. But he missed Rome terribly, and a year later he went back. While in New York, he had made inquiries about a competition the government was sponsoring for a statue of Admiral David Glasgow Farragut, and it was his plan to begin working on some sketches as soon as he returned to Italy in the summer of 1873. By the summer's end, winning the commission for the Farragut statue had become a major goal.

One sultry evening in Rome, Augustus was introduced to a young American woman whose name, in an unlikely coincidence, was Augusta. She would soon be given the nickname Gussie, to match his own sobriquet, Gus. With her brother as chaperon, Augusta Homer had come to Italy from her home in Massachusetts to study painting and, on a less happy note, to seek medical help in Vienna for her deafness, which seemed to grow worse every year. The deafness both saddened and attracted Augustus Saint-Gaudens. This young man, who devoured every sensory experience, found it hard to imagine how one could go through life with so much of its sound muffled or lost. At the same time, Augusta's lack of hearing gave her a watchful, listening air that made being with her seem unusually intimate, as if the two were closed off alone together in the busiest room.

The young people saw each other often in Rome. One night, in a flight of high spirits, Augustus bought "an inexplicably high silk hat" and, in a pouring rain, without an umbrella, marched gaily across the Piazza di Spagna to Augusta's rooms to amuse her with his

---

*Mr. Gibbs's enthusiasm for the project waned, although he continued to be a strong supporter of Saint-Gaudens. But a family friend, former Governor Edwin Morgan, saw the model in Rome and paid Augustus $800 to carve Hiawatha in marble for his own collection.

elegant new headgear. Whether it was Italy's romantic backdrop or genuine passion, the relationship intensified, and by the time Augusta was due to return to Massachusetts in June 1874, they were engaged. All that stood in the way of their marriage was Augustus's securing the Farragut commission.

Augustus returned to America to be closer to the selection process, but he was again so homesick for Rome that he left the faucet running in his studio to remind him of the sounds of the fountain in the Barberini Gardens. And the roaring vocalizing that brought Stanford White to his door was a manifestation of the nostalgia for the grand music that was so much a part of his love of European life.

In December 1876, the Farragut commission was awarded to Augustus Saint-Gaudens, and he and Gussie made plans to marry. He was free also to return to Europe, and this time he decided to go to France to begin preliminary work. Two days after their wedding, in Roxbury on June 4, 1877, Gus and Gussie sailed for Europe. Not long afterward, in one of the many letters they exchanged across the ocean, Augustus asked Stanford White to collaborate with him on the Farragut statue by designing its pedestal.

The location of the statue had been an issue of much debate and the subject of much additional correspondence between the colleagues. White, in New York, was able to explore the possible sites and finally sent word to his friend that he recommended the Twenty-sixth Street corner of Madison Square: "The stream of people walking down Fifth Avenue would see it at once. It would also have a more northerly light, and you wouldn't have any white reflections to dread."

The Farragut memorial was unveiled on May 26, 1881. Thirty-three-year-old Augustus Saint-Gaudens stood alongside his beaming father as Quartermaster John Knowles of the navy parted the canopy that hid the sculpture from view. Sailors in dress whites stood at stiff attention while the artillery fired a nineteen-gun salute.

There the admiral stood, feet planted solidly on his quarterdeck, holding binoculars to peer into the horizon, his uniform seeming to stir in a strong sea wind. The crowd, after a moment's silence, burst into appreciative, patriotic applause. The base of the statue, built of bluestone, won its own praise, though there would be some detractors who found its unconventional shape "primitive . . . a series of stone slabs on end."

Nonetheless, critical response to the Farragut statue was overwhelmingly positive. The art critic Kenyon Cox declared that there was no display of "cold conventionalism" in this work, but, rather, "a penetrating imagination which has got at the heart of the man." A long piece in *The American Architect* pointed out Saint-Gaudens's unique ability to produce a sculpture with such a "strong national accent . . . while the general canons which bind in all ages the sculptor's art have not been in the least transgressed."

This ability to combine European tradition with a singularly American style was of course the characteristic that would always mark Stanford White's architecture and designs. The two redheaded men were exuberant as they saluted the Farragut project's success. Working together had been wonderfully rewarding, and it could only lead to many more years of mutual triumph.

8

CLASHES
OF
CULTURE

———————◆———————

AUGUSTUS SAINT-GAUDENS became an overnight sensation after the unveiling of the Farragut statue. Leading society figures like Cornelius Vanderbilt immediately wanted bas-reliefs and bronzes of family members by Saint-Gaudens to display in their new mansions. More to the sculptor's liking, he was also sought out to do works of major historical and artistic significance.

Among Saint-Gaudens's commissions was a large sculpture of Colonel Robert Gould Shaw, a member of a prestigious New England family who led a regiment of black soldiers in the Civil War and was killed in battle; another was a statue of Abraham Lincoln for Chicago's Lincoln Park, which received unprecedented praise when it was unveiled in October of 1887. There would be a complex tribute to victory in war — the General William Tecumseh Sherman Memorial in Central Park — and a haunting piece of sculpture commissioned by Henry Adams in memory of his wife, Clover, who had committed suicide. The statue, which stands in Washington's Rock Creek Cemetery and portrays a seated woman with one hand held up to her shrouded face, has often been called *Grief*. As Mark Twain

Grief, *a haunting monument to memory and regret.*
The statue of Clover Hooper Adams by Augustus Saint-Gaudens.

wrote of his first glimpse of the work, "All human grief is shown in this sad figure."

Saint-Gaudens was not spoiled by his fame, though he welcomed the opportunity it gave him to meet people he admired. From the moment he had read Robert Louis Stevenson's *New Arabian Nights*, for example, he was eager to know the man whose "stories set me aflame as have few things in literature." He asked a mutual friend for an introduction to the poet and let it be known that he'd be pleased to have Stevenson sit for a bas-relief. The ailing Stevenson, in America for treatment of his worsening tuberculosis, found Saint-Gaudens immensely likable, "a splendid straightforward . . . fellow," and agreed to the sittings. To save the poet's strength, Saint-Gaudens took his easel to Stevenson's rooms at the Albert Hotel on Eleventh Street. Saint-Gaudens's experience as a cutter of cameos had made him skilled in the art of bas-reliefs, and he immensely enjoyed capturing a friend's likeness in a handsome bronze medallion.

In the decade that followed his work on the Farragut statue pedestal, Stanford White created some of America's most stunning residences — in New York City as well as in such enclaves of the wealthy as Mamaroneck, Long Island, Newport, Rhode Island, and Great Barrington, Massachusetts. He continued to collaborate with Saint-Gaudens, designing the frame for the disquieting Adams statue and the magnificent presidential chair for the sculpture of Lincoln, by Daniel Chester French, in the Lincoln Memorial.

White would go on to create many of this country's architectural treasures — New York's Washington Memorial Arch, several buildings on the University of Virginia's famous campus, the Century, Metropolitan, and Harmonie clubs in Manhattan, and the city's Judson Memorial and Madison Square Presbyterian churches. The critic John Jay Chapman would liken the Madison Square church to "a Byzantine jewel" in its lavish, polished perfection.

Saint-Gaudens and Stanford White each sang the other's praises to anyone who would listen. And they still best enjoyed each other's company. From the moment Saint-Gaudens and his wife settled in their first apartment in Paris, it was filled with visitors — usually other artists such as Frank Millet and John Sargent, who had come to Europe to paint or study. But no visitor delighted Augustus as much as Stanford White, who arrived there with Charles McKim in the spring of 1878.

Expecting an influx of Augusta's relatives, Saint-Gaudens welcomed the architects' invitation to join them on an eleven-day jaunt. A letter Gussie wrote to her parents explained her husband's absence as "a business trip. Mr. McKim wants Augustus to do some bas-reliefs on something that he's going to be the architect of."

To be sure, the three men did visit twenty towns to study local treasures, but the trip did not go quite as Gussie reported it. When the journey was over, Stanford White contentedly remembered that, along with the awesome art and architecture at Beaune, they "came across two very attractive and inseparable things — good wine and pretty women. . . . At Tours . . . we are met by the loveliest of landladies who smiled at us in the softest way. Somehow or other, three or four times, I could not find my room and had to go downstairs to ask where it was — only to meet McKim and Saint-Gaudens on the same errand."

White frequently stayed with the Saint-Gaudenses when he stopped in Paris during the ensuing months of independent travel, and the sculptor's wife enjoyed having him around. White, however, never felt that Augusta suited his dear Gus. As he wrote to his mother from Paris, "She is very kind . . . mends my clothes and does all manner of things," but he found her little more than "an animated clothes rack," and worried that her fierce concern about money would dampen Augustus's artistically extravagant spirit. "Why fate should have ordained that such a man be harnessed to such a woman, heaven only knows," White continued.

And, indeed, by the summer of 1880, when the Farragut statue had been completed and Gussie was expecting her first child, there were already signs that the marriage was not entirely satisfactory for Saint-Gaudens. Both before and after their son, Homer, was born in New York that September, Gussie traveled regularly to her family's home in Massachusetts or to some other more congenial climate to pamper her health. While his wife was away, Augustus spent more and more time with Stanny White and other friends, a practice he continued after Augusta returned for good.

Among the many clubs Stanford and Augustus belonged to was the Tile Club, which met each week in the basement of a building on Tenth Street. Most of the group were artists; the club had taken its name from a member's artistic experiments with tiles. At their meetings, the members analyzed one another's work; often they went on sketching trips that were noted as much for merriment as for productivity. On one typical excursion, aboard a barge traveling up the Hudson, the men were costumed for a Roman dinner served by "models" wearing skimpy togas.

Whatever the evening's diversion, there were always frolicsome partners available for rich and powerful men in these openly licentious years. More than France or England, America observed the double standard. The sexual appetites of men and women were regarded as entirely different, and there was almost always a distinction between the sort of woman a man married and the sort who fired his passion. And, because a woman's social status and financial security depended on marriage, she tended to be tolerant of an errant husband, as long as he remained a generous provider.

The double standard also dictated a very different code of behavior with one's own or the opposite sex. Although men now spent more time socially with their wives than they had in Samuel Ruggles's day, the almost total exclusion of women from all the important clubs in New York City reflected the general feeling that a man was most himself when he was with other men. According to the social critic Cleveland Amory, a man could act out the double standard even further by making discreet contact from his club with the other women in his life. If a paramour wished to arrange a meeting, she could bring a note of invitation to the club, where it was delivered by a "tactful servant . . . on a silver tray, butter side down; this was of course on the chance that the lady might be connected, in some fashion, with another member."

Many of the women involved in these illicit affairs were charming and refined, but they came from humble backgrounds that made them ineligible for moneyed marriages. With society offering so few occupational opportunities to women, their only route to enjoying life's luxuries was often through the merchandising of their physical charms. Along the Ladies' Mile alone, there were more than forty "temples of love," most of which advertised in the *Gentleman's Directory*, openly distributed throughout the city. In this guide, a man could find listed the addresses of the better houses of prostitution and the names of the favorite girls there, along with explicit descriptions of their charms.

The Ladies' Mile was also the territory of scores of streetwalkers, young women considered beneath the girls of "rare personal attraction" who entertained in high-priced brothels, but above the streetwalkers who worked less fashionable neighborhoods. Since the style of beauty favored by most men of the day was a soft childish face and a body that combined youthful slenderness with seductive curves, these "nymphes des paves" or "cruisers" tended to be young and innocent-looking. Thus, as they promenaded along the Ladies' Mile after dark, their slow stroll lit by gaslight, they could easily have been daughters of visiting merchants who had gone out for a breath of air while their fathers waited protectively at their hotel.

Moralists, as always, blamed social greed for the spread of vice in the city. It was even rumored that many of the brothels employed married women, who, tempted by advertising and seductive arrays of merchandise, had left respectable husbands and families to earn money for worldly goods.

In some shabbier parts of the city, men could still meet women at "concert saloons," where sidewalk barkers lured customers with promises of free music, liquor, and "the prettiest waiter girls in town." For the most part, however, in the late nineteenth century the erotic invitation to the upper-class man was more subtle. Some of the finest restaurants, such as the Parisian-styled Martin's, allowed unescorted young women, usually struggling actresses or singers, to sit in their foyers. When a gentleman arrived to dine, he might strike up a conversation with one of these ladies, and it was highly unlikely that she would refuse his invitation for supper and ensuing diversions.

This was also the age of the chorus girl, who often performed in the scantiest dress to set off her provocative turns around the stage and the double-entendres of her songs. The men in evening clothes who sat in the front rows of the theater, night after night, were more than willing to take these charming "stars" to lavish suppers at Martin's or the Café des Beaux-Arts after a performance. A popular gesture for a generous escort was to arrange for the restaurant's Gypsy violinist to meet him and his beautiful companion at the door and follow behind her, playing in time to her undulating walk as they made their way to their table. This was known as "making an entrance," and established female stars wouldn't think of entering a restaurant any other way. The girl who dreamed of becoming the next Lillian Russell tended to be well disposed to the gentleman who gave her such an opportunity to be seen by New York society.

·　　·　　·

Even in this sexually indulgent atmosphere, Stanford White's carnal appetites were considered shocking. The architect's reputation was haunted by stories, such as the one about a party he gave for Diamond Jim Brady, where every guest was supposedly given a naked girl after the guest of honor unfurled his nude companion from a broad red ribbon. One party he attended was to bring White particular notoriety, because it involved a girl barely older than a child. According to a sensational account, the assembled gentlemen were first entertained by dancing girls wearing only bands of sleigh bells around their ankles. Then a cake was wheeled in by musicians singing, "Sing a song of sixpence, a pocket full of rye" — and "a shining child of exquisite beauty . . . arose in the centre of the pie." Her seductive swaying as she emerged caused one man to leap to "the sacrificial pastry" and lift "the pink darling to the floor; then cradling her in his arms he disappeared. The storm burst. A tornado of twirling flesh, the atmosphere punctured by shrieks of laughter and growlings of wild men."

Stanford White always took the disapproval of society lightly, and even those friends who were occasionally upset by his disregard of convention defended his behavior as being typical of many other men. Indeed, many highly placed men were rumored to be heavily involved with perverse forms of sexual pleasure. Pornography was big business in nineteenth-century New York, and it was rumored that some of Manhattan's wealthiest men were avid collectors. An influential social movement called Purity Reform had as its goal the elimination of pornography. The members feared the effects that pornography would have on society (but many artists would be frustrated by the reformers' inability to tell the difference between graphic depictions of lust and art).

In any case, however much a voluptuary Stanford White was, he was also a very loving man. In fact, his resistance to marriage stemmed primarily from his observing the failures of love in the marriages of his close friends Charles McKim and Augustus Saint-Gaudens. "You no catchee me marry," he protested, and yet, during a trip west with Augustus in 1883, he unexpectedly announced that he was going to marry a young woman named Bessie Smith. Augustus was incredulous and by no means enthusiastic.

After their marriage, on February 7, 1884, the new couple took off for a six-month tour of Europe. (Augustus Saint-Gaudens would miss his friend fiercely, announcing when White returned that "it was like champagne, having him around again.") During his honeymoon trip, Stanford White bought tapestries, paintings, rugs, and furniture that he would later use in his home in Gramercy Park. White modernized the house, which had been built when the neighborhood was new, opened it up with windows, glass-walled alcoves, and skylights. In the first-floor hall, red marble pillars rose up more than ten feet. There were gilded lions, tiger-skin rugs, painted Baroque wooden ceilings, and black-and-gold Spanish-tiled doorways. It was a grand mix that stunned people when they first glimpsed its splendor, but even critics agreed that the décor was successfully eclectic.

A room of opulent display, bearing the celebrated decorative touch of the proud but often absent homeowner, Stanford White

Stanford White's theory of the placement of furniture was that no matter how many pieces went into a room, they should not serve as borders, lined up piece by piece against the walls. Instead, he placed chairs and sofas all around a room so that people could sit actively inside the living space. Chairs were also placed for the optimal view-

ing of particular paintings, with the paintings themselves often lean-
ing on easels or against walls.

Much as he loved his Gramercy Park home, Stanford White
quickly tired of the restrictions of marriage, and eventually he would
have what amounted to a second home — an apartment in the tower
of Madison Square Garden. The garden was built by an investment
group that included Stanford White, J. P. Morgan, and Andrew
Carnegie, among others; they were determined to build the "most
magnificent amusement palace in the world." When the huge arena
opened in 1891, it could accommodate more than nine thousand
people to watch full orchestras, corps of "ballet girls," elaborate cir-
cuses, and animal shows. White regularly designed artificial worlds
for the garden, precursors of the make-believe environments that
later made Walt Disney a legend. At Madison Square Garden, one
could visit replicas of the Globe Theatre in London or Dickens's Old
Curiosity Shop, or, at Christmas time, a whole village made of toys.

The real excitement of the building, however, was the tower that
rose three hundred feet above the sidewalk, dominating the skyline
above Madison Square. When he was designing the tower, White
decided that something wonderful should crown it, as a beautiful star
topped a Christmas tree. Naturally, he turned to his friend Saint-
Gaudens to create the garden's ultimate showpiece.

White knew that Saint-Gaudens had always wanted to sculpt an
idealized nude figure, and he invited him to create one for the tower.
Knowing his friend's dedication to art over money, White had no
qualms about telling Saint-Gaudens that he wouldn't be able to pay
him a fee but would pay all his expenses. Saint-Gaudens could then
give free rein to his imagination without having to worry about a
budget that sacrificed art to economy.

When White agreed that the goddess Diana would be perfect to
grace his tower, Augustus began work on the project. Diligently
studying mythology, as well as other sculpted and painted images of
the goddess, he constructed his own exquisite nude of gilded beaten
copper. Saint-Gaudens's Diana stood ethereally slim and hauntingly
graceful on the toe of one foot, seeming as nearly airborne as the bow
and arrow she held in front of her. At night, searchlights played

around the statue, silhouetting her against the dark New York sky and causing tourists at nearby hotels to wonder at the daring of this amazing city. During the day, *The Mercury* noted wryly, the building generated even more traffic. The magazine noted a "marked change in the character of the frequenters of Madison Square. Formerly this beautiful little park was the gathering place of children. . . . In their place the Square is now thronged with club men armed with field glasses."

The model for the figure of Diana was a woman named Dudie, who lived over the Tenth Street room where the Tile Club held its meetings. At the rate of fifty cents an hour (posing with her clothes on came considerably cheaper), Dudie was a popular model for many of the club's members. The model for the statue's face, however, was a woman named Davida Clark, the name Augustus bestowed on a beautiful Swedish woman whose loveliness he likened to Michelangelo's David.

Augustus Saint-Gaudens, sensualist and lover of beauty, had many affairs, but he truly loved Davida, and did not leave her after the first flush of passion cooled. Davida posed for many of Saint-Gaudens's most stunning pieces, and it is speculated that she didn't pose for Diana's body only because she was busy with her infant son, whose father was Augustus Saint-Gaudens. Augustus set mother and child up in a home in Connecticut, where he was a frequent visitor.

Even with a mistress and infant son ensconced fairly close to home, Saint-Gaudens was far less cavalier about his affairs than Stanford White, whose marriage certainly did not seem to interfere with his highly visible social life. In fact, one of the most familiar sights of New York night life was White arriving at the opera, alone or with a party of friends. Dressed in stylish evening clothes and a flowing cape lined with red silk, he took his seat in the center of the orchestra section just minutes before the curtain went up, thereby ensuring that everyone could see him. Invariably, the opera house was packed, for music was thriving in the prosperity and cultural self-consciousness of the late nineteenth century. From 1854 through the early 1880s, the Academy of Music, on Fourteenth Street and Irving Place, was the premier location for opera and concerts in the city, although concerts were also given at Steinway Hall, just around the corner. The world's most famous singers regularly appeared at the academy, from the legendary Adelina Patti — considered by many to be the greatest singer in the world — to Jenny Lind, whose loyal fans were also fevered in their enthusiasm.

George Templeton Strong had found the academy's productions uneven in his time, though he was grateful for its presence. One night in 1867, after strolling home from a less than thrilling evening at Irving Place, Strong noted one reason not to bemoan his continuing lack of spare cash. "Were I a millionaire," he wrote in his diary, "I might be weak enough to own a box at the Academy of Music, and feel bound to appear in my place two nights out of three. How dreadful that would be! . . . I sat but three acts of laborious feebleness, and then came off, with the sensations of a Norwegian who has been supping on bread made of sawdust, and no butter."

Strong may have been unsure about the joys of owning a box at the opera, but in the 1880s and nineties numbers of affluent men hungered for its social cachet. This is how New York acquired its first Metropolitan Opera House, and, consequently, why the Academy of Music declined. The Academy of Music had only eighteen boxes, and they were all held by members of those first New York families who made up the Knickerbocker aristocracy. Mrs. William Vanderbilt, wife of one of the "upstart" millionaires whose money and social power went only as far back as the Civil War, was outraged at being passed over for a box, even though her fortune was undoubtedly greater than that of any family who had one. (When William Vanderbilt's father died in 1877, he left an estate of $94 million, which had already nearly doubled in value.) Refusing to let old money triumph over new, the nouveaux riches decided simply to build their own elegant hall.

Vanderbilt quickly enlisted the support of other millionaires who had been turned down at the academy and hired an architect to build the Metropolitan Opera House. Standing triumphantly apart, on Broadway and Thirty-ninth Street, it was a clear symbol of Manhattan's expanding boundaries. The opera house was constructed of yellow brick in the Italian Renaissance style, and was called by the owner of the Academy of Music "the new yellow brewery on Broad-

*The Metropolitan Opera House, where old society and aspiring social leaders
came to hear music and appraise one another's splendor*

way." But the press duly noted after opening night in 1883 that it
had more than enough boxes for its determined and affluent subscribers: "The Goulds and the Vanderbilts and people of that ilk perfumed
the air with the odor of crisp greenbacks. The tiers of boxes looked
like cages in a menagerie of monopolists."

The managing of the opera house was uncertain, because its owners knew little about running such an establishment, and in fact probably cared little about it once they had achieved their goal, but all
New Yorkers who loved opera gained in the competition between the
Met and the Academy of Music. New York became flooded with
song as the very best performers from all over the world appeared
on its two stages. As an Italian journalist marveled, "The artists,
because of the war between the young and the old aristocracy, pock-
eted veritable treasures, and the public had the luck to hear in a single
winter all the living celebrities of the world, a luxury certainly not
afforded by any capital in Europe."

· Leopold Damrosch not only managed the Metropolitan; he

formed the New York Symphony and the Oratorio Society. His son Walter carried on the effort to present fine concerts of classical music to New Yorkers after Leopold died in 1885. Here, too, there was a new level of sophistication, though George Templeton Strong, who for several years served as president of the Philharmonic Society until his death, in 1877, might have remained skeptical about public interest in symphonic music. "Our civilization is still of low grade," he complained after a private recital given by the president of Columbia College, Frederick A. P. Barnard. To the dismay of both Barnard and Strong, the ladies and gentlemen sitting in the president's finely appointed parlor had been less than attentive. "An assemblage of New Yorkers will gossip and cackle during one of Mozart's melodies or Beethoven's symphonies," Strong later wrote disdainfully. When he formed the Church Music Association in 1870 to present choral and orchestral concerts of religious music, Strong passed out handbills and program inserts that cautioned people against talking during a performance. To his surprise, not only were the concerts successful, but his message was heeded, perhaps because the music was religious.

Another reason for improvement in audiences' behavior was the growing practice of giving private musicales. Socially ambitious citizens began to realize that they would offend their hosts by inattentiveness during an expensive musical offering and risk not being invited back. Most of these musicales were financed by wealthy men, but the city had a few women who were independently wealthy enough to support their own social lives. Many of these women found their way to Gramercy Park. The neighborhood, with its mix of intellectual and artistic residents, always seemed to value wit and accomplishment more than tradition or social conformity.

In 1850, two sisters from Ohio, Phoebe and Alice Cary, bought a house on Twentieth Street with income earned from the sales of poems to literary magazines and the popular press. Their Sunday evening receptions were attended by a variety of well-known people from within as well as outside the bounds of Gramercy Park. Horace Greeley regularly stopped by for an hour or so and drank two cups of sweetened milk before going off to the *Tribune* offices to write his

Monday morning editorial, and P. T. Barnum could often be found regaling a group of visitors with colorful stories that might or might not have been true. Invariably, there were female guests who were known outside this welcoming circle as too "advanced" or "strong-minded," such as Susan B. Anthony and Elizabeth Cady Stanton. These two apostles of women's rights had become part of the Gramercy Park neighborhood through their work at the Women's Bureau, a house on Twenty-third Street funded by a wealthy female philanthropist, where Anthony and Stanton published a weekly journal of social protest.

Emma Thursby. With her sweet, strong voice, she became one of the first American women to forge an international musical career.

Thirty years later, one of the most coveted invitations in New York City was to the receptions known as Thursby Fridays, given by another female resident of Gramercy Park, Emma Thursby. Miss Thursby was a concert singer who began her career as a church soloist in Brooklyn. By 1877, she was a major presence on the concert stage and had signed a $100,000 contract with the impresario

Maurice Strakosch, the brother-in-law and former manager of Adelina Patti. Under the guidance of her manager, she traveled all over the world, entrancing audiences wherever she appeared. When not on the road or traveling abroad, Miss Thursby lived with her sister in the luxurious first cooperative apartment building in New York City, 34 Gramercy Park (even though one of the several building regulations mandated no practicing of the piano before 8:00 A.M. or after 6:00 P.M.).

Of course there were thousands of New Yorkers who would never be invited to such a reception nor have the price of a ticket to a Thursby concert, the New York Symphony, or a Mozart opera. But the legacy of New York's patron saint helped to close this gap. Peter Cooper's institute was still dedicated to the enlightenment of all New Yorkers, and free concerts were given at Cooper Union by an orchestra called the People's Symphony. Residents of the Lower East Side could ride their shabby wagons up to Astor Place and, in the Great Hall, forget their troubles while the music washed over them.

In 1887, a group of prominent New Yorkers commissioned Augustus Saint-Gaudens to create a tribute to Peter Cooper, who had died in 1883. The statue took ten years to complete, for Saint-Gaudens was determined to honor his first patron's memory properly. The sculptor made twenty-seven designs on paper and in clay before he was ready to begin work on the actual figure, which was erected under a marble canopy designed by Stanford White.

Augustus Saint-Gaudens often wondered what Peter Cooper would have thought of life in New York in these final years of the nineteenth century. The great inventor would surely have been thrilled by the uses of electricity and rejoiced in the improvements made in daily life by the electric fan, the iron, the stove, the sewing machine, and the electric street car. He would have been overjoyed that the soon-to-be completed Brooklyn Bridge would make Cooper Union accessible to so many new students. But the proper old man would surely have raised an eyebrow at some of the habits of modern society.

Increasingly, in New York, there was a preference for novelty and style over sober convention. One of the most obvious examples at that time was a salon on Irving Place run by Elsie de Wolfe, a flam-

The flamboyant Elsie de Wolfe, awaiting the arrival of carefully selected guests, who, no matter their social station, coveted her invitations

boyant actress turned interior decorator, who eventually married England's Lord Mendl. De Wolfe had bought the house, which had originally belonged to Washington Irving, with her lover, a woman named Bessie Marbury. Miss Marbury had actually grown up in the Gramercy Park area and had gone on to make an important career as a literary agent, representing the most famous European writers in America and often serving as a producer of their work on stage. Wags soon referred to the two women, who made no attempt to disguise their relationship, as "the Bachelors." The label bothered Elsie not at all; one of the blithe mottoes she embroidered on silk pillows (which were copied and sold by shops all over the country) was "Never Complain, Never Explain."

Between 1897 and 1907, Sunday afternoons at the Irving House, which had been decorated to resemble an eighteenth-century French town house, became one of the city's chief attractions. Such stars as the opera singer Nellie Melba and the actress Sarah Bernhardt mixed with Henry Adams and the newspaperman Charles Dana. "Ordinary" New York society people who received invitations were often amazed by the Bohemian assemblage. Mrs. William Astor was so thrilled with the company that she told Elsie, "I am having a Bohemian party, too." Elsie tried not to show her amusement when she asked what guest list would provide this racy mix and Mrs. Astor replied, "J. P. Morgan and Edith Wharton!"

Elsie's style of decorating her house to serve as an elegant backdrop for her life intrigued her Gramercy Park neighbor Stanford White, and it was with his encouragement and assistance that she became the country's first female interior decorator; indeed, the first person to turn the talent into a profession. Until then, interior design had been the purview of architects like White, or of people who sold furnishings and antiques. But when White designed New York's first important club for women, the Colony Club, he recommended Elsie de Wolfe to do the interior. There was considerable resistance from the board of governors about hiring this gifted but inexperienced woman to decorate a major new institution, but White waved away their objections. "Give it to Elsie," he said shortly, "and let the girl alone! She knows more than any of us."

When it came to arranging for commissions, Stanford White was generous with all his friends. In the winter of 1890, when the Players' Club decided that an official portrait of Edwin Booth should hang in the main parlor, White suggested John Singer Sargent as the artist. Sargent, who went around to see Booth at his home in Gramercy Park, found the actor dressed for traveling, his luggage already on its way to the train station. Booth generously agreed to postpone his trip for a few days, during which time he would pose for as many hours as possible. Although the actor was cooperative, Sargent confided to White and Augustus Saint-Gaudens that he was distressed by the sadness in his subject's demeanor, and feared the final product would not please the club committee.

To be sure, as the century drew to its end, Edwin Booth did not look to the future with optimism. The bitter events of the past seemed to dominate his life, though he tried to hide his despair from his daughter and his friends. At night, after leaving other members of the club to their brandy, cards, and billiards, he climbed the stairs to his room and struggled for sleep. More often than not, he left his bed after hours of tossing and turning and sat beside the window, looking out at the silvery gates and shadowed trees of moonlit Gram-

The accumulated woes of a lifetime cast their shadow on canvas.
John Singer Sargent's portrait of Edwin Booth.

ercy Park. These were the "vulture hours," he explained with a sad
smile to friends, during which he battled with a lifetime's "vulture
thoughts."

Booth's health began a steady decline after a small stroke in 1889,
even though he continued to act until 1891. After that, he busied
himself with his grandchildren and with the running of the Players'
Club, lunching there every day when he was in town. Afternoons,
he read Shakespeare in the club parlor, sitting under the Sargent
portrait (which indeed had pleased him and the club members with
its haunting likeness) and then took a promenade around the park,
usually pausing to play a round or two of marbles with the neighborhood boys. On April 18, 1893, he suffered another, far more
severe stroke, and was in and out of a coma for seven weeks. Just
before midnight on June 6, a severe electrical storm ripped through
Gramercy Park, extinguishing all the lights. His daughter, Edwina,

who was sitting at his bedside as the room went dark, cried out in distress. When the lights flashed on again a moment later, Edwin Booth was dead.

The newspapers made much of this remarkable drama, but the death soon after of another Gramercy Park resident was even more dramatic. As the century ended and a new one began, Stanford White, who was at the peak of his career, was spending more and more time in his Madison Square Garden tower apartment, giving parties that were rumored to be as uninhibited as anyone could imagine. Among the decorative touches to aid an evening's pleasure was a red velvet swing, on which, it was said, beautiful young showgirls were encouraged to swing high, wide, and unencumbered by clothing.

For some time, White's name had been connected with that of Evelyn Nesbit, a magnificent young chorus girl in the famous song and dance group known as the Floradora Girls. After a time, the relationship ended, and Evelyn eventually married Harry K. Thaw, a millionaire from Pittsburgh with a reputation of decadence and instability. Thaw was reportedly obsessed with the need to hear every detail of Stanford White's imaginative use of Evelyn's lovely body, and some speculated that he found his wife's recollections erotically stimulating. In any event, on the evening of June 25, 1906, both Stanford White and Mr. and Mrs. Thaw attended a performance of a revue called *Mamzelle Champagne* at the Roof Garden theater of Madison Square Garden.

Perfunctory greetings were exchanged, but Thaw appeared to grow more and more agitated, jumping up from the table several times to talk to other patrons. More than once, he seemed to be walking toward Stanford White, but would stop and simply stare at him. Evelyn, dressed in a white embroidered dress and a huge black picture hat, tried to get her husband to return to her side. Suddenly, as the comedian Harry Short finished a chorus of "I Could Love a Thousand Girls," three shots rang out, and Stanford White, fifty-three years old, fell dead on the floor of the building he had designed for the enjoyment of life.

A lurid trial and even steamier newspaper accounts followed. It

The flawlessly beautiful,
dangerously entrancing
Evelyn Nesbit

Stanford White, the charming
sensualist whose appetites were as
rich and varied as his talents

became the mission of his closest friends to clear White's name of many of the scurrilous accusations that were made about his life in explanation of how he had come to such an end. In a letter he wrote to the editors of *Collier's Weekly*, Augustus Saint-Gaudens, who was by then fighting a losing battle with cancer of the colon, said, "As the weeks pass, the horror of the miserable taking-away of this big friend looms up more and more. It is unbelievable that we shall never see him again. In the thirty years that the friendship between him and me endured, his almost feminine tenderness to his friends in suffering and his generosity to those in trouble or want, stand out most prominently. That such a man should be taken away in such a manner in the full flush of his extraordinary power is pitiable beyond measure."

The loss of his friend seemed to sap the little strength left in Saint-Gaudens's gaunt body, and after a brief rally he fell deeply ill, beyond the reach of anything but death. He spent his last weeks at his farm in New Hampshire, in the house that Stanford White had remodeled for him in 1885. His son Homer described how his father, who lay watching the changing New England sky late one afternoon, said quietly, "It's very beautiful, but I want to go farther away." A few days later, on August 3, 1907, he died.

Charles McKim, the survivor of that close, bawdy, and astonishingly productive late-nineteenth-century group, heard the news while traveling in Edinburgh. In memory of his friend, he visited the Church of St. Giles, which was decorated with Augustus's bas-relief of Robert Louis Stevenson. "The pilgrimage there was the nearest I could come to him," McKim wrote, "but it was a comfort to me . . . to see his great work constantly surrounded by the public. The gulf between him and the next best man in his art will long remain unfilled."

9

LITERARY
PURSUITS

———————◆◆———————

BOTH Augustus Saint-Gaudens and Stanford White had been charter members of the National Arts Club, founded in 1898 by Charles de Kay, the literary and art critic of the *New York Times*. De Kay's original aim had been to unite all the arts — painting, sculpture, music, and literature — and to allow serious patrons to mingle with the men and women whose works they admired and collected. Admitting women as members was a revolutionary move, but it seemed particularly appropriate when the club relocated to the hospitable streets of Gramercy Park in 1906. Seventy-seven of the club's 1065 charter members were female "art workers" or energetic supporters of the arts.

The new location of the National Arts Club was next door to the Players' Club, in a magnificent building that had formerly been the residence of Samuel Tilden. Tilden, who was elected governor of New York in 1874, had resigned from office to run for the presidency, and he was back in New York on the night of the election in 1876. He spent the early hours of the evening receiving reports on voting tallies with his friend and neighbor, Abram Hewitt, at a hotel

The National Arts Club,
meeting place for artists and patrons

on Union Square. Well before midnight, it seemed certain that Samuel Tilden had won the election, and he headed for Gramercy Park, where a cheering crowd waited to congratulate the new President-elect.

Of all the city's newspapers, only the *New York Times* held back a declaration of victory the following morning. Governor Tilden had most assuredly captured the popular vote, and he had 184 electoral votes to Rutherford B. Hayes's 181 — but, the *Times* explained, 185 votes were needed for election. Florida was not yet reported, and a surge of Republican effort had successfully rallied that state's votes for Hayes. Rumors of fraud and political pressure made their unhappy way to Gramercy Park, but despite challenges and recounts, the Electoral Commission ultimately accepted the Hayes majority of one vote and declared him President of the United States. From then on, Tilden quietly but consistently referred to the decision as "the crime of 1876."

With ties to neither Albany nor Washington after the election, Tilden spent much of his time in Gramercy Park, where he kept most of his vast book collection, considered one of the finest private

Samuel J. Tilden, who lost the presidency by one electoral vote.
His house became the National Arts Club.

libraries in the country. Like George Templeton Strong, Tilden would spend freely to acquire an original manuscript, such as Thomas Jefferson's diary, or a rare, beautifully bound first edition. Tilden had a good deal more to spend than did Strong; he had established a successful practice as a corporate lawyer at a time when business was booming as never before in the country's history. His investments were shrewd and farsighted, and he died a very wealthy man, leaving an estate of more than $5 million.

During the last four years of his life, Tilden read — or had read to him — more than four hundred books, an accomplishment that gave him immense satisfaction. Since he had never married, it seemed fitting that he left most of his estate in trust for the construction of a grand new library and reading room for New York City. Unfortunately, the will was contested by relatives, and by the time adjustments had been made, the monies appropriated for the library had shrunk to $2.25 million. In 1895, when these still generous funds were added to the endowments for the Astor and Lenox libraries, the city agreed to build a huge, free public library on Fifth Avenue, on the site of the demolished Forty-second Street reservoir.

After Tilden's death, in 1886, his house was allowed to deteriorate. Without the wonderful collection of books, its forty rooms seemed to have lost their character. De Kay's decision to make the mansion the new home of the National Arts Club enabled it to recapture some of its rich literary history.

Many writers, including Mark Twain, were early members of the National Arts Club, for by the end of the nineteenth century, New York City was clearly the pre-eminent center of publishing in America. All over the country, aspiring poets, novelists, and journalists dreamed of becoming part of Manhattan's literary life — brilliant salons, writers' clubs, restaurants where celebrities routinely dined and toasted the author of a play they had just attended.

And there certainly was no better place to be than in New York if one was already a successful writer. Visiting authors, like Charles Dickens years earlier, became the toast of the city from the minute they stepped onto its new asphalt-paved streets. Henry James, back in New York after six years in Europe, was astounded by the number of invitations he received, not just for dinners and banquets, but for lavish daytime socializing. "People — by which I mean ladies — think nothing of asking you to come to see them before lunch," he complained.

The English novelist and poet Charles Kingsley was swept up in the social whirl even before he came ashore. A welcoming committee from the Lotos Club, which was then in the Gramercy Park neighborhood, on Fifth Avenue and Twenty-first Street, boarded his ship while it was still in the harbor to make plans for a banquet to be held in his honor. "But gentlemen," said the exasperated writer as he struggled for a sight of the long-awaited Manhattan skyline, "I am trying to view the approaches to New York. I cannot make any engagements now!"

The Lotos Club vied for literary influence with the Century Club, which had been founded in 1847 for a prestigious charter membership of a hundred artists and writers. The Century was seen as the more conservative of the two, less open to the "realistic" work of some of the newer writers. The club was presided over by Edmund

Clarence Stedman, a Gramercy Park resident who earned his substantial living on Wall Street but was a ranking arbiter of literary taste. Stedman produced prodigious amounts of poetry and officiated poetically at all sorts of important events. In fact, his presence at state funerals, honorary banquets, and building dedications was so certain that he came to be known by the press as America's "universal official poet."

Stedman also wrote critical articles that appeared in major magazines and were later collected into books. A major theme of his essays and regular Saturday night discussions at the Century Club was the "misguided" desire of modern writers to tell the stories of "lowly common men" in their writings. A staunch advocate of literary romanticism, he admonished William Dean Howells, editor of the Boston-based *Atlantic Monthly* and the leader of the realistic movement, not to "banish idealism entirely from our tastes."

The aspiring writer who wanted to make a name for himself as a writer in New York in the 1870s and eighties either joined Stedman's camp or hoped to be taken up by the rebels who met at the Lotos Club. There, on Saturday nights, actors and musicians gave informal performances that the general public would never see. The most celebrated evenings, however, were literary banquets where writers dominated, or more informal gatherings where important new American authors spoke off the record about their often controversial work. Over a fine meal and brandy, members heard Mark Twain, the playwright Bronson Howard, who was exciting audiences with a new realistic style of drama, William S. Gilbert and Arthur Sullivan, or Oscar Wilde, who had the whole city gossiping even before he first arrived there in 1882.

Gilbert and Sullivan's opera *Patience* was a huge success at the Standard Theater, and it was widely known that the character of the "fleshly poet," Reginald Bunthorne, was modeled on Oscar Wilde. The D'Oyly Carte Opera Company decided to take advantage of the writer's reputation and brought Wilde to the United States for a series of talks that would be sure to generate even more interest in their production.

When he arrived in New York Harbor, Wilde told the customs

officer that he had "nothing to declare but my genius." He seemed to invite being stared at as he ambled down Fifth Avenue or took a seat at the Standard Theater or a table at Delmonico's. His shoulder-length black hair and pale skin were set off by a velvet suit, black silk stockings and buckled shoes, a Regency silk hat, a long, puce overcoat, and a white walking stick in his lavender-gloved hands. Wilde had brought along with him dozens of letters of introduction to New York society, and many of the recipients were willing to avoid the troublesome question of where the line should be drawn between a person's moral values and his art. They found Wilde's outrageous reputation titillating, and his suite at the Grand Hotel was constantly filled with flowers, usually delivered with invitations to parties being given in his honor.

The literary world, however, was less immediately hospitable, largely because Edmund Clarence Stedman despised everything he thought Wilde represented in the changing literary scene. Even when Stedman's dear friend Mrs. John Bigelow, one of the literary set's leading hostesses, gave a dinner for Wilde at her Gramercy Park home, Stedman angrily declined to attend. He informed the venerable lady that any parties she gave for him in the future would be considered far less an honor, now that her courtesy had been extended to a man of Oscar Wilde's character.

But Stedman's opinion of Wilde was ignored by more and more members of New York's literary society. The newspapers even took up the "Wilde case," properly seeing it as a kind of a last struggle between realism and romanticism, between the old guard and the experimental new writers who wanted to enter the twentieth century free of the prudery and idealization they felt had deadened most nineteenth-century writing. A decade later, Wilde's writings, then represented in America by Bessie Marbury, enjoyed even greater success in the United States, despite the author's conviction in London for sodomy in connection with his homosexual affair with Lord Alfred Douglas, a conviction that had put a stop to all production or publication of his work in England.

In the midst of all this literary controversy, there was one area of neutral territory for members of both factions, and this was the home of Richard Watson Gilder. Gilder, a distinguished poet, was also the editor of *Scribner's Monthly*, which evolved into the influential journal, *The Century*. He was a strikingly handsome man, tall and slender, with fine features and large, mesmerizing eyes. The artist Cecilia Beaux first saw Gilder when he gave a lecture on poetry at Chickering Hall and remembered, "Even across the space of a lighted hall, full of people, the dark brilliancy of his eyes held one with an almost magic force." The color was beyond "black" she said, but a combination of "intense darkness and light" that seemed symbolic of his whole "luminous and richly drawn person." An immensely charming and witty man, Gilder was modest and not apt to take himself too seriously — characteristics that served him well as friend, poet, and certainly as an editor.

Richard Watson Gilder, wise editor, resolute friend, a man of candor and honesty, who would not "coddle the commonplace"

In later life, Richard Watson Gilder would commission a stunning apartment house of duplex suites to be built for his family and other tenants right on Gramercy Park. But for the first fifteen years of his marriage, which began in 1874, he and his wife, a beautiful, knowledgeable young artist named Helena de Kay, lived in a charming little house on Fifteenth Street. Affectionately called the Studio, it had been converted to living quarters from the stable of the young couple's Union Square neighbor, Samuel Ruggles.

As Gilder's daugher, Rosamund, explained, "The Studio very quickly became the gathering-place for a group of young artists and authors, many of whom subsequently won an honorable rank in their professions. It was not alone the circumstance of my father and mother being themselves artists that brought them so many and such varied friendships, but because they possessed to an unusual degree a power of sympathetic understanding which drew every type of person to them." It was true that even though Gilder was both a traditionalist and a romantic at heart, he was surprisingly open to the work of the new realistic writers. And he did his best to encourage friendly relations among people who might disagree on literary matters by bringing them together in the benevolent atmosphere of the Studio.

Walt Whitman was a frequent visitor to Fifteenth Street, where the Gilders unself-consciously included him in conversations with people who were known to find him too eccentric for their tastes. After fame made him more socially acceptable, Whitman recalled to Horace Greeley how dearly he had treasured the early friendship and staunch support of Richard and Helena Gilder: "At a time when most everybody else in their set threw me down, they were nobly and unhesitatingly hospitable . . . they just asked me along in the most natural way. It was beautiful — beautiful. You know how at one time the church was an asylum for fugitives — the Church, God's right arm fending the innocent. I was such an innocent and the Gilders took me in."

Augustus Saint-Gaudens and Stanford White had both experienced this sympathetic friendship, for the Gilders were just as concerned about innovation and tradition in art and architecture as they were about literature. Together, Saint-Gaudens and Helena de Kay Gilder founded the Society of American Artists to compete with the conservative Academy of Fine Arts. Gilder offered enthusiastic encouragement to the project, even volunteering to serve as the group's unpaid "humble secretary."

Richard Watson Gilder was born in Bordentown, New Jersey, in 1844, and later moved to Flushing, New York, where his father, a minister, served as headmaster of a girls' school. Until he was

Walt Whitman, iconoclast and revolutionary poet, celebrated the commonplace along with the greatness of the nation. "I believe a leaf of grass is no less than the journey work of the stars."

fourteen, Richard received his education in his father's school as its only male pupil. The Reverend Gilder's death forced Richard to abandon plans for college, and without hesitation he looked to journalism as the place to start a career. It was a world that had intrigued him since he was twelve years old and spent every minute of his free time at the *Long Island Times*, where he helped out in exchange for lessons in publishing procedures. The publisher even allowed the quick-witted boy to put out a newspaper of his own to take home and read to his family. Gilder remembered with amusement that his paper "was dedicated to no less a purpose than 'the Promotion of Literature, Morality, Religion and Science," and promised it would "on all occasions . . . observe a proper degree of dignified decorum," although never being "governed by fear or favor." Gilder may have been amused by his own youthful earnestness, but the pledge he made to his readers then was one that guided his editorial role forever.

·   ·   ·

Early in his career, Richard Watson Gilder helped Robert Newton Crane, the uncle of Stephen Crane, launch the *Newark Morning Register.* He also took a second job with a monthly publication called *Hours at Home,* published by Charles Scribner, and commuted back and forth endlessly between Newark and New York. In the fall of 1870, his split existence ended. *Hours at Home* was absorbed into a new publication, *Scribner's Monthly,* and at twenty-six Richard Watson Gilder was named assistant editor. The senior editor was Josiah Gilbert Holland, an established writer who, the publishers hoped, would persuade other major writers to publish in the magazine.

One needed clout to make a magazine succeed in the late 1800s. In the immediate postwar years alone, about a hundred new magazines were put out every year, each attempting to satisfy the newly diverse tastes of American readers without offending their still largely conventional values. Holland, while dedicated to treating important issues seriously and to maintaining high literary standards, was still determined not to offend the traditional moral code in any way. When, on one occasion, Gilder objected to a negative editorial on women's rights (an issue that, along with housing reform, claimed a great deal of his attention), Holland insisted on having the final say. Holland also hated Walt Whitman's work and repeatedly rejected it, against Gilder's passionate conviction that to argue about the worth of Whitman's poetry was as foolish as approaching the "roaring ocean confused by arguments concerning it."

Gradually, however, Holland began to step back from the magazine, and Richard Watson Gilder gained more control. To some extent, this shift had to do with Holland's discomfort with the literary battle that still raged between the new and old guard. Most of the new crop that Holland found so alarming were friends of Gilder's. William Dean Howells was fond of telling about one evening when Holland joined him, some other men, and Gilder in a discussion of literature. After an hour or so of heated debate, the older editor could take no more and reached for his hat. "I have been listening to the conversation of these young men for over an hour. They have been talking about books. And I have never before heard the names of any of the authors they have mentioned," he said with a bewildered shake of his head.

By 1876, Gilder had nearly complete control over the content of *Scribner's Monthly,* and the difference between his and Holland's literary taste and goals was readily apparent. Now, instead of authors like Margaret Oliphant and George MacDonald and the work of somber theologians, there were pieces by Bret Harte, William Cullen Bryant, Henry James, and Ivan Turgenev. By 1880, the magazine's circulation had climbed to almost 150,000, and Gilder complained that he could hardly walk down the street, since all those he passed seemed to be harboring "concealed manuscripts" that they thrust at him in hope of publication.

In 1881, as a result of a controversy between the publishers of *Scribner's Monthly* and the parent company of book publishers, the two concerns split and a new company was started by the magazine's former business manager, Roswell Smith. Richard Watson Gilder was appointed editor of Smith's new publication, *The Century Magazine,* a name Gilder borrowed from the Century Club, although there was no affiliation between the two. "I expect now to lose my friends," Gilder said, smiling, as he took over the job.

The new *Century Magazine* offices, which were spread over an entire floor of a brand-new office building on Union Square, were decorated with oriental rugs and original art. The magazine was immediately successful, and quickly became both more profitable and more popular than its two major competitors, *The Atlantic Monthly* and *Harper's Magazine.* Indeed, William Dean Howells resigned as editor of *The Atlantic* in 1880 to come to New York and write, largely supporting himself by regular contributions to *The Century.* From 1881 to 1885, Howells was the chief contributor to *The Century* — writing prose, poetry, and drama — an association that ended only when he began writing a regular review column for *Harper's* in 1886.

Howells, who lived with his wife and daughter in a sedate brownstone on Seventeenth Street in the Gramercy Park neighborhood, was a plump man with sparkling eyes and a ready smile. He was a rambler, and was as likely to be found exploring the teeming streets of lower Manhattan as taking tea with an industrial baron in a Fifth Avenue mansion. Howells delighted in riding the elevated train to the Upper West Side, where new streets and apartment houses were

William Dean Howells, an early leader of realism in literature. His criticism and encouragement spurred the efforts of many of America's most important writers.

Mark Twain's seventieth birthday dinner at Delmonico's was given by Harper & Brothers.

being built, scattering the pigs, goats, and chickens that still ambled about. He enjoyed watching the bustle of shoppers on Broadway, and visiting the dime museums on East Fourteenth Street, where people with relentlessly humdrum lives could find excitement by viewing freaks or human monsters, or watching daring shows by sword swallowers and fire eaters.

Since one of the new literary theories Howells fervently espoused was that character was far more important to fiction than action, the diversity of New York's citizenry enraptured him. New York City, said William Dean Howells, was a place where "one gets life in curious slices." It was from the slices of life he observed on his walks around New York that Howells would write *A Hazard of New Fortunes*. Published in 1890, it was the first novel that offered America a realistic view of its most astonishing city.

Richard Watson Gilder always considered William Dean Howells, Mark Twain, and Henry James the three greatest fiction writers in America, and was willing to publish anything they wrote, no matter how controversial it might be. When Howells's early novel about divorce, *A Modern Instance*, was serialized in *The Century* in 1882, Gilder wrote an editorial defending the writer as an "artist [whose art] lays bare the springs of human conduct." No matter how provocative the theme of the novel, Gilder argued, it was an important work because it was true to life.

Howells's close friend Mark Twain was a far more controversial author for *The Century* to publish, although Howells's laudatory reviews in *The Atlantic Monthly* were credited with making Twain palatable to cultivated audiences who might otherwise not have taken seriously his colloquial, humorous writings. Even so, Richard Watson Gilder knew that Twain offended many readers, who found his use of words like *sweat* and *rot* crude, and his poking fun at churchgoing and marital fidelity irreverent and even obscene. Letters from indignant readers about a Twain piece in *The Century* were always personally and patiently answered by its loyal, imperturbable editor.

When a superintendent of public schools wrote that Mark Twain's writing was "destitute of a single redeeming quality" and was "hardly worth a place in the average country newspaper which never assumes any literary airs," Gilder called such criticisms "singularly untrue," and added, "The literary judgment of this country and of England will not sustain you in such an opinion." Furthermore, Gilder insisted, "Mark Twain is . . . a good citizen and believes in the best things."

On the other hand, Gilder had, by his own admission, "carefully edited" parts of *Huckleberry Finn* before serializing the book in his magazine. Although the deletions were minimal, both serious readers and other writers were outraged that the editor had tampered with even the smallest section of a novel they considered the first truly American classic. Twain himself had made no objections to Gilder's editing, and continued to publish in *The Century* and to defend Richard Watson Gilder's liberalism. Like many other *Century* authors, Twain respected Gilder's dedication to literature and to the cultivation of American writing. He knew that the editor would often publish the work of lesser-known American authors over that of more established British names, even though the latter might be more attractive to his readers. On the other hand, the red-haired, ebullient Twain enjoyed challenging his friend's liberality with dismaying off-color stories and wildly scatological allusions.

The Century paid its writers generously. According to Walt Whitman, Richard Watson Gilder was the only editor in America who not only took everything Whitman sent him, but always paid the price he asked. Out of his deep concern for the sanctity of literature, Gilder helped form the American Copyright League, which strove to establish an international copyright treaty. The cause became so important to him that he sent his associate editor, Robert Underwood Johnson, to Washington, D.C., for three years to lobby on its behalf. The passage of copyright laws in 1891 put an end to the established practice of pirating American writing in England, and the publication of English authors over Americans in America, because local publishers did not have to pay royalties to foreign authors.

Gilder took very seriously the responsibility of the editorial role, which is why the criticism of his work on *Huckleberry Finn* distressed him. To his mind, "the care of manuscripts is the care of literature." He summed up his feelings about sitting in judgment on a writer's work in a deceptively lighthearted poem he wrote in 1875:

When I am dead and buried, then
There will be groaning among men.
I hear one sighing thus, "Alack!
How oft he sent my poems back."
And one, "He was too sensitive
To take the essays I could give."
Another, weeping, "Ah, how few
Of my poor stories seemed to do."
I think I never will forget
The way in which he said to me
"We're loaded down with poetry."
"In fact," said one, "there is no doubt
That contributions wore him out."

Certainly, during *The Century*'s heyday the numbers of contributions it received was prodigious, making the magazine astonishingly rich fare for its cover price of twenty-five cents. For example, readers of *The Century*'s February 1885 issue were able to find substantial sections of William Dean Howells's *The Rise of Silas Lapham*, Henry James's *The Bostonians*, and Twain's *Huckleberry Finn*.

Many of the writers published in *The Century* lived in Gramercy Park; others spent much of their time in the neighborhood as members, along with Richard Watson Gilder, of the Players' or National Arts clubs. But one Gramercy Park author would never know of the publication of his work in *The Century*, for the magazine did not publish him until after his death. In 1891, when Richard Watson Gilder learned that Herman Melville had died, he asked Melville's widow, Elizabeth, for some writing to publish as a memorial. Mrs. Melville chose some poems from her husband's final collection of privately printed verse, saying to the editor, "I do not know of any publication in which I should be more pleased to see his name."

Melville had become a resident of Gramercy Park in 1863, after several years of going to sea and extended stays in the country town of Pittsfield, Massachusetts. His New York home, on one of the first streets laid out by Samuel Ruggles, was built of yellow-painted brick with brownstone trim, standing, according to Melville's grand-

Herman Melville's early popularity diminished as he turned to bewildering themes that later generations would recognize as existential, psychological, and darkly satiric.

daughter, among a "long row of houses on East 26th Street, each exactly alike except for the number on the door."

That early Harper & Brothers fire, in which the writer had lost some of his original manuscripts, must have seemed a bitter omen of a literary career that would never fulfill its promise. When Herman Melville moved to Gramercy Park, he was forty-three years old and had written *Typee*, *White-Jacket*, *Moby-Dick*, and *Pierre*, among other works, all with little financial or critical reward. In New York, he was forced to take a job as a customs inspector; in a customs house uniform, he inspected the cargo of freighters that docked at Gansevoort Street on the Hudson River Pier. It was a job he described as "a most inglorious one; indeed, worse than driving geese to water."

During the more than twenty years that he worked for the customs house, Herman Melville wrote little in comparison to his early output. The years of literary rejection, and the personal tragedy of one son who committed suicide and another who became estranged from the family, turned the essentially solitary Melville into a virtual recluse. Few people visited the gloomy, old-fashioned Melville home, with its shabby exterior and dark, uninviting rooms.

When Melville's wife came into an inheritance in 1885, the author was finally able to retire from the customs house, and he spent his last six years writing. Tall and still gravely handsome, he would walk around the neighborhood, lost in private reflection, apparently still uninterested in socializing, even with his literary peers. Edmund Clarence Stedman, Melville's neighbor and admirer, tried to get Melville to join another new club he had started for authors, but after attending only one meeting, Melville politely declined to return.

What no one knew was that in his bleak bedroom, with its brown wallpaper and black iron bed, Herman Melville was writing his last novel. He had no illusions about its commercial success, but he was driven to write the story of a man who is sacrificed in the name of maintaining order aboard his warship, yet manages to reconcile himself to his fate and even to forgive his persecutors. The book thus ends on a more peaceful note than much of Melville's earlier work, as if the author had come to terms with the despairs and injustices of his own life. In fact, he had scribbled across the opening of the manuscript, "Here lies a story not unwarranted by what happens in this incongruous world of ours." The book was *Billy Budd*, and Melville completed it only five months before he died, in 1891.

Despite the posthumous publication of his poems by Richard Watson Gilder, Melville received little public notice even in death. The *New York World* described him in its obituary as "Herman Melville, formerly a well-known author," and other newspapers gave him even less credit for his achievements. In this atmosphere of obscurity, *Billy Budd*, a book that many Melville scholars consider one of his greatest works, lay undiscovered for more than thirty years. Mrs. Melville, who thought the book was still unfinished, had packed the manuscript away with some of Melville's other papers, and it was not until 1924 that the work was finally published.

·   ·   ·

Melville often sat musing about his characters and themes on the back porch overlooking his rose garden. During the year 1875, if he had glanced up, he might have seen the young writer who was living in the house directly opposite, on Twenty-fifth Street. Henry James vastly preferred living in Europe, and would soon return to make his permanent home there, but in New York City his choice of a residence in Gramercy Park was undoubtedly due to the neighborhood's resemblance to a London square.

James had sold several stories to *Scribner's Monthly,* and when Richard Watson Gilder became editor of *The Century* he sought out the much-admired author for new contributions. They were already friends: James was a frequent guest at the Studio, and Gilder particularly enjoyed talking to him about literature. To his great discomfort, however, Gilder soon discovered that Henry James's writing, especially his fiction, was not very appealing to *The Century*'s largely middle-class readership. This became particularly clear when James's novel *The Bostonians* was serialized in the magazine in 1885.

After four installments had appeared, to the increasing irritation of the magazine's readers, Gilder wrote to James with suggestions for editorial changes. Although the move made Gilder uncomfortable, he asked James to try to abbreviate future sections, because "the movement of *The Bostonians* is so slow that people seem to be dropping off from it." It was evident that his friend's suggestions dismayed James, because thirty years later he said to a critic who was praising this early novel, "Your good impression of *The Bostonians* greatly moves me — the thing was no success whatever on publication in *The Century* . . . and the late R. W. Gilder of that periodical wrote me at the time that they had never published anything that appeared so little to interest their readers."

Another writer who lived in Gramercy Park at the time was never published in *The Century* while Gilder was editor, although Gilder was a friend of his family. Stephen Crane's father had been a Methodist minister in Newark, New Jersey, and his mother lectured for a women's temperance union. It was clear to Gilder that twenty-one-year-old Stephen, though a loving son, did not share his parents'

Stephen Crane, keen observer of real life. He helped set the tone of naturalistic writing and considered himself an impressionist who "believed in irony."

view of life. He was irreverent, often cynical, and startlingly unconventional.

The novel Crane submitted to *The Century* in the fall of 1892 was entitled *Maggie: A Girl of the Streets.* He seemed concerned, as were many of the new realistic writers, with enriching literary realism through a writing style that was both impressionistic and symbolic:

> She went into the blackness of the final block. The shutters of the tall buildings were closed like grim lips. . . . Afar off the lights of the avenues glittered as if from an impossible distance. . . . At the feet of the tall buildings appeared the deathly black hue of the river. . . . The varied sounds of life, made joyous by distance and seeming unapproachableness, came faintly and died away to a silence.

The style made Richard Watson Gilder uncomfortable, even though he recognized the gifted mind that had created it, and he tried to soften his rejection of the book he found too "cruel" with a careful explanation of his reasons. The writer angrily interrupted. "You mean that the story's too honest?" he asked, and the editor, after a painful pause, agreed.

While Richard Watson Gilder continued to champion realism in writing, and was able to face both his own and his era's literary limitations, he could not give up the deep-rooted belief that some idealism and gentility belonged in literature. Crane's Maggie, a helpless girl with an abusive mother and a brother who arranges her seduction into prostitution, led a life so grimly hopeless that it offended Gilder's romantic nature, and he certainly knew it would offend his readers' sensibilities. Stephen Crane deplored Gilder's conservatism and was sure that it would be shared by other publishers, so he borrowed money from his brother to publish the book himself under a pseudonym. The paper-bound book sold only two copies, and one wintry night, in a gesture that was both pragmatic and cynical, Stephen Crane used a pile of the books to start a fire in his frigid room.

The slim, pale young writer had written *Maggie* because of his intense absorption in the darker side of New York life. Like William Dean Howells, whom he greatly admired, Crane spent as much time as possible wandering the city's streets. For Crane, the most compelling streets were those where the downtrodden lived and tried to forget their hopelessness through drink or sex.

Along the Bowery, in those years, the ugly streets were filled with decaying rooming houses and tawdry saloons. At night, the once-elegant Union Square would fill with tired women with painted faces and weary, beaten men. Crane often sat and talked to them long into the night, horrified and enthralled by the different routes people took in their desolate lives. Was it society's fault or some intrinsic weakness, a proclivity "to willingly be knocked flat and accept the licking"? If the latter was true, what was it in our culture that produced such passivity? The more he saw, the more Crane was determined to defy the sanctimonious myths of "respectable" society and to write novels that would "show people to people as they seem to me." How, though, would he get people to read his work if editors like Richard Watson Gilder, who was less conservative than many, refused to publish him?

When William Dean Howells, by now considered the dean of American letters as well as the leading figure in the crusade for literary realism, read *Maggie*, he lamented the decision of his friend Gilder to favor gentility over reality. Inviting the young writer to tea, Howells praised Stephen Crane in language that made the author forget for a moment how penniless and desperate he was. Howells called Crane's voice more powerful than Mark Twain's, and declared him an author who appeared to have been born full-blown to his art. Unfortunately, even Howells's reputation did not help him convince any other publisher to reprint the "shocking" and "sordid" novel.

Stephen Crane's Gramercy Park studio, which he shared with three artist friends, was on Twenty-third Street. The multistory building had formerly housed the Art Students' League, and, appropriately, its rooms were almost all rented by aspiring painters and authors. Their passionate impatience with convention and artistic restraint, so like Crane's own, seemed to be summed up by the quote from Emerson he discovered chalked on a beam of one of the "topmost and remotest" studios: "Congratulate yourselves if you have done something strange and extravagant and broken the monotony of a decorous age."

At this point, Stephen Crane could afford only to think extravagantly. Three of the four roommates shared one bed, taking turns sleeping in the middle. On a rotating basis, the fourth person slept alone on a rickety cot. They had only one good set of clothes among them, which they wore when looking for work or embarking on important social occasions, as when Stephen Crane went to William Dean Howells's home for tea. They ate their meals, such as they were, mainly at a delicatessen called Boeuf-à-la-Mode, nicknamed the Buffalo-Mud, where cheap, filling foods like potato salad could be had for breakfast or dinner.

Delicatessens were relatively new in Manhattan and, according to visitors from other states, unique to the city, where so many Germans had settled. There were other places a struggling writer might go for food, such as bars that served free lunches along with the price of a drink. One establishment, on University Place near Fourteenth Street, was named for its owner, Billy Mould, and was popular because it doled out huge quantities of wonderful bean soup, "on the house, like a tin roof." Billy Mould especially liked writers, and was generous about extending credit when their stories and poems went unpublished. In more affluent moments, regulars celebrated publication with a round of Billy Mould's special drink. Called the Razzle-dazzle, it was a powerful concoction of brandy, ginger ale, and the most popular liquid refreshment of literary men, absinthe.

For poor and rich alike, dining out in restaurants was a vital part of New York life in these postwar years. By the 1870s, New York already boasted more than six thousand restaurants of every price range and description. Delmonico's, which was then on Twenty-sixth Street, was considered the finest and most beautiful restaurant in Manhattan, if not the world. A modest dinner, without wine, cost $4.00 or $5.00 for two people, an extravagant sum at the time, and an elaborate meal cost much more. In 1892, a French journalist was somewhat amused at the "palazzo Delmonico's" exaggerated luxury, but nonetheless judged it "better and more sumptuous than the finest Parisian restaurant." He saved his highest praise for the "baked ice" invented by the restaurant. Given the name Alaska, the dessert was also favored by the fashionable women who arrived by carriage day and night with their well-dressed, often much older, escorts.

In the chaotic lower reaches of the city, there were scores of restaurants where a lady rarely ventured; if she did, she would be seated in a separate women's section. Between the hours of noon and three, merchants and clerks from Wall Street and Park Row thronged into huge dining rooms with long counters and rows of tables, and the noise of slamming doors, shouted orders, and clattering dishes was thunderous. More than fifteen hundred men might be served every day at a particularly popular establishment, with the bar providing a substantial portion of the owner's revenue.

There were chophouses throughout the city, where the specialty was a huge mutton chop and a baked potato. Cheaper versions were the "fifteen-cent houses," where the sum bought a hefty slab of meat cut from a joint, along with bread, butter, potatoes, and pickles. As you turned the windy corner of some busy intersection, the rich smell of chicken turning invitingly on a spit in a rotisserie window might lure you inside for lunch. For something lighter, there were confectionery shops and Viennese coffee houses near the shopping and theater districts, and oyster parlors seemed to dot the entire city.

At the turn of the century immigrants continued to stream into New York, and their ethnic restaurants attracted the adventurous. Lüchow's, the famous German restaurant, suddenly found competition from smaller, less expensive places — where simple food was washed down with tall glasses of Rhine wine and seltzer — and from the growing number of beer gardens that served heavy platters of wurst and tankards of cold beer. It was also possible to get a table d'hôte dinner for fifty or sixty cents in the Italian kitchens along MacDougal and Sullivan streets, and a veritable feast for the same price in the dense Chinese quarter between Mott and Pell streets.

All this gustatory diversity helped make it possible for the struggling writer or artist to survive, albeit precariously, in late-nineteenth-century Manhattan. There were terrible low points that could drive a writer like Stephen Crane to tell one of his mentors, Hamlin Garland — the western writer of social protest — that he would give away all his work for $30.

Crane left his studio apartment for a while in 1893 to try other living arrangements, but he showed up again one rainy night, soaking wet and shivering with cold. His former roommates took him in and insisted that he stay on with them at least until he finished the novel he was working on. *The Red Badge of Courage* was based on the Civil War. For research, Crane had been studying the series of articles, printed in *The Century*, called "Battles and Leaders of the Civil War." What seemed to be missing from these pieces, as well as from the other histories he read, was any description of what the individual experienced in war. In his early drafts, Stephen Crane called Henry Fleming, his protagonist, Everyman, just as in the first drafts of *Maggie* he had referred to the central character as Everywoman. In both cases, he saw the character as the victim of social forces beyond his or her control.

By April 1894, the novel was finished, and Crane asked Hamlin

Garland to read the manuscript. In Garland's uptown apartment, while his "sallow, yellow-fingered" guest hungrily ate the lunch he had been offered, the established, successful author began to read. So lifeless did his young friend seem that Garland was almost "unable to relate him to the marvelous . . . images so keen and phrases so graphic and newly coined. . . . Each page presented pictures like those of a great poem, and I experienced the thrill of the editor who has fallen unexpectedly upon the work of genius."

The Red Badge of Courage was published by D. Appleton in New York the following year, to great acclaim and attention. Shortened versions appeared in hundreds of newspapers across the country. *Maggie* was republished commercially, reaping all the acclaim Howells and Garland had always thought it deserved. Its acceptance seemed a triumphant harbinger of what lay ahead for American literature. Americans were finally ready to abandon the simpler depiction of life that lingered from the early nineteenth century and to accept twentieth-century writing, with its bold realism, its fearless questioning, and its decidedly brash manner. Clearly, Stephen Crane's powerful novels, which celebrated truth over the ideal, had given dramatic birth to what twentieth-century America would recognize as modern American fiction.

The tumultuous birth of modern American writing did not bode well for *The Century*. The magazine had been a steady voice during the early years of literary ferment, and Richard Watson Gilder was, as its editor, a singularly powerful figure in American letters. Gilder had ample reason to finish the century with pride in both his accomplishments and the vision that was often ahead of its time. Farsighted as he was, however, he could not help wondering whether he and the magazine could retain their foothold — whether *The Century* was ready for the heady pace and the unabashed modernism that marked the changing climate of the approaching era.

III

A Thousand and One
Mechanical Conveniences

---◈---

1900-1920

10

THE
NEW REALISM
IN LETTERS

━━━━━━━━ ✦ ━━━━━━━━

IN THE EARLY PART of the new century, Richard Watson Gilder
began to withdraw from editorial responsibility for *The Century*.
The dilemma facing him — compromising his own literary sen-
sibility to accommodate the great contemporary writers or publishing the work of lesser writers to provide the fare his readers preferred — had grown too great for him, and he no longer enjoyed the
editorial role.

Instead, Gilder turned to his own poetry. In 1907, he said, "I
have written more freely and more in quantity than in any year of
life since I wrote *The New Day* [his first book of poems, published
in 1875]. Indeed, in 1908, the Boston publisher Houghton Mifflin selected him to be the first living poet in their series "Household
Poets," placing him in the company of such prestigious writers as
John Greenleaf Whittier and Henry Wadsworth Longfellow.

Unfortunately, Gilder paid a price for not taking full responsibility for the contents of *The Century*. Just as in his youth, when he had
worked as Josiah Holland's assistant on *Scribner's Monthly*, Gilder
was forced to battle more conservative impulses than his own. Over

and over again, the associate editor, Robert Underwood Johnson, took issue with a writer's work, protesting that it was too realistic or liberal for *The Century*'s already declining readership.

One conflict that caused Gilder particular distress concerned Edith Wharton. From the moment he first read her stories, Gilder had been captivated by her work and wanted to publish everything she wrote. In a letter to Johnson in 1904, Gilder implored, "I'm sorry you don't feel as I do about Mrs. Wharton's position as a story writer. In her . . . stories touching on divorce she is very strong and human; as well as being a writer — which few of our novelists are. . . . She is on the eve of a great popular success . . . I think, and I fear that we will not then be able to get her. I had an idea that we could develop her fame and make a good thing in every way out of serial and book publication."

In fact, it is unlikely that Edith Wharton would have wanted to link her name with *The Century*, even early in her career. The magazine's reputation and influence were waning, and its genteel tone may have been a painful reminder of the passionless life she had tried so hard to escape.

Edith Wharton's parents lived for many years on East Twenty-first Street in the heart of Gramercy Park, and then moved to an almost identical brownstone nearby, 14 West Twenty-third Street, where Edith was born on January 24, 1862. Her father, George Frederic Jones, had been one of George Templeton Strong's college classmates; her aloof, aristocratic mother was Lucretia Rhinelander Jones. Wharton would later say, "I was never free from the oppressive sense that I had two absolutely inscrutable beings to please — God and my mother . . . and my mother was the most inscrutable of the two."

What Edith longed for in her mother, she found — perhaps to some degree invented — in her father. He was remembered by others as a quiet, mild-mannered man, but to Edith he was a hero. In recalling influences on her own literary development, she wrote that "the new Tennysonian rhythms . . . moved my father greatly; and I imagine there was a time when his rather rudimentary love of verse might have been developed . . . but my mother's matter-of-factness must have shrivelled up any such buds of fancy. . . . I have won-

Edith Wharton. With acute and piercing intelligence,
she exposed the foibles of culture, class, and morality.

dered . . . what stifled cravings had once germinated in him, and what manner of man he was really meant to be."

Whatever regret she felt for her father's wasted potential, Edith spent the happiest times of her childhood in his company. In her autobiography, *A Backward Glance*, she offered her very first childhood memory — taking a walk around the Gramercy Park streets on a winter day with her "tall handsome father." Referring to herself in the third person, Wharton wrote, "She had been put into her warmest coat . . . and her hands were encased in white woolen mittens. One of them lay in the large safe hollow of her father's bare hand . . . who was so warm-blooded that in the coldest weather he always went out without gloves, and whose head, with its ruddy complexion and intensely blue eyes, was so far aloft that when she walked beside him she was too near to see his face. It was always an event in the little girl's life to take a walk with her father."

Other happy childhood memories of Gramercy Park were associated with her dearest friend, Emelyn Washburn, whose father was rector of the neighborhood's Calvary Church. The two girls spent many cold winter days in the Washburns' home on East Twenty-first Street, curled up in big chairs in the Reverend Washburn's library, reading from his collection of Old Norse and Icelandic literature. In better weather, they would sneak up to the roof of an adjoining building and read Dante aloud to each other.

To her mother, Edith's intellectual and literary interests were a kind of aberration. Unlike many of the families who lived in the brownstones of Gramercy Park, the Jones led a highly traditional life, and their daughter was not expected to pursue an education, let alone a career. Edith was not even granted the pieces of foolscap she asked for, and, she remembered, "was driven to begging for the wrappings of the parcels delivered at the house. . . . I always kept a stack in my room . . . and I used to spread them on the floor and travel over them on my hands and knees, building up long parallel columns of blank verse."

To Edith Wharton, her staid brownstone home symbolized all that was wrong with much of New York society. "I have often sighed, in looking back at my childhood," she wrote years later, "to think how pitiful a provision was made for the life of the imagination behind those uniform brownstone facades." And indeed, the Jones household, full of polite conversation and social convention, was, like that of many other society families, devoid of a glimpse of what Wharton would call "the high gods. Beauty, passions, and danger were automatically excluded."

Wharton used the "safe" brownstone world as the setting for much of the social criticism in her novels, and it was this level of realism which offended Robert Underwood Johnson and kept her out of *The Century*. By revealing the coldness and hypocrisy of families who valued social form above genuine feeling, she mirrored the conceits of fashionable New York life.

In *The Custom of the Country*, for example, she paints the scene:

As Ralph . . . passed into the hall, with its dark mahogany doors and
. . . black and white marble paving, he said to himself that what [is]
called society was really just like the houses it lived in: a muddle of
misapplied ornament over a thin steel shell of utility. . . . Ralph
sometimes called his mother and grandfather "the aborigines" . . .
doomed to rapid extinction with the advance of the invading race.

Twentieth-century life was changing so rapidly that those who wor-
shiped tradition, in life as well as in literature, may very well have
felt bewildered and beleaguered. A combination of invention, impatience, and energy was transforming almost every aspect of the
social order. Not since the years of ferment just before the Civil War
had Manhattan seemed so ebullient and vigorous. Its standard of
living was far higher than that of any city in the Old World, and
visitors were astounded by its "10,001 conveniences."

"Steel-cage" buildings soared above the sprawling metropolis,
looking, said Henry James, like "extravagant pins in a cushion already overplanted." The Flatiron Building, built in 1902, was an
immediate tourist attraction because of its amazing twenty-one
stories.* Taking up the block between Twenty-second and Twenty-
third streets, the triangular building dominated Madison Square,
wrote the journalist John Corbin, like "an ocean steamer with all
Broadway in tow." On the other hand, the Russian novelist Maxim
Gorky, who came to New York in 1906 to raise funds for the Russian Revolution, found the Flatiron Building and other skyscrapers
"dull, heavy piles [of] monstrous height," with a look of "cold and
haughty presumption." Two years later, the Flatiron Building was
eclipsed by the forty-seven-story Singer Building. It was very clear
that in the coming years the city would continue to grow beyond the
wildest dreams of earlier generations.

In keeping up with the rapidly expanding population, New York
City's telephone system had become the best and the largest in the

---

*The slang expression "Twenty-three skidoo" originated with the Flatiron Building.
Young men enjoyed loitering outside the building to view women's skirts as they were
tossed up by the building's strong downdraft. The men were sternly warned by the
policeman stationed there to "skidoo" from Twenty-third Street if they wanted to avoid
trouble with the law.

world by the turn of the century. In 1896, there were already fifteen thousand subscribers, and it was possible to make calls to cities as far away as Boston, Washington, and Chicago. Of course, most New Yorkers still didn't have their own phones, and went instead to the nearest hotel or one of the many stores that had installed telephones for their customers' convenience. It was exciting but hardly intimate, to speak to someone this way, for the phone was usually hung on a wall out in the open, and shoppers or hotel guests unabashedly eavesdropped.

At this time, the Edison Company, the city's largest supplier of electricity, serviced six thousand customers, and street lamps were changing from gas to electric light all across the city. Gone from many neighborhoods was the familiar figure of the lamplighter, who came at twilight with his torch and returned at dawn to put out the flame. One British journalist tried to describe how the city looked when the electric lights flashed on automatically at dusk: "The effect of the light in the squares of the Empire City can scarcely be described . . . so weird and so beautiful it is."

Nowhere was this fairy-tale atmosphere more apparent than in the theater district. The splendor of Broadway, which had been an outstanding feature of New York's mystique in Edwin Booth's time, had been somewhat overshadowed in recent years by the elegance of Fifth Avenue. With electric lighting, New York's Rialto once again became a major attraction. Electric signs flashed advertisements all night long, turning the theater district into what became known worldwide as the Great White Way. As early as 1903, when electricity was still rather primitive, a French visitor marveled at Broadway's "multicolored bouquets of luminous advertising," and by 1910 the signs were not just colorful; they moved. One travel writer described a stroll down these streets, lit with an "immense blaze of legends and pictures, most of them in motion," as "the finest free show on earth."

·   ·   ·

The elevated steam locomotive railway system, first introduced in the 1870s, was also rapidly expanding. By 1900, there were several lines crossing the city, including the Sixth Avenue and Third Avenue els. The cars whizzed along the elevated tracks at two- and three-minute intervals, "so near to the houses," it was reported, "you might

Above: The first head-quarters of the New York Telephone Company. People from all over the United States and Europe came to visit the "long line of busy young women in action."

Above: Under the direction of the city's first street-cleaning commissioner, appointed in 1895, white-coated crews tried to usher in a cleaner century.

Left: Around the intersection of Broadway and Thirty-fourth Street stood the New York Herald Building, the Times Tower, the Metropolitan Opera House, the Hotel Astor, and Macy's department store.

shake hands with the inhabitants and see what they had for dinner."

By the end of the century, cable cars, which ran at eight miles an hour, had also begun operating on Broadway and Lexington Avenue. William Dean Howells found the cable cars particularly alarming, and described how a car would "rush wildly over the track, running amuck through everything in its way, and spreading terror on every hand." Cable cars did frequently derail, causing serious accidents and even deaths. A particularly hazardous corner at Fourteenth Street and Union Square was nicknamed "dead man's curve." Extra policemen were always stationed there; their principal job was to warn passersby of approaching cable cars. Their booming voices, mixed with the shrieks of frightened ladies as they tried to cross the street and with the wildly ringing cable car bells, created an unbelievable cacophony.

Despite the less tranquil moments on cable cars, New Yorkers flocked to them, and in the summer, when open cars were available, the five-cent trip provided pleasant relief from steaming weather. In the farther reaches of the city, there were electric trolley cars that ran on under-trolley systems rather than underground cable, and a popular pastime was to rent one for a neighborhood outing or a private party. The incandescent lamp had recently been perfected, and the trolleys could be strung with pretty lights while a German band, hired for the occasion, set up its instruments in the front seats and sent rollicking Bavarian music into the night.

All the elevated trains, cable cars, trolleys, and even the horse cars that were still running couldn't meet New York City's transportation needs. William Barclay Parsons, a prominent engineer, was dispatched by the Rapid Transit Board to study the underground transportation systems of London and Paris. When he returned, he drew up plans for a subway system that he estimated would cost $60 million. The plan aroused great controversy before it was finally accepted, but digging began in 1900 so that the city's expansion would now, amazingly, even go underground.

The first subway line opened in 1904, running up the East Side from City Hall to Grand Central Terminal, turning west at Forty-second Street and continuing back up north along Broadway, all the way up to One hundred and forty-fifth Street. Construction immediately began on the Upper West Side, and when the Eighth Avenue subway was completed in 1905, developers went wild. The vacant land on Riverside Drive, Central Park West, Broadway, and West End Avenue was suddenly lined with lavish new apartment buildings, some containing individual apartments of as many as twenty rooms. Many, like the Turrets, on Riverside Drive and Eighty-fourth Street, offered their tenants such amenities as swimming pools, gymnasiums, billiard rooms, ballrooms, banquet halls, bowling alleys, and basketball courts. According to the architectural historian M. Christine Boyer, "These exaggerated twentieth-century proportions far outstripped the nineteenth century's concept of luxury and comfort."

While mass transportation crisscrossed the city above and below, a bicycle craze was sweeping through the streets of New York. This new sport was more alarming to traditionalists than many other new developments, because it caused a profound change in dress and manners, particularly among young women. Until the advent of the bicycle, women seldom engaged in sporting activities, with the excep-

SUNDAY MORNING ON THE ROAD

The bicycle craze sweeps through New York. Adventurous cyclists abandon church and family gatherings for a Sunday outing.

tion of an occasional game of croquet or a demure round of tennis on summer weekends in Long Island. Now, girls from even the very best families spent their mornings bicycling through Central Park, instead of shopping along the Ladies' Mile.

Sunday was the most popular day for cycling, and spirited adventurers of both sexes would ride up to the Bronx to picnic in such newly developed recreational areas as Bronx and Pelham Bay parks. Chaperoned groups of young people also rode through Central Park up to Riverside Drive, where they dined at the fashionable Claremont Inn before riding down along the drive again at night, the stream of their bicycle lamps making the bordering trees seem ablaze with fireflies.

A number of ministers denounced the fad that was robbing their churches of Sunday parishioners, and the more conservative press printed their tirades, including a piece by the Reverend Asa D. Blackburn, who warned New Yorkers that "you cannot serve God and skylark on a bicycle." The same newspapers never tired of printing photographs of young women from important families aboard their "bikes," attired in the latest bicycle costumes — and it was the costumes that outraged the old guard most of all.

Fashion had already become more relaxed as the nineteenth century drew to an end. Young men had abandoned frock coats and stiff-fronted shirts for "soft shirts" with detachable starched cuffs and collars. Female fashion was undergoing far more drastic changes. Among the most popular articles of clothing for women of the early twentieth century was the "rainy-daisy" skirt. Designed ostensibly for wearing in bad weather, these skirts ended a full six inches from the ground, making them practical gear for traversing wet and snowy streets. Now that young women were bicycling or skating on ice and roller rinks, they sported rainy-daisy skirts even on sunny days. The skirt complemented the Gibson girl look, which was all the rage and which critics found disturbingly "mannish." With its boater hat, shirtwaist, and close-fitting skirt, the new style gave women an air of competence and self-assurance as they rode their bicycles or strolled about the city.

Without doubt, the most elegant bicycle costume in New York

City belonged to Lillian Russell, who, with her friend Marie Dressler, pedaled regularly around Central Park to keep her figure. Her dress was made of white serge with leg-of-mutton sleeves, magnificently tailored and trimmed. And it was only fitting that she be dressed so beautifully, for she rode a bicycle that was the talk of Manhattan. A gift from Diamond Jim Brady, the bicycle was gold-plated, with mother-of-pearl handlebars that were monogrammed in diamonds and emeralds. The wheel spokes and hubs were set with jewels that flashed in the sun as Miss Russell rode jauntily through the park.

New Yorkers were also getting their first look at the "horseless carriages" that operated on either gasoline or steam. William Dean Howells once again commented unsympathetically on this latest development in modern transportation, which, by 1908, could no longer be considered a passing novelty. "The motorist whirs through the intersecting streets and round the corners, bent on suicide or homicide," he wrote in his column in *Harper's Magazine*. "The kind old trolleys and hansoms that once seemed so threatening have almost become so many arks of safety from the furious machines replacing them."

Horses were rapidly fading from the transportation scene, and the streets of New York began to get a little cleaner. The "pulverized manure" that made up so much of the swirling dust around the city finally diminished. A street-cleaning commissioner had been appointed in 1895, and he assembled a crew of aides who wore long white coats as they swept and washed the streets. But the relentless noise, continuous movement, and constant change that had always characterized New York life struck visitors more forcefully than ever before.

H. G. Wells came to New York City in 1906, and many believe that what he saw there inspired him to create his wonderful tales of the future. Indeed, the visit resulted in *The Future of America*, which Wells wrote and published later that year. In the book, he describes how his "first impressions of New York . . . enhance the effect of . . . material progress . . . as something inevitable and inhuman, as a blindly furious energy of growth that must go on."

Wells described a sensation that was close to fear as he watched people coming and going to work: "They arrive marching afoot by every street in endless procession; crammed trolley cars disgorge them; the Subway pours them out . . . they are clerks and stenographers, shopmen, shop-girls, workers of innumerable types, black-coated men, hat-and-blouse girls, shabby and cheaply clad people. . . . The distinctive effect is the mass . . . rippled with unmeaning faces, the great, the unprecedented multitudiousness of the thing, the inhuman force of it all."

Other writers, in the tradition of William Dean Howells and Stephen Crane, found that the enormous swirling mix of city life did not destroy the individual, but, instead, produced a million separate stories every day. One of these writers was the man whose name is perhaps associated most closely with the literary history of Gramercy Park. William Sydney Porter, who wrote under the pseudonym O. Henry, was to earn his reputation as America's most popular short-story writer by spinning magical tales from everyday life. His characters were usually the men and women who made up the "four million" in a city that was not Wells's harsh, obliterating metropolis, but rather an enchanted "Little Bagdad on the Subway."

Manhattan was like Bagdad to O. Henry, because, as he put it,

> If you have the right kind of eye — the kind that can disregard high hats, cutaway coats and trolley cars — you can see all the characters in the "Arabian Nights" parading up and down Broadway at midday. . . . The twin spirits Romance and Adventure are always abroad seeking worthy wooers. . . . At every corner handkerchiefs drop, fingers beckon, eyes besiege, and the lost, the lonely, the rapturous, the mysterious, the perilous changing clues of adventure are slipped into our fingers.

One must always be open to romance and adventure, the author cautioned, or risk arriving "some day . . . at the end of a very dull life, to reflect that our romance has been a pallid thing of a marriage or two, a satin rosette kept in a safe-deposit drawer, and a lifelong feud with a steam radiator."

William Sidney Porter (he later changed his middle name to Sydney) began his own adventurous life in Greensboro, North Carolina, in September 1862. His father, Algernon Sidney Porter, was a prominent physician, and his mother, Mary Jane Virginia Swain, was the daughter of a successful newspaper editor. A college graduate, she was gifted in languages and artistic in temperament, qualities that, along with a basic shyness, she somehow passed on to William, though she died when he was only three. After her death, Will, his brother, and his father moved in with his grandmother and a maiden aunt. Dr. Porter became withdrawn and dependent on alcohol, and Will began to feel that he had no parents at all.

His aunt encouraged Will's interest in literature. As a pupil in her small private boys' school, he read the classics and acquired an impressive vocabulary, a true respect for language, and a talent for witty epigrams. At fifteen, when Will was too old for his aunt's school, his education ended, a fact he would regret all his life. To earn necessary income, he went to work as an apprentice pharmacist in an uncle's drugstore.

Even after he became a licensed pharmacist four years later, the profession held little appeal for him. For Will, the best part of the job at Porter's Pharmacy was chatting with the local men, who used it as a kind of club, gathering around the potbelly stove to smoke cigars and drink the whiskey that he kept in a decanter behind the counter.

One man remembered the young drug clerk as "holding court" — engaging men more than twice his age with his easy wit and mischievous smile. He was slight, about five feet, six inches tall, with brown hair and pale skin. Sometimes he seemed feverish and had a hacking cough, which troubled people who knew that his mother had died of tuberculosis; they tended to nurture him, a task made easier by his good humor.

One of those people was a physician, who invited Will to join his family at a ranch he owned in southwest Texas. It was a place where Will could build himself up, and the dry Texas air might ward off tuberculosis. The nineteen-year-old boy leaped at the chance to seek adventures that small-town life in North Carolina would never offer him.

After a while on the ranch, Will Porter moved to the growing city of Austin, where he worked at a series of jobs and enjoyed the life of

William Sydney Porter, who wrote as O. Henry. His stories preserved the city's atmosphere and myriad dramas.

a sporty young western bachelor. He even grew a bushy mustache, which he twisted up at the ends in the style of a Texas gunfighter. At a dance, Will Porter met Athol Estes, the stepdaughter of a prominent Austin grocer. Immediately convinced that he loved her, he conducted a relentlessly romantic courtship — to the great annoyance of Athol's family. But their objections couldn't counteract his charm, and when Will, then twenty-five, decided that he and Athol — who at nineteen was past the age of consent — should elope, it didn't take much to convince her. It is testimony to Porter's extraordinary personality that he was able to win over his in-laws. They not only forgave him; they became his strongest supporters during the most stressful times of his life.

Athol encouraged her husband's writing, which he was working at every spare moment, and he soon began to sell some of his work to newspapers and small magazines. Nothing would have pleased Athol or Will more than for him to be able to devote himself entirely to writing, but misfortune quickly began to dog the young couple. Their first child died at birth in 1888, leaving Athol considerably weakened, and after she gave birth to their daughter, Margaret, two years later, she fell victim to tuberculosis. Thus, when Will was offered a job as a teller in the First National Bank in Austin, he accepted quickly, though he had neither banking experience nor any interest in the profession.

Predictably, William Porter found the bank as boring as the drug store, so he amused himself behind the bars of his teller's cage by drawing sketches of his customers or dreaming up stories about their lives. At night, he let off steam by playing poker or drinking prodigiously at a local bar, often in the company of a socially unacceptable woman. Unfortunately, even when Athol was in remission, she did not have enough energy to keep her husband company, and soon they began to quarrel over the ways he found to amuse himself. Will loved his wife, but he felt "owned" by her demands. "In all matters of the heart, the word o-w-n-e-r-s-h-i-p should be expunged," he opined in one of his many critiques of marriage.

In 1894, Porter was suddenly forced to leave his job because of discrepancies in his bookkeeping. Although the bank examiners were building a strong case against him, bank officers refused to believe that their engaging colleague was guilty and declined to press charges when he was brought to trial in 1895. Will's defense was helped considerably by the revelation of the relaxed manner of Texas banking at the time. Apparently, depositors were free to go behind the counter and help themselves if no teller was on duty, leaving only a personal memo indicating the amount of their transactions.

Although he was exonerated, Will thought it best to leave Austin after the trial, and he accepted a job with the *Houston Daily Post*. In six months he wrote fifty-nine short stories and sketches, based on his own experiences and observations. He wrote about important people in Texas, and people no one ever paid attention to, like ailing newspaper boys and courageous tramps; he wrote about harried Christmas shoppers and New Year's celebrations, about gamblers and embarrassed lovers and frustrated husbands and wives. The stories were unabashedly sentimental, but they all celebrated the heroism of the common citizen, and many of them served as models for the stories Porter would later write in New York. The themes of mistaken identity and the heavy hand of fate, both to be found in so many O. Henry tales, have their roots in this early Texas writing, and he would return to western settings long after he had moved east.

His Texas stories are noted for their realistic description, capturing the natural beauty, the vastness, and the stark simplicity of people's daily lives in clear, simple prose:

> They swept out of the little town and down the level road toward the South. Soon the road dwindled and disappeared, and they struck across a world carpeted with an endless reach of curly mesquite grass. The wheels made no sound. The tireless ponies bounded ahead at an unbroken gallop. The temperate wind, made fragrant by thousands of blue and yellow flowers, roared gloriously in their ears.

In early 1896, William Porter heard that the Austin bank examiners had reopened his case, and on February 14, he was indicted for embezzlement. On his way to Austin to face the charges, he impulsively changed trains and fled to New Orleans, setting out shortly afterward for Central America.

William Porter led an idyllic existence in Honduras, "a life full of music, flowers and low laughter," but news of Athol's serious decline brought him home in 1897. In Texas, the courts postponed his trial because of his wife's condition, and he devoted himself to her care, reading to her, feeding her, carrying her out to the carriage for their daily outing; but she continued to waste away, and in July 1897 she died. Porter spent the time between his wife's death and his upcoming trial writing. The one bright spot in this long, bleak period was his first sale of a story to *McClure's Magazine*, a relatively new and adventurous journal dedicated to mirroring the concerns and activities of everyday people.

At the trial, it was revealed that William Sydney Porter had borrowed some money from the bank — a fairly common practice among bank employees — but there was every indication that he intended to pay it back. Unfortunately, his flight to Central America weighed heavily against him; it was generally believed that his case was also used to set an example to other bank employees, who might have continued to help themselves to company funds. On March 25, 1898, Porter was sentenced to five years in the Ohio Penitentiary, which was taking a share of federal prisoners. He was thirty-five years old, and along with other vital statistics listed in his prison record, his education was described as "good" and his personal habits as "intemperate."

Porter was intensely depressed in prison. The prison physician, who like many others before him befriended Will, recalled that among the thousands of prisoners he had seen, he had "never known a man who was so deeply humiliated by his prison experience." The doctor also recalled that Porter soon began to write stories about the other prisoners. Because he was working as the prison pharmacist, and was "unusually good" at his job, Porter was allowed "to look after the minor ills of the prisoners at night. He would spend two or three hours on the tiers of cells every night and knew most of the prisoners and their life stories."

Writing became Porter's salvation. Although he personally was treated well, the atmosphere was brutal and harsh, and he never came to terms with it. He spent most of his spare time writing, sending numerous letters full of self-reproach to his in-laws, who were taking care of their granddaughter. His letters to Margaret perpetuated the fiction that he was working at a demanding job out of town.

Many critics rate the fourteen short stories Porter wrote in prison as among his finest work. There is a decidedly autobiographical quality to them. As Gerald Langford has written in his analysis of O. Henry's life and work, eight of the tales are based on the idea of "the vindication of a character who has in some way forfeited his claim to respectability or even integrity . . . and the plot invariably turns on the regeneration of an admitted delinquent, not on the vindication of a character who is blameless." By the time he was released from prison, he had become a disciplined master of the short-story form. Three stories, which he submitted for publication through a friend in New Orleans, were printed while he was still behind bars, and the others appeared after he was released for good behavior in 1901.

The name he signed to his stories was O. Henry. It is obvious that he intended to avoid the stigma of a criminal's name, but opinion varies as to the origin of his pseudonym. The two most popular theories are that he borrowed the name of a prison guard, Orrin Henry, or that the name was a variation on that of a celebrated French pharmacist, Étiene-Ossian Henry, which Porter saw abbreviated in the *United States Dispensatory*, a reference book that he used while working in the prison pharmacy.

According to accounts of his release from prison, it was enormously important to Will that he return to the world in as much style as he could muster. The well-tailored tweeds he had worn to jail had been misplaced by his keepers, but he recoiled at wearing the standard cheap suit given to all discharged prisoners. He had made so great an impression on everyone in the prison — from officials to guards to inmates — that they assembled a wardrobe for him from their own clothing. So, attired in a fine brown worsted suit, a black derby, and pigskin gloves, the now stocky, round-faced man in his fortieth year walked out the prison doors without a backward glance.

After a short stay in Pittsburgh, where his in-laws and daughter were living, O. Henry went to New York. His response to the city, which he had never seen, was profound. It was as if, after wandering aimlessly all his life, he had finally come home. To a newcomer, he said, New York City immediately became an enemy or a lover. Without doubt, to O. Henry Manhattan was a lover: Manhattan "woos you to its heart with the subtlety of a siren."

O. Henry's attention to detail, his heightened sensitivity to nuance in word and experience, made him Manhattan's most astute and faithful biographer. But he did not romanticize what he saw; he drew on many of the same inequities and injustices as Stephen Crane had for his work. Like Crane's *Maggie*, many of O. Henry's stories feature young women who turned to prostitution as a desperate escape from twelve-hour-day, $8.00-a-week jobs in sweatshops. He describes such a girl, in his story "The Trimmed Lamp," as having a "look of silent but contemptuous revolt against cheated womanhood; of sad prophecy of the vengeance to come. When she laughs her loudest the look is still there. The same look can be seen in the eyes of Russian peasants; and those of us left will see it on Gabriel's face when he comes to blow us up."

Prostitution continued to be a major theme of writers who wished to expose the more shameful aspects of city life. New York, as the country's most powerful city, threw glaring light on the problems that arise from unbridled ambition, avarice, and a lack of social conscience. In O. Henry's day, Manhattan was considered a "wide open" town. There were an estimated twenty-five thousand prostitutes on the streets, and hundreds of "cadets" regularly roamed the ethnic neighborhoods, looking for young girls to "recruit" for police-protected houses of prostitution. One victim was the daughter of a rabbi, and it is symbolic of the extent of the city's corruption that although the newspapers reported the story, which involved the girl's being drugged and beaten by her captors, not one paper suggested that she be rescued from the brothel. The newspapers, and many citizens, obviously accepted the fact that the brothel enjoyed complete — and expensive — police protection.

At this time, the lower reaches of Manhattan were patrolled and, in a sense, ruled by street gangs, whose dangerous existence fed O. Henry's imagination. Many of these groups of young men can be found in his stories, such as the Stovepipe Gang, whose turf was Hell's Kitchen, and who made their living by mugging visitors unwelcome in their terrain. The Stovepipe Gang and their leader, a fierce young man called Kid Brady, appear in O. Henry's story "Vanity and Some Sable." "The chefs in 'Hell's Kitchen' are many," O. Henry wrote, "and the Stovepipe Gang wears the cordon blue."

O. Henry himself had no qualms about visiting Hell's Kitchen or any other mean street in the city. He'd explain to a reluctant companion that if a fellow minded his own business and "didn't butt in," he would be left alone. One of his few intimate friends, the journalist William S. Williams, remembered going with O. Henry to "some of the riskiest dives in the toughest sections of New York." Once there, they would seat themselves in a corner, "apparently interested in nothing that was going on about us." In truth, O. Henry was taking in everything, every gesture and conversation, all the physical details.

While O. Henry incorporated these people into his stories of city life, he never considered himself a social reformer. Unlike Stephen Crane, William Dean Howells, and writers like Theodore Dreiser, Frank Norris, and Jack London, he did not use realistic and naturalistic fiction as a moral platform. O. Henry was, he insisted, simply a "storyteller," who wrote primarily to make a living. "Writing is my business," he would say when asked about his artistic goals. It was his "way of getting money to pay room rent, to buy food and clothes and Pilsner."

Yet to the millions of people who looked for his stories every week in the *New York World* or in magazines, his voice rang out against social injustice, against the terrible gap between the lives of the "four hundred" and the "four million." But it was not a despairing voice; O. Henry's stories were optimistic. "It was O. Henry's special gift," the critic Lloyd Morris has written, to portray what politicians would call "the little people [as] they saw themselves. . . . His myth was the one . . . Americans wanted to believe. In an age of wealth for the few and poverty for the many, it asserted that all things were still possible to the common man, and that most of them would turn out to be good."

The tales O. Henry spun for his appreciative readers often showed ordinary people triumphing over the daily struggle and escaping from the despairs of real life to realize their heart's desire for a happy ending. This search for fulfillment, according to the critic Carl Van Doren, is at the heart of almost all fiction. No matter what name it goes by, "something must furnish the element of wonder and the desired miracle. . . . It is O. Henry's most powerful aid, brilliant in his endings, everywhere pervasive." The surprise ending that to many readers is the hallmark of an O. Henry story stems from the writer's own sense of wonder at the ability of everyday life suddenly to make one's heart skip a beat.

In 1904, O. Henry had been hired by the *New York World* to write a weekly story, for each of which he was paid $100. This income allowed him to move to a Gramercy Park apartment with a fireplace and a big bay window looking out onto Irving Place. He loved the neighborhood's serenity and grace and its sense of history. Gramercy Park would often appear in his stories; "The Discounters of Money" is about an aristocratic family named Van der Ruysling that receives the very first key to the park.

In "The Trimmed Lamp," Nancy and Lou, two young working girls who have traveled diverging paths, meet again outside the park gates. Nancy, who has come to value honesty and kindness more than money, is engaged to Lou's humble, cast-off suitor. Lou has gone astray and become a rich man's mistress. When they meet, Lou, dressed in furs and jewels, is heartbroken at the news of Nancy's engagement and realizes the terrible mistake she has made. She crouches "down against the iron fence of the park sobbing turbulently." A young policeman passes by, "pretending not to notice, for he was wise enough to know that these matters are beyond help so far as the power he represents is concerned, though he rap on the pavement with his nightstick and the sound goes up to the furthermost stars."

O. Henry also loved being close to Healy's Café on Irving Place and Eighteenth Street. Although the Players' and the National Arts clubs were also nearby, Healy's was the only kind of club he wanted to join, and the tavern was actually called "the Club" by its regular customers.* The other patrons were closely studied by the quietly convivial O. Henry, who used them, of course, in his stories. There was a voluble hack driver, and a Sicilian shoemaker who gave advice on Italian wines and the good Italian restaurants around town, and a small German man who was called "the Professor," though he supplemented the income he earned teaching German by working as the janitor for a Lutheran church.

O. Henry's cohorts at Healy's respected him not only for remaining untouched by his growing fame, but for the way he could hold his liquor. O. Henry drank constantly. One friend estimated his intake at two quarts of whiskey a day, in addition to the wine and beer he drank at meals. The bartender at Healy's was often telephoned by O. Henry and asked to send a bottle of Scotch across the street to his apartment, or the writer would drop by at ten in the

---

*Healy's Café is now Pete's Tavern, and remains very much as it was during O. Henry's time. There is a plaque over the front booth informing customers this is the table where O. Henry wrote "The Gift of the Magi."

morning for a Sazerac cocktail, a favorite drink made with absinthe, to warm the morning muse. He never seemed drunk; his behavior, like his dress, was faultless.

The money he spent on liquor did diminish his income, as did his unrestrained spending on the good clothes and food he adored. He was unfailingly generous to anyone short of cash, even strangers. He kept a running account with a physician named Colin Luke Begg, and if he saw a man or woman who looked in need of medical care, he'd hand that person one of his calling cards, on which he'd write a whimsical note to Begg: "Dear Doctor, this unfortunate is in need of your assistance; see that she gets it and bill me." When friends cautioned that he was taken advantage of by those with hard-luck stories, he'd wave the advice away: "Anyone can have my money any time; they don't have to lie to me to get it."

During the two years that O. Henry worked for the *World*, the 113 stories he wrote were syndicated all over the country, reaching nearly a million people. Since he was also writing for most of the magazines, he developed various devices, used over and over, that became characteristic aspects of O. Henry tales. The literary critic Eugene Current-Garcia has described these as "the chatty, short-cut opening; the catchy, piquant descriptive phrasing; the confidential, reminiscent narrator; the chance meeting of old pals; and half a dozen or more versions of the surprise ending." Although some would later attack these "formulas," arguing that they made his stories contrived and superficial, Professor Current-Garcia has said that O. Henry's faithful audience "marveled at his astonishing inventiveness of plot, always the same old sentimental themes of sacrificial devotion, recaptured dreams, integrity restored, and love triumphant; but they were ever in new combinations, settings, and situations."

More often than not, his editor at the *World* had to pick up the stories at Irving Place himself, for they were almost always late. O. Henry carried fully formed stories around in his head, but he wrote at an uneven pace, sometimes finishing a whole story in an hour, sometimes writing only a few lines a day. The editor finally got so tired of the constant battle to get material on time that he refused to pay O. Henry until each story was delivered. The author managed a compromise: he was paid half the fee for delivering the first part of a story and received the second $50 on its completion. Some critics have commented that certain O. Henry stories appear to have introductions that have little bearing on what follows, apparently the result of this arrangement. Pressed for money, O. Henry would hand in any introduction that came to mind, often ignoring that opening when he finally sat down to write the story.

His most famous tale, "The Gift of the Magi," about the sacrificial devotion of a young husband and wife, was written when the *World* asked for a special Christmas story. Since the paper planned to print it with full color illustrations, the text and pictures had to be at hand before the rest of the magazine was set in type. After O. Henry repeatedly missed deadlines, the illustrator, Dan Smith, was dispatched to Irving Place. There he found the author, who cheerfully admitted that he had not produced a word and had no idea at all of what to write.

Mr. Smith was distraught and tried to make the writer understand that he could not deliver the artwork he was being pressed for until he knew the story's theme. O. Henry stood at his bay window, looking out at the snow falling quietly on Irving Place and at the well-dressed shoppers on their return home, carrying prettily wrapped gifts. After a few moments, he turned to the unhappy artist, and smiled encouragingly. "I'll tell you what to do," he said. "Just draw a picture of a poorly furnished rooming house over on the West Side. In the room there is only a chair or two, a chest of drawers, a bed, and a trunk. On the bed, a man and a girl are sitting side by side. They are talking about Christmas. The man has a watch fob in his hand. He is playing with it while he is thinking. The girl's principal feature is the long, beautiful hair that is hanging down her back. That's all I can think of now," he said, turning from the window. "But the story is coming."

Once a story was written, O. Henry rarely revised it, and he had little patience with writers who took themselves or their craft too seriously. When a young author asked his advice on writing a short story, O. Henry answered, "The first step is to get a kitchen table, a wooden chair, a wad of yellow foolscap writing paper, one lead pencil, and a drinking glass. They are the props. Then you secure a flask of Scotch whiskey and a few oranges, which I will describe as the sustenance. We now come to the plot, frequently styled the inspiration. Combining a little orange juice with a little Scotch, the author drinks to the health of all magazine editors, sharpens his pencil, and begins to write. When the oranges are empty and the flask is dry, a salable piece of fiction is ready."

O. Henry's only other theory of writing was just as easily summed up to an interviewer: "I'll give you the whole secret of short-story writing. Here it is. Rule 1: Write stories that please yourself. There is no Rule 2."

As much as he liked the regulars at "the Club," O. Henry enjoyed the company of only a few other famous writers. Franklin P. Adams, Christopher Morley, and George Jean Nathan were among the authors who liked to tag along when he planned to spend the night wandering. But when the Lotos Club wanted to honor him at a literary evening, he hastily declined, explaining that there would be far too many people there for him to study and try to guess "what is going on in the minds behind"; hence, there was no point to his attending.

When he was accused of being primarily a New York writer, O. Henry argued that the location of his stories could be altered to fit any place in the country: "Rub out the Flatiron Building and put in the Town Hall, and the story will fit just as truly in any up-State town." His universal popularity substantiates his claim that human nature was the same wherever you find it, but New York remained the only place where he was ever comfortable, and he was reluctant to leave it, even for a few hours. When a friend insisted on taking him fishing in Port Washington, O. Henry said at day's end, "The thing I like most about this place is the railroad that runs out of it towards Manhattan."

He was a completely sedentary man, who grew pudgier as he got older. Tennis, golf, and walks in the country were wholly without appeal; the only activity he cared about was watching people. Toward the end of his life, when he was ailing, he went to Asheville, North

Carolina, for several months in the clean mountain climate. When he returned, he told a friend that "there was too much scenery and fresh air. What I need is a steam-heated flat and no ventilation or exercise."

The quality that everyone was most conscious of in O. Henry was his air of mystery. He had a fundamental reticence that made few people, even those who were fondest of him, feel they really knew him. And he had many odd quirks, such as always taking a chair against the wall in a restaurant, and refusing to have photographs of himself published in the *World* or any other publication he wrote for, no matter how much the editors emphasized the publicity value. A few people knew his real name, and many knew that he had spent time in Texas, New Orleans, and Honduras, since the places appeared in his stories, but as Richard Duffy, the editor of *Ainslee's* magazine, explained, "Anyone who endeavored to question him about himself would learn very little."

O. Henry made no secret, however, of his intellectual or moral beliefs. He was an outspoken advocate of women's rights, and was particularly sympathetic to the tired young women who worked at joyless, underpaid jobs. He hated the term *shopgirl*, and protested that "there are girls who work in shops. . . . But why turn their occupation into an adjective? Let us be fair. We do not refer to the girls who live on Fifth Avenue as 'marriage-girls.'" (Theodore Roosevelt always credited O. Henry's stories with bringing the plight of the shopgirl to his attention.)

He was also intensely interested in what the newspapers were calling "the New Woman." Independent females challenged their circumscribed role in society by doing everything from smoking in public to deliberately staying single to seeking careers that were more interesting, if not more financially rewarding, than the shopgirl could hope to know. At his request, Anne Partlan, a writer who worked in an advertising agency, arranged small parties where he could meet some of her friends. He never revealed who he was, and, recalled Miss Partlan, "they never dreamed that this Mr. Porter, who fitted so well into our queer makeshift life, was a genius. He had absolutely no pose."

O. Henry's romantic involvements with women were always

cloaked in mystery. He was famous enough to gain entry into Stanford White's world of extravagant sex, but he never did. Nor did he mix with the social elite, who might have introduced him to well-bred young women. O. Henry treated all women with courtesy and compassion, but the women he slept with were generally of "easy virtue," content with a one-night companion. He once even advertised in the personal column of the *New York Herald*, a guide to "love" in New York City that was popularly called the "Whore's Daily Guide and Compendium." Under yet another pseudonym, he asked to meet an attractive, unconventional young woman who was "interested in artistic ideas with a view to mutual improvement and entertainment."

On September 11, 1907, on his forty-fifth birthday, perhaps tiring of his subterranean adventures, O. Henry arranged formally to meet Sara Lindsay Coleman, a woman he had known in his boyhood and with whom he had begun a correspondence. Although he confessed the story of his past to her, she did not weaken in her resolve to marry him. And, to the surprise of almost everyone who knew O. Henry, they did marry.

Irving Place, O. Henry's residence and favorite resting spot

He had already moved to East Twenty-fourth Street, because his Irving Place landlady, to whom he had become very attached, had purchased a house there. After his marriage, though his energy was flagging, he moved several times more, to the Chelsea Hotel, to Washington Place, and even to a lavish home on Long Island. But the intensely private writer found the intimacy of marriage oppressive, no matter how large a space he shared with his wife. He told Sara that the "door to the cage" had to be kept open so that he could slip in and out when he needed to, and he took a separate apartment at the Caledonia Hotel, on West Twenty-sixth Street, in which to work.

The problems of his marriage seemed to exacerbate his failing health, as well as adding to his financial woes. He worked ferociously to maintain his new standard of living, producing twenty-nine new stories in 1908, but he found it difficult to work up the enthusiasm that had always fueled his creativity.

By the summer of 1909, it was clear that O. Henry's marriage, like his health, was in serious decline. Sara went to Asheville for an extended visit, and O. Henry, remaining behind, tried to recapture the pleasures of his bachelor days, but he could not rise out of the mental and physical doldrums. Toward the end of the year, he took his recuperative trip to North Carolina, but when he returned, alone, to the Caledonia, he was an invalid, unwilling to see anyone and rarely leaving his room. Only in his forties, O. Henry had advanced diabetes, an enlarged heart, and cirrhosis of the liver. To those who did manage to visit him, he seemed, at times, uncharacteristically hopeless; to one friend he said, with a sigh, "The train's too late for happiness."

On June 3, 1910, O. Henry collapsed and was taken to the hospital. At midnight, when the nurse turned off the lights, the writer called out a paraphrase of the words from a popular old song: "Pull up the shades so I can see New York; I don't want to go home in the dark." These were his last words, although, according to his doctor, Charles Hancock, he was conscious until his death, early on the morning of Sunday, June 5.

O. Henry's past was not discovered until well after his death, and it was relatively meaningless in relation to the place that he had established for himself in American letters. His popularity was extraordinary. During his life, more than five million copies of his books were sold in the United States, and his work had been translated into a dozen languages.

The range of his popularity is perhaps best illustrated by a scene that took place in the fall of 1906, outside a bookstore near Harvard Yard. Two men were looking at a display of O. Henry books in the window; one, a Harvard freshman, the other a distinguished elderly man. Smiling, the men discussed their passion for the man who was their favorite author. The freshman was John Reed, who became a leading figure in the radical movement, went to Russia, and wrote *Ten Days That Shook the World;* the older man was William James.

II

THE
NEW REALISM
IN ART

⸱⸱⸱⸱⸱

IN 1910, a young artist named George Bellows moved with his wife, Emma, into a small, three-story red brick house on East Nineteenth Street. Bellows was proud of owning a home in such an artistically congenial neighborhood. How wonderful to be so close to the Gramercy Park studio of his mentor, Robert Henri, as well as to the Players' Club, where he spent many companionable hours, and the National Arts Club, where his work was often exhibited!

Funds were in short supply, so the Bellowses rented out the ground floor of their new house, using the second floor as their living quarters and the third floor as a spacious studio and gallery. There, for the next fifteen years, George Bellows produced a prodigious number of drawings, lithographs, and oils.

"I arose surrounded by Methodists and Republicans," George Bellows was fond of saying. He was born on August 12, 1882, in Columbus, Ohio, to parents older than most. His mother, Anna, was forty-three and his father, George Sr., a contractor and builder, was fifty-five when the baby was born, and they were dedicated to both the Republican Party and to the Methodist faith. The austere rules of the religion were strictly observed by the Bellows family, to

George Bellows, a quintessentially American painter of powerful messages — and a star shortstop

the frustration of their restless, energetic son. Church attendance was a somber constant of family life, with rigorous preparations every Sunday morning, and stiff, uncomfortable clothes for George to put on before climbing into the family carriage for the solemn ride to church.

Sunday afternoons were dismally boring. After an enormous meal, his parents would rest while George sat quietly, drawing pictures of things that excited him in the outside world, like parades and steam engines. His mother and father received these drawings with limited enthusiasm, for it was Anna Bellows's fervent wish that her only child would grow up to achieve life's ultimate success by becoming a Methodist minister. Only George's young aunt Fanny, who lived with the family for several years, and who provided some youthful lightness to the atmosphere, praised his drawings and encouraged the plan George had begun to form before he was five years old — to become an artist.

At school, the skinny boy whose blue eyes lit up when he talked about art was derided for being a "sissy." It didn't help that George's mother insisted on dressing him in white suits instead of the sturdy gray and brown clothes the other boys wore. The white suits were regularly stained with the bloody marks of battles.

Happily, around his tenth birthday George discovered a passion for baseball that helped improve his social standing. He adored the grace and deftness of the game the whole country had come to love, and with his usual determination he set about becoming skillful on the ball field. In time, he also learned to play the newly invented game of basketball, which perfectly suited his gangly frame; by fifteen the sandy-haired boy was close to his full adult height of six feet, two inches. George loved playing ball and adored the gruff camaraderie of the games. Closing the door on the pious atmosphere of his home, the boy would race off to the ribald give-and-take of the ball field, where he cultivated a vocabulary of profanities that became an inherent and colorful part of his personality as an adult.

By the time he entered high school, his life was quite full. Not only was he playing ball; he was singing in the glee club, acting in the dramatic club, and producing all the illustrations for the school's monthly newspaper. By the time George entered Ohio State University, in 1901, he knew he had moved far away from the expectations of his parents. There wasn't the slightest possibility that he would enter the church, nor did he evince any interest in his father's occupation; neither building nor business would ever claim George Bellows as one of its own.

The only things that mattered to George Bellows when he entered college were art and baseball, but Ohio State gave him more opportunity to play ball than to study artistic technique. Art courses were closed to freshmen, which bothered George until he enrolled in a literature course taught by a young man named Joseph Taylor. Taylor welcomed George into his home, where they spent captivating hours together discussing the work of Walt Whitman, whom many Americans still found strange, and of the Irish playwright George Bernard Shaw, whose "radical" values were even more disturbing to conventional readers.

To Bellows, the ideas Taylor introduced were intriguing, although, or perhaps because, they differed dramatically from the principles on which he was raised. Beside Taylor's fireside, George for the first time sympathetically examined the controversial issues of humanism, socialism, and even anarchy. In middle-class Middle America at the turn of the century, anarchism was fiercely despised, and no distinction was drawn between anarchists who advocated violence and those who accepted the ideology as a political philosophy. George could vaguely remember hearing about the bloody Haymarket Riots in Chicago in 1886, and when he began his freshman year the country was rocked by the news that an anarchist had assassinated President William McKinley. (This made Theodore Roosevelt, who was born in Gramercy Park, the youngest President of the United States.)

While George Bellows never supported violence then or later, he soon came to understand that savagery was not the province only of revolutionaries. When a wave of lynchings swept through the South after his second year at college, George's liberal convictions deepened. The newspapers of Columbus printed vivid accounts of the brutalities, and the stories haunted George Bellows. (Later in life, he would draw on them for one of his most compelling lithographs.) The need for fairness and equity in a country of diverse people and broad opportunity became a continuing preoccupation for the young college student. He lacked only an environment where his concerns would be recognized as valid so that he could shape them into what would become the powerful underpinnings of his art.

George's political consciousness added to his dissatisfaction with life in Columbus. Family battles over his plans were frequent, often ending with Anna Bellows in tears over the quarrels between father and son, and George storming out the door for a furious bicycle ride to the more sympathetic home of Joseph Taylor. Finally realizing that he could never convince his father that art was a reasonable — indeed, necessary — choice of career, George stacked the cards against himself by skipping his final exams at the end of his junior year. This meant that he would not be able to return to school in the fall and so could proceed with the plan he had never abandoned, to move to New York and study art.

"Arrived in New York, I found myself in my first art school under Robert Henri having never heard of him before. . . . *My life begins at this point*," George Bellows once wrote about his artistic beginnings.

Robert Henri, a charismatic man, was only in his thirties but was well on his way to becoming one of the most important figures in the history of American art. Trained in Europe and at the Academy of Fine Arts in Philadelphia, Henri had been elected to the National Academy of Design, and his paintings already hung in important collections all over America. The bulk of his income, however, came from teaching, for which he possessed extraordinary gifts. When

Robert Henri, a man of extraordinary dynamism and a teacher of magnetic power, who helped transform American art

Bellows arrived in New York, Henri was the most popular teacher at the New York School of Art, on West Fifty-seventh Street. Owned and administered by the artist William Merritt Chase, the school was just a short walk from the Fifty-seventh Street YMCA, George Bellows's first home in the city.

The initial meeting between George Bellows and Robert Henri was not a particularly auspicious one. Warmly welcoming Bellows into the men's life drawing class, the tall, handsome teacher asked to see the work that George had brought with him from Columbus. After his freshman year at Ohio State, George had taken courses in color theory and water color, but he had been given no help in developing a style of his own. The drawings he had turned out for the school paper and yearbooks were delightful, but they were unquestionably derivative of such fashionable artists as Charles Dana Gibson, Howard Chandler Christy, and John Singer Sargent.

As Bellows waited eagerly for Henri's reaction, the teacher looked carefully at the adept imitations of other artists' work and then innocently inquired, "Haven't I seen these before?" George quietly reached for the drawings and put them back in his portfolio. If he was embarrassed by Henri's unmistakable rejection of his work, George quickly forgot it as he listened to Henri address the class. "An artist who doesn't use his imagination is a mechanic. . . . Don't belong to any school. . . . Don't tie up with any technique. . . . A drawing is not a copy but an invention."

The Methodist boy from Ohio was dizzy with new ideas when he returned to the Y that evening, and he ate his forty-five-cent dinner alone. The other residents were nice enough fellows, but not the kind of people who would appreciate the ideas he was excitedly replaying in his head. George didn't feel lonely, however, for there were a number of people at the school he had already guessed would make wonderful companions — companions who could understand and share the excitement of Robert Henri's inspiring approach to teaching art.

Among George Bellows's classmates at the New York School of Art were several who showed exceptional promise. There was a shy, unassuming young man named Edward Hopper and a confident for-

mer architectural student from Columbia named Rockwell Kent. The
same strong camaraderie existed among Henri's students as George
had first experienced on the ball field. Indeed, encouraged by Henri,
George formed a school team that played boisterous games against
the Art Students' League and the School of the National Academy of
Design. Bellows earned money through baseball, by hiring himself
out to semiprofessional teams in the New York area.

This extra income allowed him to take an apartment with another
student on West Fifty-eighth Street, which, though crowded with
paints and easels, made George feel that he was finally, and happily,
becoming a professional artist. Columbus seemed very far away, although George exaggerated his mild midwestern drawl for no apparent reason except to distinguish himself. Perhaps in memory of
the white suits of his childhood, he also went out of his way to dress
untidily, with rumpled collar and necktie askew and paint specks all
over his shirt and jacket.

Ethel Clarke, a friend of Emma Storey, the girl George Bellows
would eventually marry, remembered her first sight of the unkempt,
volatile George Bellows when they were both invited to Emma's family home in New Jersey. Miss Clarke "heard musical rumbling from
afar, growing louder and louder as the song developed — 'Rolling
Down to Rio' — his current favorite. . . . Emma had said George
was as big as all outdoors, and when he came plunging up the front
steps, he seemed to fill the whole horizon." Dinner table conversation
was loudly argumentative; George and Emma's father shouted the
virtues of socialist versus Republican politics between every swallow.
In fact, George appeared to be "violent and argumentative about
almost everything," recalled Miss Clarke. He was "lacking in all
small courtesies. . . . Different from anyone I'd ever met. He irritated and shocked me." Yet when George yelled to Emma to play
"real music" instead of the ragtime she was tinkling out on the piano
for an afternoon sing, his renditions of "Mandalay," "Jeanie with the
Light Brown Hair," and "Hills of Home" were so beautiful that
Ethel Clarke was deeply moved and began to understand Emma's
contention that George Bellows really was a gifted and sensitive man.

If the full range of George Bellows's behavior seemed excessive at the Storeys' home in New Jersey, New York was a city able to accommodate it, just as George would always be able to accept the city's amazing mix of squalor and splendor. It was Robert Henri who taught him that the wild array of styles in Manhattan should be celebrated by any artist who truly wanted to capture life. Henri's conviction was that people must be painted as they really were — living in every possible environment, reflecting not just the lovely and the elegant, but the most mundane, vulgar, and often bleak aspects of everyday life.

Years later, the group of artists who held this view would be labeled the Ash Can School, suggesting that they preferred to depict what was ugly rather than beautiful in life. In truth, one of Robert Henri's most fervent beliefs was "There is beauty in everything if it looks beautiful to *your* eyes. You can find it anywhere, everywhere." Smiling, speaking in his distinctively mellow voice, he told his students that the artist in New York was blessed by being able to have "delightful days of drifting among people . . . stopping as long as he likes — no need to reach any point, moving in any direction following the call of interests. He moves through life as he finds it, not passing negligently the things he loves, but stopping to know them, and to note them down in the shorthand of his sketch-book, [with] a box of oils . . . or on his drawing pad."

Henri, who profoundly influenced a generation of important American artists, encouraged his disciples to take risks, to break free of convention and notions of "acceptable" subjects. "Like any hunter," he said, the artist "hits or misses. He is looking for what he loves, he tries to capture it. . . . Those who are not hunters do not see these things." Perhaps more than any of his classmates, George Bellows immediately and continuously lived by this advice. Like O. Henry, Bellows was almost obsessed with New York, and he explored it hungrily, creating his stories in a sketchbook.

The rising height of the city alone fascinated the man from Columbus. He would join the crowds who had stopped to marvel at the grandeur of the Flatiron Building, and he often paused to watch the finishing touches being put on that amazing marvel of steel construction, the New York Times Building, on Forty-second Street and

Broadway. The Queensboro Bridge was also under construction, soon to link yet another borough with Manhattan, and he loved to amble along the riverfront to watch it going up. Like O. Henry, Bellows also found the city's slums absorbing, and he would make quick sketches of rough gang members and oddly garbed immigrant children, or weary men pushing peddlers' wagons through the crowded ghetto streets.

By the turn of the century, the population of New York City had reached almost four million, and more and more were immigrants who had escaped the poverty and lack of opportunity in their native countries. The waves of immigration would eventually lead to the establishment of quotas, in 1924 and 1929, but while the gates were still open, there was a dramatic flow of new arrivals.

Crowds of astonishing numbers surround the noisy pushcart commerce of the Lower East Side.

Perhaps the most controversial group of immigrants was the Jews. For one thing, they numbered 600,000 by 1903, ten times their number only twenty years earlier. (By the 1920s, there would be nearly two million Jews in Manhattan, making New York City "the largest Jewish city in the world.") They were also a people whom many established New Yorkers found too determined to move into positions of power. As the twentieth century began, Jews already dominated the tailoring and jewelry trades, and more prosperous Jewish immigrants had begun to establish their own banks and investment houses and were controlling much of the city's wealth. Others had started businesses that made them fortunes, and were playing an important part in Manhattan's cultural life.

An Englishman who visited New York in 1910 reported that wealthy Jews were the major audiences for New York's concerts and opera performances. And the amazing new invention of moving pictures had been developed by creative, ambitious Jews from the ghetto into the most popular inexpensive amusement in the city. A garment worker, William Fox, managed to get together enough money to open a series of "nickelodeons," and a fur cutter, Marcus Loew, was building his own chain with a partner, Adolph Zukor. Zukor soon went on to open an independent moving picture house on Fourteenth Street, where he planned to show longer movies than the traditional few-minute "flickers"; he wanted to compete with the Broadway plays that had made so many theatrical producers wealthy. The tenement dwellers who had toiled alongside these entrepreneurs in downtown factories marveled at their achievements, but no one predicted that they would soon become millionaire leaders of entertainment empires, or that their motion pictures would play a vital role in American culture.

For the majority of people in the ghetto, entrance into the mainstream of American life seemed unlikely. Despite the popular thesis that New York was a "magic cauldron" in which people of diverse nationalities could shape themselves into a common persona, ghetto life was remarkably insular. In the Jewish ghetto, which ran between the Bowery and the East River, the shop signs were in Yiddish, written in Hebrew letters, and Yiddish was the language spoken in the streets. An Italian writer visiting Little Italy was amazed to find that many Italians "hardly know they are outside their native land because they have everything Italian: friends, churches, school, theater, banks, businesses, daily papers, societies, meeting places. And they can travel for many kilometers without hearing spoken any language except the Italian or Italian dialect." In Chinatown, as in China, one

rarely saw a woman on the streets — only older men wearing traditional costumes and their hair in pigtails. North of the Bowery were
streets inhabited mainly by Germans, and near St. Mark's Place were
the pleasant Gypsy cafés of Little Hungary.

The Bohemians — from Bohemia — lived a little farther up Second Avenue and worked mainly in the neighborhood's enormous cigar factories. By working eighteen hours a day, a husband and wife
could turn out three thousand cigars a week, bringing in a combined
salary of $15. New York City had also become the country's center
of the growing industry of ready-made clothing, and it was the tenement dweller whose labor kept it functioning. All night long, lights
in the ghetto neighborhoods shone on men and women huddled
over sewing machines or pressing tables, the heat of the apartments
suffocatingly exacerbated by the clouds of moist steam. By day,
they continued their work in enormous, crowded ill-ventilated
sweatshops.

As George Bellows "hunted" out his subjects on walks around
Manhattan, his socialist and anarchist sympathies were stimulated
anew. He would stroll along upper Fifth Avenue, where nursemaids
shepherded properly dressed children into Central Park, and then
head down to the ghetto, where he would gaze up at a six-story tenement and know that the average two-room apartment might house
a father, mother, ten children, and six lodgers to help pay the rent.
Privacy was nonexistent in the ghetto. In some other rundown areas
of the city, there were still vestiges of dignified living, such as door-
bells and janitors to maintain the buildings, but in the ghetto there
were no such symbols of privacy and respect and care. Any gang
member or bum could enter the dank hallways of a tenement house,
thereby forcing its residents to stay inside even if they may have
wanted to step out for a moment's respite, or if the children had no
other playground but the teeming streets or the tenement roof.

George carried his outrage back to Robert Henri and his circle of
friends, who had accepted Bellows because of Henri's obvious fond-
ness for him. In Henri's spacious studio, decorated by the bright
colors of his newest paintings, the air pleasantly fragrant with the

smell of coffee, beer, and tobacco, Henri held forth at his Tuesday evening, weekly open houses for painter friends and his more talented students. Four men from Henri's days in Philadelphia were always there: John Sloan, much rougher in manner than Henri, but an inspiring teacher when he took over his friend's classes while Henri was traveling; the glamorous Everett Shin; the short, hearty George Luks, who helped support himself by drawing a daily comic strip, "The Yellow Kid," for the *New York World*. Luks's often abrasive manner was balanced by the quiet gentleness of William Glackens, who was making impressive experiments with painting in the style of the French impressionists. Added to this core group were three men Henri had met soon after he arrived in New York in 1900. They were Arthur B. Davies, Ernest Lawson, and Maurice Prendergast, and together with the Philadelphia contingent they constituted what would soon be called, with varying degrees of praise or derision, "the Eight."

These artists, who made Robert Henri's studio the center of their social and intellectual life, were, like Henri, strongly socialist in their politics. As they discussed the cruelty of the ghetto and the sweatshop, they helped George place his moral indignation into both a political and artistic context. To them, art and social change were inextricably related. And, just as it had in literature, the harshness of life in urban America was inspiring a creative rebellion in art, complete with dramatic new forms of expression. The everyday experiences of the tenement dweller could not be captured as they were by George Luks in his 1905 painting *Hester Street* without acknowledging how unfair and debasing life could be in that mean environment. To Robert Henri's circle, such acknowledgment was not merely an artistic abstraction; it called for devoting considerable energy to liberal activist causes.

Yet Henri's Tuesday evenings were not all serious discourse. High spirits often interrupted the impassioned conversation. George Bellows, with his gift for mimicry and his spontaneous wit, shone at the extemporaneous skits — complete with choreography and costumes — that the group regularly put on. Henri's Tuesday group also liked to engage in a kind of artistic race, lining up at drawing boards and starting to sketch at the same moment to see who could first complete a drawing of another or most swiftly commit to paper some shared experience. But when the games were over and discussion began again, Robert Henri was the natural leader, throwing out a provocative question or probing for a more substantive response.

Two issues were central to the Tuesday evenings. The first had to do with the development of a truly American art. Robert Henri has been credited with introducing French impressionism to America. In an introduction to Henri's classic book, *The Art Spirit*, Forbes Watson wrote, "One can hardly believe now . . . that many of the young men and women who studied under him, although so passionately interested in painting, first heard the names of Daumier, Manet, Degas . . . and a host of others from the lips of Robert Henri." On the other hand, he explained, "The blond beauties of sunlit landscapes had no special appeal for him. What he did take from the impressionists . . . was the idea of looking at contemporary life and contemporary scenes with a fresh, unprejudiced, unacademic eye." Thus, according to Watson, Henri "showed them the Frenchmen, but he did not encourage them to imitate the Frenchmen. Without jingo, Robert Henri taught them artistic self-respect. It was not a crime to look at American material with American eyes."

The second issue that preoccupied Henri's Tuesday evenings was how to bring to the attention of important collectors art portraying social realism so that American artists would not feel compelled to imitate Europeans in order to sell their work. Henri, the only member of his group who was also a member of the National Academy of Design, did his very best to champion the liberal cause within its conservative walls, but the results were disheartening. In 1907, his patience finally gave out when the academy rejected paintings by Luks, Shinn, and Glackens for its spring show, and failed to appoint Henri to its exhibition jury for the coming year.

His response was immediate and absolute: "The Academy is hopelessly against what is real and vital in American art. What outsiders must now do is hold small or large group exhibitions, so that the public may see what the artists who have something important to say are doing." Plans were immediately set in motion to hold such an exhibition for the Eight. William Macbeth, a gallery owner, was persuaded to rent the group his Fifth Avenue space, and the exhibition opened in February 1908 to great public and critical attention. In two weeks, some seven thousand people came to see the work of the "revolutionaries," and a considerable number of paintings were sold to more progressive collectors.

Henri went on from the success of this first show to a grand design for bringing the new art to the attention of the broader public. In 1910, he put together the Exhibition of Independent Artists, which numbered more than five hundred works by a hundred artists, many of whom, like George Bellows, were current or former pupils. This time two thousand people came on the very first night, causing such a crush that the police had to be called in. Bellows, in particular, was singled out by the press as a stellar representative of the nontraditionalist movement. Several of his drawings were sold at the show, and the National Arts Club invited him to become a lifetime member, with the proviso that he give the club an original painting for its collection. The painting he chose was *Summer City*, reflecting, as always, the environment that fed his growing talent.

All aspects of urban physical and emotional life fascinated Bellows. In 1907, he was caught up in the excitement and artistic possibilities of the project that was the talk of Manhattan — the construction of Pennsylvania Station. With whole streets dug up and huge tunnels being carved under the Hudson to reach New Jersey, the project was a symbol of the twentieth-century's phenomenal uprooting force.

George came to the worksite almost every day and studied the men and the machines and the rocks they were attacking to dig their gargantuan hole. He soon produced *Pennsylvania Excavation*, the first of several paintings depicting this dynamic city theme. Another was *Excavation at Night*, with stunning contrasts of light and dark as the workmen's torches cast reflections on the blackened ground. He would appraise this painting as "the best attempt I have made to locate the center of interest by strong light. Those tenement houses behind the excavation always give me the creeps. They're just ordinary houses — but there is something about them that gets me." The

New York Times called his Pennsylvania Station paintings a "slice of New York keenly observed, keenly transcribed," and added that, while the subject might not be conventionally beautiful, "when you paint a crab apple, you don't give us a luscious peach."

Another urban setting that Bellows returned to again and again was the boxing ring. Although his paintings of boxers are few in proportion to his total output of more than seven hundred works, George Bellows is perhaps most closely identified with pictures of men caught in the grip of a boxing match. His best-known painting of all in this genre, *Stag at Sharkey's*, painted in 1909, came out of his experiences at Tom Sharkey's Saloon near the Lincoln Arcade, close to where Bellows was living at the time. Prize fighting was illegal in 1909, so Sharkey, a retired fighter, turned his bar into a "club," where, on certain nights, boxing matches were held in his small back room. The price of tickets to a match was called "dues," and when the opponents were introduced from the ring, it was as "members of this club."

George Bellows was entranced as much by the atmosphere — the clouds of thick cigar smoke and the smell of cheap, stale beer — as by the rough, loud men who seemed to lust for blood and primitive release. His boxing paintings appear to burst with ferocity and ten-

In his famous painting Stag at Sharkey's, *George Bellows captured the fierce struggles and pulsating rhythms of the "manly art."*

sion as the figures curve and lunge around each other in the blue light of the hot, sweaty ring. Later, a critic commented to Bellows that some of the positions of his boxers could never work effectively inside a real ring. The painter waved off the comment: "I don't know anything about boxing. I am just painting two men trying to kill each other."

On the strength of his growing success, George Bellows applied for a job as an instructor at the Art Students' League and, to his amazement, was hired for the 1910 academic year at a salary of $1000. With this income assured, and his paintings beginning to sell, it seemed time to press the elusive Emma Storey into agreeing to marry him. He had been seeing Emma on and off for five years, ever since they had met during his first summer in New York, when she was briefly enrolled as a student at the New York School of Art. George had been captivated by the loveliness of the young woman who seemed the very personification of the Gibson girl. Emma was tall and extraordinarily graceful. Her head was small, and she held it high under her careful pompadour. She was smart and felt sure of her own powers. If she still believed in the need to honor the values of her father, a wealthy businessman who wore a high hat and gloves to work every day, she also championed the feminist causes of Lucy Stone and Carrie Chapman and did not hesitate to let anyone know that her life would not be defined by her relationship with a man.

This was, after all, the beginning of the heyday of the "new woman," who constantly challenged conventional limits on her life. While most female workers were still employed as maids or shop-girls, the 1905 census revealed that New York already had seventy-three women who were members of the clergy, seventy-eight who were dentists, sixty-seven working as bankers and brokers, and seventy-eight practicing law. Only three women had gained entry into the relatively hazardous profession of street-car conductor, but other occupations that were just as physically demanding numbered women among their ranks. Forty-eight women were registered carpenters, thirty-seven were masons, forty-five were plumbers, and sixty-six were electricians.

As it happened, although Emma Storey had many talents and a fiercely independent spirit, she was less a revolutionary than she liked to appear. She dabbled in many fields, but did not establish herself in a career. And, while she boldly visited George in his apartment and flirted outrageously with every man who came her way, her virtue was resolutely intact, in keeping with the code of the day. One summer evening, after a marvelous outing in Staten Island, George got carried away by the moonlight and attempted a far more passionate embrace than was the couple's decorous custom. Emma was outraged that he would "think me that kind of girl" and threatened to break off their relationship entirely. When George confided his despair to William Glackens, the other painter sympathetically revealed that when his sister confessed to their mother that she had kissed her fiancé, Mrs. Glackens furiously replied, "I should think you would leave something until after marriage!"

Emma was also far less comfortable around really seductive men than her snappy retorts suggested. For a short time, one of George Bellows's roommates was a young man named Eugene O'Neill, who had been summarily dismissed from his family home in Connecticut for playing too hard and showing too little ambition. Through a mutual friend, he had found his way to Bellows's studio, where he paid his share of the rent by selling the ugliest sort of cheap jewelry, door to door, when he wasn't too hung over to get up in the morning. O'Neill was fascinated by George Bellows's apparently endless dedication to his work. George was astonished at his new friend's willingness to waste on whiskey and women what was clearly a brilliant mind. The only productive thing Gene did was read endless numbers of books and scribble poems in front of the studio's stove. To be sure, George and Gene were an unlikely pair, but they enjoyed each other's company immensely. Emma, on the other hand, was terrified of the striking, unabashed womanizer. If she arrived at the studio to meet George and he hadn't shown up yet, she would not remain alone with Gene, and when the roommates went off to New Jersey for a stay in the O'Neills' empty vacation home, Emma addressed her letters to "Decadence Manor."

Yet, despite Emma's willfulness and unpredictable behavior,

George never gave up wanting her: "I decided I'd marry you or bust. Well, I haven't bust yet." Thus, when he found out that he could afford to marry, he wrote Emma a letter that passionately pleaded his case, even though, unlike his friend Gene, he did not think the written word his most successful method of expression. "My song is awkward and I use blundering words. Can I tell you that your heart is in me and that your portrait is in all my work?"

Emma still seemed to find it immensely difficult to set a date for a wedding, but the letter impressed her. Or perhaps she was just finally wearying of the chase. In any case, Emma Storey at last agreed to marry George Bellows. Ecstatic, he went out looking for a home for them, and when he found the perfect little house on Nineteenth Street, he borrowed $10,000 from his father for its purchase and eagerly set about doing all the renovations by himself. Indeed, he was so busy with his carpentry that Emma, in a reversal of roles, had to fetch him on the day of their wedding, because he had lost track of time. She prodded him into bathing and changing into clothes free of wood shavings and sawdust. Then, with a few friends, the couple took a subway and bus to the Bronx, where a friend who was a minister married them in his church. Afterward, they went back down to Gramercy Park and the National Arts Club for a reception with a menu ordered by the groom. Bellows's tastes were not very sophisticated: his guests were served coffee, cake, and ice cream.

George and Emma's Nineteenth Street house was always filled with people, mainly artists, but with enough other friends to make a glittering mixture. Many parties included the painter Leon Kroll, with whom George disagreed on almost every principle of art. They had met at another party just days after George's wedding and had parted in anger. All the way home on the subway, George had grumbled about the arrogant young artist who had been so opinionated, but as soon as he opened the door, he bounded to the phone and called Kroll at the party. "Stay right where you are. I'm coming back!" Leaving his bride, Bellows headed back uptown to pick up an argument that would last through a lifetime of friendship.

Robert Henri was always present at the Bellowses' parties, as were the other members of the Eight; and Eugene O'Neill (whom Emma, even as a worldly wife, still found quite decadent), frequently came by. Other regulars were Gertrude Vanderbilt Whitney and the anarchist Emma Goldman. Mrs. Whitney was a very important and progressive patron of the arts, and though Emma Goldman had little interest in art, she recognized its value. Indeed, she had talked George Bellows, Robert Henri, and John Sloan into donating a few hours a week to teaching art to the underprivileged children who attended the school she had started in the city. Bellows was fascinated by Miss Goldman's passionate commitment to emancipating the individual from every kind of oppression, whether inhumane working conditions or government censorship. In George Bellows's Gramercy Park studio, Goldman generally found as much sympathy for her views as she did in the Lower East Side cafés where she regularly joined other radical émigré intellectuals.

Influenced perhaps by Goldman, George Bellows began drawing regularly for *The Masses*, a radical magazine of which John Sloan was art editor. The traditional press detested everything about the journal. One disdainful newspaperman appraised *The Masses* artwork:

> They draw nude women for *The Masses*,
> Thick, fat, ungainly lasses —
> How does that help the working classes?

George Bellows cared not a whit about how his drawings were received by conventional colleagues. He loved the intellectual fellowship he found through his work for the magazine. After the monthly issue was "put to bed," the staff held informal parties, where editor-in-chief Max Eastman read poetry and John Reed engaged in intense arguments about politics or literature and drew Bellows out on the place of social realism in art.

Bellows donated his work to *The Masses*, but he was beginning to sell drawings to other magazines. In 1912, *Collier's* commissioned three drawings to set off a romantic little story, and paid him $150. From that assignment, many others began to come in, from *Collier's* and other journals. These commissions made life on Nineteenth Street much more comfortable.

In 1913, shortly after a triumphant return to Columbus, where he was given a one-man show in the city's Carnegie Library, George Bellows returned to New York to find it in an artistic turmoil. Arthur B. Davies, one of the Eight, had rented the Sixty-ninth Infantry Regiment Armory on Lexington Avenue and Twenty-fifth Street for a month. It would house the exhibition that the group had been planning for a year, ever since the new Association of American Painters and Sculptors had been formed under Davies's leadership. The group's goal was to mount a show that would build on the success of Robert Henri's earlier Exhibition of Independent Artists.

When Davies was elected president of the Association, he had asked that the show include examples of European art, and the request was granted by the planning committee. Alfred Stieglitz, who had shown the work of Picasso and Matisse at his famous gallery, "291," lent the committee drawings by both artists as well as a bronze bust by Picasso.

But Robert Henri, who was one of the initial organizers, began to draw back from the show, in part because he felt that the European section was becoming too large. He had worked long and hard and passionately to establish the merits of American artists, and he feared that so much emphasis on European artists would set back his cause.

George Bellows, on the other hand, grew more and more enthusiastic as the show's opening approached. He was a member of the executive, reception, and publicity committees, and in the five days allotted by the Armory to mount the thirteen hundred paintings and sculptures, he was kept busy hammering and hanging. Despite his mentor's unhappiness with the European contributors, Bellows was intrigued by some of the European avant-garde paintings, including one that the press seized on to attack, *Nude Descending a Staircase*, by Marcel Duchamp. *Cubism*, *futurism*, and *postimpressionism* were the new terms tossed around by the bemused critics and the public, who flocked to the Gramercy Park neighborhood to see the exhibit when it opened on February 17, 1913. Conservative New Yorkers were outraged, and many even demanded that the show be closed for obscenity. Theodore Roosevelt was, at best, puzzled and, at worst, was heard to call the artists a bunch of lunatics. Enrico Caruso found it all terribly funny, and drew his own caricatures of cubist paintings on scraps of paper, which he scattered to the delighted viewers.

But even those who hated what they saw sensed that the show was an extraordinary event. In one exhibition, the visitor saw the works of Van Gogh, Cézanne, Gauguin, Braque, Kandinsky, Brancusi, Picasso, and the work of Americans of the Ash Can School. Together they formed a developing history of modern art. How fitting that the show should take place, as had so many other major cultural events, in America's greatest city.

George Bellows was so immersed in the Armory show that he went there every day. Very little art was actually purchased there, so he might well have spent his time at his easel on Nineteenth Street, yet he did not regret the lapse in productivity. His career, so clearly ascending, had been profoundly affected by the connection of his own experience to the wider world of modern art. As America's relationship with Europe became increasingly troubled, Bellows knew that his future work would reflect concerns that were more socially, and universally, relevant than ever before.

12

WORLD WAR I
AND ITS
AFTERMATH

B<small>Y THE TIME</small> America had reluctantly entered the war in 1917, George Bellows was a major name in American art. His paintings were selling well, he was serving on important artistic juries, and he continued to win coveted and often financially rewarding prizes. Bellows's growing prosperity accommodated the birth of two daughters, Anne, in 1911, and Jean, in 1915. George and Emma were loving parents, but their approach to child care was, at best, casual. Even when George devoted an afternoon to taking the girls to the park to jump rope or skip along the planted paths, he might forget them completely if he chanced on an acquaintance there and became engaged in heated conversation. Despite his haphazard caretaking, however, he enjoyed the atmosphere of the park, and captured it perfectly in a 1920 painting. The mood of *Gramercy Park* is gentle, full of soft light shining on children at play and dappled shadows beneath the trees.

Not many of the Bellowses' friends had children, particularly those who were members of what had come to be known as the "Washington Square crowd." Indeed, the Henris and Bellowses were among the few traditionally married people who socialized with that colorful, rebellious group. Marriage and monogamy had not been entirely abandoned in "the Village," but they were largely ignored by the Bohemian set, who aimed to shake up all aspects of conventional behavior. Max Eastman listed his wife's maiden name and his own on the mailbox of their apartment on Charles Street, giving the titillating impression that they were not married. The other editor of *The Masses*, Floyd Dell, went a scandalous step further by not marrying the woman with whom he lived.

Just about everyone in the Washington Square crowd passionately protested against America's entering the war, and for a long time George Bellows shared their views. But as he read the terrible stories coming from Europe, his thinking began to change. In April 1917, when President Woodrow Wilson finally asked Congress for a declaration of war, George Bellows supported the need to defend democracy. "I am a patriot for beauty," he wrote in an article for the journal *Touchstone*, explaining his change of heart. "I would enlist in any army to make the world more beautiful. I would go to war for an idea far more easily than I could go for a country. Democracy is an idea to me, it is the Big Idea."

At the same time, Bellows continued to support the right of others to oppose the war. In the patriotic zeal that was sweeping the country, *The Masses* was put out of business by the Department of Justice, and

Edna St. Vincent Millay, the lyric spokeswoman of Bohemian life in Greenwich Village. She became a symbol of postwar rebellion against convention.

its editors, George's friends, were indicted under the Espionage Act. Pacifists who refused to serve in the military were regularly brought to trial for their resistance, and another member of the Washington Square crowd, Edna St. Vincent Millay, often came to the courtroom to offer comfort by reading her poems aloud while the juries debated.

Once America was in the war, even formerly neutral New Yorkers plunged headlong into war activity. Fifth Avenue became the Avenue of the Allies and was hung with the flags of England and France along with the Stars and Stripes. Restaurant or theater patrons stood at attention when the orchestra began an evening's entertainment with the anthems of the Allies. According to a British correspondent, William George Fitzgerald, it "was New York . . . that mobilized the impulsive generosity of the continent." And, indeed, feverish bond drives became twentieth-century versions of the Sanitary Fairs that had raised money for the Civil War. Dramatic gestures of support were made everywhere: the sweatshop worker threw a few precious coins on the platform as a speaker finished his emotional appeal, wealthy women tore off their jewels, and the multimillionaire Jacob Schiff once added $100,000 to an evening's coffers.

One did not have to attend a rally to be asked to give to the war effort. On busy street corners, bands of musicians blared patriotic songs like "Over There" while banners urged New Yorkers to buy Liberty bonds or make contributions to the Red Cross. Every office in every building in the city was visited at least once a week, and sometimes more often, by a military nurse, a Boy Scout, a sailor, or an important bank official asking for money. There were large wood coffins on the sidewalk, accompanied by a hammer and pile of nails. Passersby were urged to put "nails into the Kaiser's coffin," for which privilege they were charged $1.00. These combined efforts raised billions of dollars to help support America in her first world war.

The role of women in American society had been steadily evolving, but now, as during the Civil War, many were able to put aside their traditional roles and behavior. Women began routinely dining out on their own, and many even smoked in public. The application of makeup, traditionally a secret female ritual, was now openly done in restaurants and hotel lobbies. A tantalizing new pastime for women with time and money was the *thé dansant*, at which they could dance away the afternoon with handsome young men who had been hired by the hotel management to amuse female guests.

As the needs of war became more demanding, most women turned to more purposeful activities. At the war front, the country needed them as nurses, stretcher bearers, and ambulance drivers; at home, they filled the jobs in factories and offices left by men who had become soldiers.

Everything about these women began to change to suit their new lives. One discovery women made very quickly was how impractical their enormously complicated hairdos were in their new, busier lives. With patriotic abandon, they untwisted the nineteenth-century chignons, removed the combs and "rats," and cut their hair short. When the very popular dancer Irene Castle was forced to cut her hair because of an infection, the look became fashionable as well as utilitarian.

The dance team of Irene and Vernon Castle, her husband, was revolutionizing New York's social life by turning the dance craze that had swept through the city into a permanent aspect of its culture. Not only were hotels like the Plaza holding their dansants; many important restaurants had closed down to make way for dance halls and cabarets. At these new gathering places, wrote one entertainment reporter in amazement, was "a social mixture never before dreamed of in this country — a hodgepodge of people in which respectable young married and unmarried women, and even debutantes, dance, not only under the same roof, but in the same room with women of the town."

A wholesome, engaging couple without a hint of decadence in their often acrobatic dance routines, the Castles softened some of the moral outrage felt by many city leaders and clergy about public dancing. Always the entrepreneur, Bessie Marbury was so taken with the Castles that she persuaded a group of society matrons, among them Mrs. Stuyvesant Fish of Gramercy Park, to open a dance school. Across from the Ritz-Carlton Hotel, the Castles taught the rich to dance the Lame Duck, Innovation, Half and Half, and the exaggerated Castle

Walk. These newly invented dances were often introduced at private balls, and there was dancing now at every fashionable dinner party, with guests footing it lightly between every course. (Etiquette dictated that partners sit down with each other at the end of a dance instead of returning to their previous places at the table.)

If Irene Castle's hair style and light, easy clothes mirrored changes in women's fashion, men's fashion was changing as well, reflecting new modes of behavior and new social values. Style and comfort had suddenly become as important as dignity and durability. In 1900, men's suits were invariably worn with derby hats and shirts that were pulled on over the head and held together at the neck by studs. Despite the great variety in New York's climate, there was no difference in weight between summer and winter suits. Between 1900 and 1925, men's clothing evolved from the darkest shades to lighter hues of gray, brown, and blue; derby hats gave way to soft felt ones; and lighter weight suits were sold, particularly in the appropriate season. Shirts were buttoned, and gone was the uncomfortably confining high-top boot. Emancipation from social constraints was evident everywhere in New York, from upper Broadway to Wall Street, and only the most steadfast traditionalist could believe that the world would return to its old ways once the war ended.

The war officially ended on November 11, 1918. Fifth Avenue, which was closed to traffic, was thronged with thousands of joyous people, who kissed, blew horns, and formed riotous snake lines that danced in and out of the dense crowds. Boats on all of New York's rivers blew their horns in continuous sound while storms of ticker tape were thrown from office windows. The celebrations continued for weeks; there was one each time a regiment of soldiers returned from abroad. Two British journalists, Sir Philip Gibbs and W. L. George, who visited Manhattan at the end of the war, were overwhelmed by the "colossal scale [of its] height, spirit and emotion." New York seemed, more than ever before, a city of people "conscious of their own power," of their "glory and splendor."

And, indeed, life in Manhattan had never been more brilliant. New York was well on its way to becoming what Ford Madox Ford would soon call "the city of the Good Time," where "the Good Time is so sacred that you may be excused anything you do in searching for it." Hedonism prevailed, in spite of the new law against drinking that took effect with the start of 1920.

On the evening before Prohibition became official, every bar, café, and hotel supper room was filled to capacity for one final, outrageously immoderate public party. People claimed champagne glasses, ice buckets, and empty gin bottles to take home as souvenirs. Around the elegant Waldorf-Astoria bar, patrons burst into a chorus of "Auld Lang Syne" as the clock struck midnight, and one of the older bartenders began to weep. But it didn't take long for the speakeasies to be born; these establishments were more reckless and giddy than any New York had ever known in its legal drinking days.

The lowest of these enterprises were called "clip joints" or "cab joints," because the owners paid taxi drivers a commission to lure tourists there with promises of drink and accommodating girls. When the bill came, it was preposterously high, but if the customer objected, he was persuaded not to complain by husky employees of the establishment. The midtown speakeasies were more genteel; housed in brownstones, they were easily identified by the long lines of empty cars parked in front of their deceptive façades. The locked doors were opened only after the caller had been thoroughly scrutinized through a small, grill-covered opening. After drinking in a speakeasy, New York society usually went on to one of the new nightclubs — one that hadn't been recently raided by Federal agents for selling something more than ginger ale to its customers. Manhattan's most famous nightclub proprietor was Texas Guinan, who covered herself with diamonds and sequins and welcomed customers with a raspy "Hello, Sucker!" It could cost a party of five over $1000 to spend an evening at a club like Guinan's, but night after night the "suckers" kept coming.

For women, the double standard was dramatically and rapidly crumbling. The Nineteenth Amendment to the Constitution, which was passed in 1920, gave women the right to vote — and, it seemed to some, the right to dance all night, swigging gin from delicate purse flasks. The 1920s were a brand-new age, and the flapper,

Queen of the speakeasies, Texas Guinan.
New Yorkers' ten-year thirst brought her a royal income.

Europe found Texas Guinan and her troupe of entertainers too racy for its blood.
France refused to allow the ladies to step on shore.

who, according to the newspapers, was determined to live "her own life," had arrived to make the most of it.

Flappers not only kept their hair short; they changed its color with peroxide or henna. Their eyelids were painted and glittering, and their cheeks and lips were rouged. The ten yards of material it had once taken to make a dress had shrunk to barely three, and knee-length hems caused constant controversy. "Give feminine fashion time enough and they will starve all the moths to death," quipped one journalist. Another guessed that the reason women wore their skirts "at half mast" was out of respect to long-gone modesty. Cotton stockings just about disappeared, even for office wear, and were replaced by sensuous silk hose that were rolled below the knee, calling attention to the ankle-high, unfastened, flapping galoshes that gave this new generation its name. Visitors from other parts of the country were shocked to see ladies' leather-goods shops carrying something called an overnight case, implying a freedom that made traditionalists shudder.

George Bellows, painting and making lithographs in his studio on Nineteenth Street, may have found little to interest him in the frenzied, changing social scene of the 1920s; one of his neighbors embraced its every bold nuance. The brash antics, extravagance, and often foolish pretensions of the 1920s captured the imagination of the man whose personal stationery bore the motto "A little too much is just enough for me." This freewheeling atmosphere, in which people avoided commitment and celebrated change, allowed Carl Van Vechten to feel perfectly comfortable about pursuing three consecutive and distinguished careers during his lifetime: music criticism, novel writing, and photography.

Carl Van Vechten, like George Bellows, had come to New York from the Midwest. He was born in Cedar Rapids, Iowa, in 1880, and like Bellows, was born to older parents. Although the Van Vechtens were cultured people who encouraged their young son's precocious interest in music, literature, and writing, Carl often felt alien in the country of his birth. "There was no one quite like me in Cedar Rapids," he recalled; "I couldn't wait to get out."

There was no question that Cedar Rapids found Carl Van Vechten peculiar as he grew into young manhood. He even looked odd. In adolescence, he was already over six feet tall, with protruding front teeth that his friend Mabel Dodge would later say gave him the look

Carl Van Vechten, irreverent, amused, urbane observer

of a "domesticated werewolf." In a conscious gesture of eccentricity, he had grown one fingernail on each hand to talonlike length. He rode around town on the latest model of bicycle, dressed, as the argot had it, like a "dude," in a derby hat and patent-leather boots, with an ascot at his neck, shoulder pads in his jackets, and trousers tighter than anyone in Cedar Rapids had ever worn.

Carl Van Vechten left Iowa for the University of Chicago in 1899, with a sense of relief that probably matched O. Henry's when he was released from jail. He studied music and English, wrote for school publications, and regularly and enthusiastically attended performances of the Chicago Symphony. Under the progressive direction of Theodore Thomas, the orchestra offered American audiences programs of "new music" by such European composers as Ravel, César Franck, and Debussy, even before they were heard in New York. This armed Van Vechten with a sophisticated taste that stood him well when he arrived on Manhattan's music scene. He also heard ragtime in the clubs where black musicians played deep into the night, and found its syncopated rhythms both enormously exciting and totally compatible with his love of opera and classical music.

After graduation, Carl was hired as a reporter by the *Chicago American*. His assignments covered subjects ranging from disasters to social events, and his accounts were often satirical. His proclivity toward satire deepened as he grew older, and led Dorothy Parker to describe him as always "having his tongue in somebody else's cheek." In 1906, when he was twenty-six, his derisory approach got him into trouble with the *Chicago American*'s still rather conservative readers, and he was fired for writing about clothes horses rather than show horses in a story on Chicago's annual fashionable horse show.

The dismissal hardly unsettled Van Vechten. Chicago held no lasting attraction, and he had long been intrigued with the idea of life in New York City, which must surely be the antithesis of Cedar Rapids. After borrowing money from his father, he went to find out whether all the stories were true, and knew immediately, with the thrill of homecoming akin to that experienced by O. Henry, that New York was the place for him. His long-time friend, the editor Emily Clark, once observed that Carl Van Vechten was "the most successful New Yorker of my acquaintance. . . . For him Manhattan never loses its 'Arabian Nights' glamour, and all the hanging gardens of Babylon are its sky-line." Carl himself wrote, after thirteen years of residence in the city, "I shall never be able to do New York justice. I love her too much and I am too inconstant to any one part of her."

After settling into temporary quarters on West Thirty-ninth Street, Van Vechten was hired by *Broadway Magazine* to write about the controversial opera *Salomé*, by Richard Strauss, based on Oscar Wilde's play. If Van Vechten was nervous about the assignment, he relaxed when he met the magazine's still relatively unknown editor, Theodore Dreiser, who was even more nervous. The author of *Sister Carrie* kept "folding and refolding his handkerchief until it was a nest of tiny squares," Van Vechten remembered. "When it could fold no more, he opened the handkerchief and started all over again." Van Vechten's article, "Salomé: The Most Sensational Opera of an Age," appeared in the January 1907 issue of *Broadway*, coinciding with the opening at the Metropolitan Opera House. The piece contained provocative samples of Wilde's text — "Wilde at his wildest" — as well as the personal asides that would always be part of the charm of Carl Van Vechten's criticism. When he wrote of Salomé's sensational dance in the opera, for example, he happily recalled first seeing the "species of contortion" by Little Egypt at the Chicago World's Fair.

Some of the Metropolitan's directors were so outraged by the opera that *Salomé* was cancelled after only one performance. J. P. Morgan offered to refund the entire cost of the production if that was what it would take to stop further performances of the "revolting and degrading" spectacle. Meanwhile, Carl had gone on to other writing assignments for *Broadway* and for the *New York Times*.

In November 1906, Van Vechten had been hired by the *Times* as a staff reporter, and a few weeks later was appointed assistant to Richard Aldrich, the paper's music critic. Carl was allowed to write a fairly regular column on his own, combining music news with chatty bits of gossip about the artists: Caruso had shaved off his mustache; Emma Eames was divorcing her husband. At the same time, Van Vechten was developing a theory of music criticism that he would later explain as having two major purposes ("beyond the obvious and most essential one that it provides a bad livelihood for the critic"). The first purpose was to "entertain the reader, because criticism, like any other form of literature, should stand by itself and not lean too heavily on the matter of which it treats; the other is to interest the reader in music . . . or in musicians."

As much as Carl enjoyed his position with the *Times*, writing about music in New York only made him the more eager to see and hear European performances, so he planned a summer excursion abroad. In what seemed an impulsively romantic move, he decided to marry an old friend from Cedar Rapids, Anna Elizabeth Snyder, because she, too, was planning to travel in Europe. Borrowing more money from his indulgent father, Van Vechten sailed for England. By the summer's end, after a blissfully musical honeymoon, he had to borrow yet again to return to New York with his bride.

Although he returned to Europe in 1908 as Paris correspondent for the *Times*, by 1909 Carl was firmly back in his post as assistant music critic. Naturally, he reviewed productions that were not of primary interest to his boss, Richard Aldrich, and he was also given the task of interviewing performers whom the essentially conservative Aldrich found too flamboyant or controversial, like Mary Garden and Sergei Rachmaninoff. With these and other performers as his subjects, Van Vechten began writing a series, "Monday Interviews," that emphasized the art of performance more than any critic had done before. These witty, intimate, and enthusiastic pieces, later called "Interpreters," were collected in a book of that name in 1917, and other collections would follow.

The essays express the importance of personality in creative expression. "There is an *au-delà* to all great interpretative art, something that remains after story, words, picture and gesture have faded vaguely into that storeroom in our memories where are concealed these lovely ghosts of ephemeral beauty. . . . This quality cannot be acquired, it cannot even be described, but it can be felt." Similarly, Van Vechten believed that "criticism should be an expression of personal feeling. Otherwise it has no value."

How Carl Van Vechten felt about hearing a piece of music was far more important to him than academic analysis; his approach to critical writing had few supporters among musical scholars of the time. On the other hand, in a recent evaluation of Van Vechten's contributions to the field of music criticism, Francis Robinson, associated with the Metropolitan Opera for nearly forty years in various managerial roles, is reported to have said "No photograph can duplicate Van Vechten's *Interpreters*. But of course no music critic today writes like Van Vechten either. He wasn't afraid to say so when he liked something."

Carl Van Vechten's fervent praise of favorite performers was often attacked by more traditional music critics, who believed that critics should put some distance between themselves and their subjects. Van Vechten found that idea absurd, just as he derided the unwritten rule that a critic should not socialize with the artists whose work he wrote about. "I may say that if my profession kept me from knowing anybody I really wanted to know, I should relinquish the profession without hesitation," he declared, and went on to say that it was ridiculous "to feel that you cannot dine with a singer without praising her performances. Many days in each month I dine with authors whose works I abhor. I find their companionship delightful. Should I be deprived of their society because I happen to be a critic?"

In 1910, Van Vechten discovered a new art form to write about, as well as a new group of people to enjoy. The Met invited the Russian ballerina Anna Pavlova for a limited engagement, and at the same time Isadora Duncan made a second appearance in the city. Neither artist particularly appealed to Richard Aldrich, so he dispatched his assistant to cover their performances.

A major reason for Aldrich's lack of interest was that until this time, most Americans considered dance a minor art, confined to chorus lines in operettas and an occasional corps de ballet at the Metropolitan Opera House. Van Vechten was more enthusiastic about dance, because he had seen several virtuoso performances while living in Paris. Although he had little real knowledge of the art, he had enjoyed the performances immensely, and when he saw Pavlova make her turns on the Metropolitan's stage, he was overwhelmed.

Pavlova did not begin to dance until after midnight, after the end of the scheduled Massenet opera. When the curtain rose again, she stood alone on stage, as small and as delicate as a porcelain figurine, and she began to move into a waltz that stunned the audience with its grace. At the conclusion of her recital, well over an hour later, the audience rose to their feet in thunderous ovation. The following day, Carl Van Vechten told *Times* readers that "her technique is of a sort to dazzle the eye," and after a second performance, when the house was filled to capacity, Carl tried to describe that technique: "With her left toe pointed out behind her, maintaining her body poised to form a straight line with it, she leaped backward step by step on her right foot. She swooped into the air like a bird and floated down. She never dropped. At times she seemed to defy the laws of gravitation."

Van Vechten's enthusiastic writings about dance not only encouraged an audience for the art form, but established him as America's first dance critic. He set a standard for the genre that remains a valuable reference point for those following in his path. Others may write with more erudition about dance history and technique, but, according to one scholar, "Van Vechten is the most literary, the most successful in matching a writing style to the grace, movement, and effects of ballet."

With dance, as with other arts, Carl Van Vechten was drawn primarily to the expressive qualities of the form. When he wrote about Nijinsky in 1915, he found in the Russian's compelling dance statements "the unbroken quality of music, the balance of great painting, the meaning of fine literature and the emotion inherent in all these arts." He wrote, with varying degrees of enthusiasm, about the distinctive dance personality of Isadora Duncan. For a while, Duncan had a studio near Gramercy Park, where she taught a group of young disciples, called the Isadorables, how to enrich their spirits by emancipating their bodies from restrictions and inhibitions. Van Vechten appreciated Isadora's brand of interpretive dance, but he criticized her tendency to leave the audience bewildered. In a recital where she danced to the "Liebestod" from *Tristan and Isolde*, Van Vechten described the result as neither pantomimic drama nor dancing: "She puzzled those who knew the drama, and did not interest those who did not."

On the other hand, Isadora amused him immensely. During her closing night party at the Plaza Hotel, she told Walter Damrosch, the Met's conductor, "For you, Mr. Damrosch, I shall dance nude!" and promptly proceeded to do so. Mr. and Mrs. Damrosch made a hasty retreat, but Carl Van Vechten and a few other tireless guests stayed until dawn, when they crowded boisterously into a taxi and took Isadora to the pier to sail for Europe.

Carl Van Vechten often attended as many as three theatrical and musical events in an evening, and spent the better part of every day interviewing, lunching with his subjects, and writing up his stories at his office. This left little time to be with his wife, Anna, and the marriage, always more amiable than passionate, began to erode. In the legal gameplaying of the time, Carl arranged to be "caught" in an adulterous episode that allowed Anna to sue him for divorce in 1912. The court ordered him to pay his former wife $25 a week, a sum he could not possibly afford, but Anna seemed perfectly content to consider the judgment a mere formality, since money had always been one of their problems.

A lack of personal income had never limited Van Vechten's social relationships. One of his most long-lasting friendships was with the fabulously wealthy and flamboyant Mabel Dodge, who had returned from a long stay in Europe to take up residence on Washington Square. In Mabel Dodge's stunning white drawing room, hung with a shimmering Venetian chandelier and the finest modern art, Van Vechten first met George Bellows, Robert Henri, and many of their artist friends.

Indeed, it was in Mrs. Dodge's apartment that plans had first been drawn for the 1913 Armory show. Any revolutionary idea fascinated Mabel Dodge, and on the advice of Lincoln Steffens she often chose a controversial conversational theme for her much-talked-about Wednesday evenings. Modern art was only one of the heated topics. In the lustrous salon her lover, John Reed, and Emma Goldman preached anarchism; Margaret Sanger denounced sexual repression and advocated birth control; and A. A. Brill, who had been trained by Sigmund Freud, explained Freud's theory of the subconscious in such shocking detail that even this liberated crowd was startled.

Like Mabel Dodge, Carl Van Vechten found no idea too outrageous to consider or embrace; and they both liked to quote Walt Whitman's sally "Do I contradict myself? Very well, then, I contradict myself." Mrs. Dodge recalled how much her friend enjoyed himself when controversy arose, whether between people or ideas, for it "took him farther away from Cedar Rapids. . . . How Carl loved the grotesque! He loved to twist and squirm with laughter at the oddity of strong contrasts."

It was through Mabel Dodge that Van Vechten met a woman who personified the delights of contradiction and contrast — Gertrude Stein. They met in Paris when Van Vechten was visiting there in the summer of 1914, before starting a new job as dramatic critic for the *New York Press*. He would write of this new and lasting friend (in her will Miss Stein named Carl Van Vechten beneficiary of all her unpublished work), "The English language is a language of hypocrisy and evasion. How not to say a thing has been the problem of our writers from the earliest times. . . . Miss Stein . . . has really turned language into music, really made its sound more important than its sense."

In 1914, Carl Van Vechten married Fania Marinoff, a beautiful Russian Jewish émigrée who was a talented and fairly successful actress. Although the marriage would be richly enduring, it got off to an unusual start. When Van Vechten's first wife, Anna, learned about the marriage, she demanded all the back alimony owed to her. Unable and, in truth, unwilling to pay, Van Vechten accepted a prison sentence of four months, and did his very best to make it amusing. His cell was filled with flowers and exotic food and drink brought to him by his exuberant friends, and he was somehow given a piano so that visitors, often celebrated artists, could entertain him. His colleagues from the press made much of the story. As one newspaper typically headlined: CARL VAN VECHTEN HAPPY IN JAIL. . . . RESENTS THE INTRUSION OF THE TURBULENT OUTER WORLD. . . . REVELS IN TURGENIEFF. . . . RECIPIENT OF MANY GIFTS. . . . AROUSED IN HIS EPICUREAN CALM THE ENVY OF THOSE WHO MUST TOIL AND SPIN.

When his prison term was over, Carl found himself temporarily out of work again, but the combined income from his writing and Fania's acting allowed them to begin married life in new quarters, at 151 East Nineteenth Street, directly across the way from George Bellows. They papered the living room of their top-floor apartment in Chinese red with gold dots, creating an exotic atmosphere for the parties that would soon make Carl Van Vechten one of Manhattan's most famous hosts.

A New York host of some notoriety lived immediately next door to the Van Vechtens. Robert Chanler, a very wealthy occasional painter, owned a house in which he gave riotous parties. The center of the merriment was always on the top floor, practically adjoining Carl and Fania's apartment, so even if they had not enjoyed the carryings-on, they would probably have attended, since sleep was not too likely with the uproar from next door. Carl and Fania often ran into George Bellows at Chanler's parties. (Emma Bellows rarely came after she called the police one evening to protest the noise, only to have the police sergeant accept an invitation to join the party, and drunkenly present Chanler with his officer's cap as a token of appreciation.) After another of these evenings of highly imaginative "entertainments," Ethel Barrymore commented, "I went there in the evening a young girl and came away in the early morning an old woman."

As the twenties approached, and Carl Van Vechten neared his fortieth birthday, he began to tire of writing music criticism, even though collections of his work were selling well and his essays were much in demand by *Vanity Fair* and other major magazines. To his mind, forty was an age that was not really compatible with being a critic. One begins to experience, he said, an "intellectual hardening of the arteries," and he teased that he could feel himself beginning "to prefer Johann Strauss waltzes to the last sonatas of Beethoven; Chopin pleased me more than Brahms." In any case, he had really always been "a writer who apparently at heart was . . . creative rather than critical." And so, Carl Van Vechten decided, he would greet the 1920s primarily as a fiction writer.

In the seven novels he wrote during the next decade, Van Vechten created characters and narratives that perfectly captured what it was like to live in what he named "the Splendid Drunken Twenties." In his previous career, Van Vechten had once noted that a music critic "must not be afraid to say to-day what [he] may regret to-morrow," and this summed up his approach not only to art, but to life. The moment at hand was the moment to celebrate, and it could be as outrageous as a gin-soaked imagination could make it. Tomorrow was not a concern as long as sex and liquor and cleverness and freedom were present.

That the long party of the 1920s would end with a thunderous collapse in only a few short years was not even suspected at the beginning of the decade. Later, it was Carl Van Vechten who would write the era's obituary in his final novel, appropriately titled *Parties*. But collapse and depression and fatigue and disappointment were a long way off. For now, the night was young, and Carl Van Vechten, with his prematurely silver hair and a glass in hand, stood at the door of his Gramercy Park apartment, inviting the restless pleasure seekers to come inside and play.

IV

How Bright the Night,
How Bleak the Morning

———◆———

1920-1939

13

PARTIES
UPTOWN
AND   DOWN

———————— ✦ ————————

eter Whiffle: His Life and Works, Carl Van Vechten's first novel, was published in 1922. The book purports to be the true story of a man who has spent his life trying to be a successful writer. At his death, he requested that his literary executor, Carl Van Vechten, write his biography.

As the first-person narrator, Van Vechten recalls how Whiffle experimented endlessly with new and sensational ways of experiencing life, as well as with finding the perfect approach to writing. Whiffle finally decides that no literary experiment can be successful unless the author expresses how he really feels. Clearly using his own experience, Van Vechten, through Whiffle, asserts that writers should take a tip from the grand performance artists on the importance of personality in creativity. "The great interpreters . . . Duse, Bernhardt, Paderewski and Mary Garden are all big, vibrant personalities," says Whiffle. "If you cannot release your personality, what you write, though it be engraved in letters an inch deep on stones weighing many tons, will lie like snow in the street to be melted away by the first rain."

This reference to the theatrical and musical worlds associated with Carl Van Vechten's name was not lost to readers. Alfred Knopf, Van Vechten's young publisher, advertised the book as a "curious, gossipy chronicle," deliberately suggesting that it was a roman à clef, in which readers could learn "inside" news about a most exclusive and exotic group of people. The dust jacket of the book reinforced that message by declaring that the characters in *Peter Whiffle* were based on real people, wearing only "thin, epithetical masks."

Certainly no one who had ever read any gossip about Mabel Dodge could miss her in the character of Edith Dale. No one who had ever wondered what went on in her salon could resist peeking at the "strange salad of capitalists, revolutionists, anarchists, artists, writers, actresses, feminists" that Edith Dale mixed together in her fictional drawing room.

In the book, Van Vechten also shared the wonder of his initial visit to Paris with readers who had only heard about the city's gloriously gay life. "An American youth's first view of Paris," wrote the critic Robert Morss Lovett in his autobiography, *All Our Years*, "is an unforgettable experience, a favorite theme of Henry James, but nowhere touched on so happily as by Carl Van Vechten in *Peter Whiffle*."

This invitation to readers to share vicariously in a life more glamorous than their own undoubtedly accounted for the novel's enormous success; it went into eight printings during its first year. The *Herald Tribune* called the book "the smartest thing of its kind done by an American," and the *New York Times* declared it "sparkling and delightful." Nearly every reviewer commented on its stylishness, wit, and modernity. From Paris, Gertrude Stein applauded her friend Carl as being "indeed the most modern the least sentimental and the most quietly persistent of the romantics."

Practically the only negative response to the brash, decidedly modern *Peter Whiffle* came from Van Vechten's father, who, at the age of eighty-two, understandably found the novel's sophisticated artifice bewildering. Other older Americans may have been alarmed by the unabashed enthusiasm for everything new that characterized this postwar era, but the search for innovation and novelty swept New York like a fever. Whatever was new was worthwhile — fashion, invention, ideas. Tradition seemed obsolete, because there were hints everywhere of a fantastic future, bigger, better, and happier than any the world had ever known.

Despite his father's distress, Carl Van Vechten, at forty-two, found himself introduced by *Peter Whiffle* into a literary career that kept quick pace with the twenties. His next book, *The Blind Bow-Boy*, was published only a year after *Peter Whiffle*. It deals with a young man launched by his father on the high seas of New York's most sophisticated society. The father hopes that his son will recognize the decadence of this world and return to traditional values, but his plan backfires when the son embraces the wildly uninhibited social scene.

The dust jacket first planned for the novel featured unattributed notes by Carl Van Vechten, declaring, "This book is not . . . 'realistic' or 'art' or 'life' and no ideas are concealed beneath its surface." On the other hand, Carl told his friend Emily Clark, "My formula at present consists in treating extremely serious themes as frivolously as possible." It is not clear whether this formula was a calculated attempt to benefit from the temper of the twenties, or whether he was simply so perfect an exemplar of the current mood that it came to him instinctively. There's little question, however, that Van Vechten's light literary touch was the secret to his vast popular success. In an age when people constantly sought new, and preferably shocking, ways to be amused, Carl Van Vechten was enormous fun to read.

The twenties and thirties are generally regarded as a highly important era in the history of American letters. Born around the turn of the century, writers like Ernest Hemingway, John Dos Passos, John Steinbeck, William Faulkner, and F. Scott Fitzgerald were the first true generation of American modernists. Their values reflected the kaleidoscopic quality of twentieth-century life, and the themes of their novels were based on modern values and concerns. They had grown up with war, the birth of psychology, extraordinary advances in science and technology, and upheaval in the foundations of morality and social behavior. An air of cynicism and a brooding introspection frequently pervaded their writing.

Carl Van Vechten was older than most of these writers. By 1922, when *Peter Whiffle* was published, he was already famous as a music critic, had lived well, traveled widely, and enjoyed himself immensely through the period when these younger men were facing the matchless challenges of the modern coming-of-age. Van Vechten's views on life were, in comparison with the views of the others, much more positive; as he himself indicated, he tended to laugh at rather than anguish over the foibles of society. Thus, while the serious modernist was appreciated by critics and more thoughtful readers, Van Vechten's novels provided a light, escapist antidote to the literary scene. *The Blind Bow-Boy*, Sinclair Lewis wrote to Carl after reading the book, is "impertinent, subversive, resolutely and completely wicked. . . . I didn't believe any American could do that — I know my own wickedness is so feeble and apologetic. . . . I think you slap the tradition that highbrow American novels must be . . . lugubriously and literally 'realistic.'"

Despite the difference in his perspective, Van Vechten was intimately acquainted with most of the important writers of the period, particularly those who had achieved any degree of celebrity. The literary set met often, and almost always at parties. As Van Vechten contentedly recalled, "The Twenties were famous for parties; everybody both gave and went to them; there was always plenty to eat and drink, lots of talk and certainly a good deal of lewd behavior."

The careless abandon that marked the decade was best expressed at a party. No type of behavior was too bizarre to be accepted; no amusement was too dear to be capriciously abandoned if a more outrageous adventure offered itself. Van Vechten himself seemed never to tire of going to or giving parties, and completely enjoyed his reputation as one of New York City's best-known hosts. In his Nineteenth Street house, and later, when he moved uptown to larger quarters, entrancing combinations of people came together to amuse and sometimes astonish each other.

Carl would move among his guests, smiling expansively, dressed in clothes that were as colorful as a gathering that might mix George Gershwin, Theodore Dreiser, Elinor Wylie, and Paul Robeson. As Van Vechten grew older, his taste in clothes became even more eccentric. He took to wearing bracelets, some of heavy gold links, others of jade, and rings on several fingers, and his hair fell over his fore-head in a poetic fringe. His exquisite taste in furnishings did not keep him from garbing himself in outrageous combinations of colors and designs — a brown-and-green-striped shirt with a wide orange-and-red-flowered necktie.

Van Vechten parties, like the era that spawned them, became more intense with time. When the hour grew late, sparkling discourse often gave way to uninhibited play that, if not as abandoned as the entertainments of Van Vechten's neighbor Bob Chanler, was still worthy of its own celebrity. Langston Hughes remembered a night that turned into "a gossip party, where everybody was at liberty to go around the room repeating the worst things they could make up or recall about each other to their friends on opposite sides of the room — who were sure to go right over and tell them about it."

On another occasion, when Carl's banker brother Ralph came to New York, Carl booked him into the Algonquin Hotel and gave a large and progressively drunken party to celebrate the visit. At one point in the evening, H. L. Mencken fell asleep with a young actress sitting on his knee. When he woke up, he discovered that the girl had been replaced by another young lady of the theater, Tallulah Bankhead, which led Mencken to congratulate delightedly Van Vechten for being so resourceful that "he has his first set of girls beheaded or baked, only so he can enjoy a second set later." As the mood grew more feverish, recalled Emily Clark, "total strangers began to drift in. Dancing began. Conversations rose and fell: about sex, about the theater, about Prohibition, about Sigmund Freud, about kissing parrots, about the liquor. A popular novelist began to cry . . . and another, of slight build, was invited by the president of the Chicago Athletic Club to jump up and down on his stomach." And all the while, Carl's brother from Cedar Rapids gazed incredulously at New York's outlandish notion of a social gathering. Finally he slapped his knee and cried, "My God, isn't it wonderful to see all these interesting people here together!"

The Algonquin was, of course, the center of much of New York's literary life and the site of the famous Round Table. The group, including such writers as Alexander Woollcott, Robert Benchley, and

Robert Sherwood, met regularly at the Algonquin for lunch and the sharpest of conversations. Carl Van Vechten and Scott Fitzgerald were frequently asked to join the core group, along with any other literary luminaries who might be passing through New York. It was a time when every important writer seemed to know and generally to appreciate the others, and the Algonquin was their favorite watering hole. Noted one regular, "If the Algonquin exploded, American literature would stop dead for twenty-four hours."

The literary set also met at publishers' teas, which were intended to provide a congenial setting for writers to discuss their work. More often than not, these too generally turned into merry "Prohibition parties." One literary tea given by the otherwise dignified publisher Horace Liveright ended with his playfully pulling Carl Van Vechten off a piano stool and breaking the writer's collarbone. With rare exceptions, writers and liquor seemed inextricably mixed. In his memoir of the twenties, the writer Dwight Taylor recalled that when Prohibition struck, "our national heritage of freedom seemed in jeopardy, drinking became a patriotic duty, and the average American writer's reaction to the passing of the Eighteenth Amendment was to embark upon a prolonged Boston Tea Party, in which he very often found himself acting like an Indian."

Under Prohibition, not only writers but most of Manhattan's population were drinking astonishing quantities of liquor. Although speakeasies were constantly being raided and shut down, there were usually as many as 100,000 in operation, all trying to keep up with a city that seemed determined to be perpetually and defiantly drunk. New Yorkers in the "splendid, drunken twenties" were pushing both federal restrictions and their own inhibitions to the absolute limit. Decadence, not decorum, was the social norm, and the Dionysian goal was achieved on bootleg gin.

Van Vechten's own drinking was prodigious during this bacchanalian period. When his brother Ralph died in 1928 and left Carl a sizable part of his very large estate, Carl's taste for excess could be lavishly supported. But he had never tried to restrict his thirst for liquor even before the inheritance. Fania, as liberal a companion as any pleasure seeker could ask for, nonetheless often grew angry with her husband in the wee hours of a party and demanded that he stop drinking and go to bed. She rarely convinced him. His favorite drink was a sidecar, but he would willingly accept anything his bootlegger or a party host could supply. As Van Vechten explained, this was a decade when someone was always giving a cocktail party, and "a man with an extensive acquaintance . . . could drink steadily . . . from the beginning of cocktail time until eleven in the evening without any more expense than that entailed by car or cab fare."

After cocktails, the "real" drinking began, often for Carl with companions even more thirsty than he, like Scott and Zelda Fitzgerald. At one Gramercy Park dinner party, given by the critic Ernest Boyd, the Fitzgeralds arrived well after everyone had finished eating. As soon as they were served their soup, they put their heads down on the table and fell asleep. Someone picked up Zelda, her diaphanous gown draped over her slim body, and carried her to a bedroom, and Scott was helped to the living room sofa. But only moments later, he woke up with a start and telephoned an order for two cases of champagne and a string of taxis to come to Nineteenth Street and take all the guests to a nightclub.

No one intimately involved with the Fitzgeralds seemed to find their behavior particularly outrageous. Mixing excess and brilliance, they were simply extreme examples of the way everyone in their set seemed to live. After the decade ended, they would appear as David and Rilda Westlake in Van Vechten's final novel *Parties*, and their antics, like the era's, would seem more tragic than appealing. At one point in the book, the Westlakes awaken to a midafternoon sun and face each other with unwelcome sobriety. David says:

> "We're swine, filthy swine, and we are Japanese mice, and we are polar bears walking from one end of our cage to the other, to and fro, to and fro, all day, all week, all month, ever to eternity. We'll be drunk pretty soon and . . . we'll get drunker and drunker and drift about nightclubs so drunk that we won't know where we are, and then we'll go to Harlem and stay up all night and go to bed late tomorrow morning and wake up and begin it all over again."
>
> "Parties," sighed Rilda. "Parties!"

That Van Vechten, like Fitzgerald, was able to continue writing in this recklessly dissolute atmosphere attests to his inherent creativity and fundamental strength of will. "Carlo," as his close friends called him, once advised Langston Hughes to write three hundred words every day, no matter how physically or emotionally bankrupt he might feel. "You will find this method hard at first and very easy after a week or two," he assured the gifted young black poet.

Langston Hughes was only one of Carl Van Vechten's many black friends. In 1925, *Time* magazine announced that "sullen-mouthed, silky-haired author Van Vechten has been playing with Negroes lately, writing prefaces for their poems, having them around the house, going to Harlem."

The thinly veiled derision was typical of the prevailing attitude toward blacks. In the press, blacks were always referred to as "negroes," with a small *n*. More colloquially — and very openly — in the old-time minstrel shows that were still popular, they were called "coons" or "niggers." It was almost impossible in New York for a black person to buy an orchestra seat in a theater or to get a table in a leading restaurant, and the producers of Eugene O'Neill's play *All God's Chillun Got Wings* had to segregate their juvenile casting because the public refused to accept black and white children together on a stage. Few white New Yorkers knew what went on uptown — how people lived, the range of their interests and achievements — and they had no interest in finding out.

Carl Van Vechten, on the other hand, had always been deeply attracted to Negro culture. It was an interest first fed by his being raised in an atmosphere of racial respect. Carl's father had made it a point to address the Van Vechtens' black laundress and gardener as Mr. and Mrs. rather than by their first names, as was common practice. The senior Van Vechten had also helped found a school for Negro children in Mississippi when he learned that there was no school open to blacks. As his own artistic interests developed, Carl's belief in racial equality made him receptive to Negroes' contributions to the arts. Indeed, he acquired a major collection of photographs, manuscripts, and recordings that documented the race's gifts to American life.

As early as 1917, Carl had begun writing articles on the various forms of music that had their origins in black society. Since his days in Chicago, he had loved and respected ragtime: "It is the only American music on which the musicians of our land can build." His enthusiasm spread to jazz and the blues. "Jazz may not be the last hope of American music, nor yet the best hope, but at present, I am convinced, it is the only hope," he wrote in 1924. As for the blues, he adored nothing more than listening to its dark rhythms, on one of his four hundred recordings of Negro music or when visiting a late-hours jazz club in Harlem or, better still, when he had brought together a small group of appreciative friends to hear the music live in his apartment.

Bessie Smith was a great friend of Carl's from the time they met in 1925, when he crossed the river to New Jersey to hear her sing in a Newark theater. In an article for *Vanity Fair*, written the following year, he noted his admiration for her artistry, as well as for that of Clara Smith and another rising talent, Ethel Waters. Van Vechten remembered how beautiful Bessie Smith looked when he first saw her stride onto the stage, dressed in crimson satin, "with the rich ripe beauty of southern darkness, a deep bronze brown, matching the bronze of her bare arms." When she opened her mouth to sing, it was with a voice "full of shouting and moaning and praying and suffering."

Like Bessie and Clara Smith, Ethel Waters was a regular guest at Carl's parties, though she recalled her discomfort the first time she found the "little gray balls" called caviar, and borscht with sour cream — "beet soup and clabber . . . enough to curdle your gizzard."

Van Vechten counted many important black writers among his friends, and was instrumental in bringing attention to their work. When Langston Hughes won a poetry contest sponsored by a Negro journal, Carl asked the young writer to send him a sheaf of his poems so that he could bring them to his publisher, Alfred Knopf. The poems were published as *The Weary Blues*, in 1926, with an introduction written by Van Vechten. Similarly, Carl wrote the introduction to *The Autobiography of an Ex-Colored Man*, by James Weldon

Johnson, a distinguished Negro diplomat and author who was a very close friend for many years. In fact, the two men agreed that whoever survived the other would take charge of all the deceased man's literary works. When Weldon died, Carl established a James Weldon Johnson Memorial Collection of Negro Arts and Letters at the Yale University Library, to which he contributed his own collection of items relating to the Negro's contribution to America's cultural history.

Van Vechten's enthusiastic interest in the blacks' place in American culture is credited with being a major impetus for the Harlem Renaissance of the 1920s. Some early signs of the movement had introduced the writings of James Weldon Johnson, Paul Laurence Dunbar, and the singularly important Jean Toomer to readers outside the black community.

In 1921, the Renaissance further flowered after a Harlem revue, *Shuffle Along*, came downtown to play for white audiences. The show featured the remarkable jazz piano playing of Eubie Blake, the singing of Noble Sissle, and a spectacular singer-dancer named Florence Mills. White audiences had never seen anything like this array of talent, and they wanted more. Miss Mills was immediately booked into the Plantation Club on Broadway, went on to a triumphant tour of Europe, and then returned to New York with two new revues, *Dixie to Broadway* and *Blackbirds*, for her clamoring downtown fans. It was in these elaborately conceived, fast-paced productions that white Manhattan was first stunned by the haunting sounds of Ethel Waters singing the blues and the acrobatic footwork of Bill (Bojangles) Robinson tap-dancing up and down a staircase. Meanwhile, as Harlem flooded Broadway with its music, playwrights were turning out major works that called for the talents of black actors. Charles Gilpin starred in Eugene O'Neill's *The Emperor Jones*, Paul Robeson in O'Neill's *All God's Chillun Got Wings*.

Certainly Carl Van Vechten did not create the Harlem Renaissance. He is widely credited, however, with starting the recognition of the movement by calling the public's attention to Negro talent in the articles he still wrote from time to time — when he felt a subject was important enough for him to take time away from his novels. As

James Weldon Johnson explained it, Van Vechten's magazine articles and "personal efforts in behalf of individual Negro . . . artists did more to bring about the appreciation of Negro talent than anyone else in the country."

Although from today's perspective Van Vechten's behavior might be seen as self-consciously liberal, indeed patronizing, he was one of the first prominent people to mix the races socially. Because his parties were commonly reported in the press, the notion of an integrated guest list was introduced to people who would normally never have entertained such an idea. His guests were, as always, remarkably diverse in background and occupation; a dinner party might include Somerset Maugham, Salvador Dali, and Bessie Smith.

In 1926, Van Vechten's novel *Nigger Heaven* was published. It was his most serious and controversial work, and he worried about achieving his goal of depicting Harlem's artistic and intellectual vigor. "I'm very unsettled about *Nigger Heaven*," he told Langston Hughes. "I get too emotional writing it, and what one needs in writing is a calm, cold eye." Van Vechten's insistence on the shocking title is indicative of his penchant for both irony and accuracy. To critics, he explained straightforwardly, "'Nigger Heaven' is an American slang expression for the topmost gallery of a theater, so called because in certain of the United States, Negroes who visit the playhouse are arbitrarily forced to sit in these cheap seats. The title of this novel derives from the fact that the geographical position of Harlem, the Negro quarter of New York, corresponds to the location of the gallery in a theater."

In the novel itself, the leading character, who wants to be a writer, returns to Harlem after a fruitless day downtown and despairs, "Nigger Heaven! That's what Harlem is. We sit in our places in the gallery of this New York theater and watch the white world sitting down below in the good seats in the orchestra. Occasionally they turn their faces up towards us . . . but they never beckon. It never seems to occur to them that Nigger Heaven is crowded, that there isn't another seat, that something has to be done."

Reviews of *Nigger Heaven* were decidedly mixed, in both the white and black press, but there were enough important positive responses for Van Vechten not to be too despairing. His close friends in the Negro community, like Langston Hughes, James Weldon Johnson, and Walter White, a novelist and, later, head of the NAACP, were supportive. Johnson, who had seen the book in manuscript, wrote a long review for a Negro magazine, *Opportunity*, praising the book as "the most revealing, significant and powerful novel based exclusively on Negro life yet written. . . . The author pays colored people the rare tribute of writing about them as people rather than titles." Johnson ended his defense by saying that those Negroes who were attacking the novel must have judged the book by its title and never even opened its pages.

Ellen Glasgow, a white novelist, contributed her opinion to a debate in the magazine *The Bookman*, and praised Carl Van Vechten for finally liberating himself from the "gloss of dilettantism. . . . The roots of this book cling below the shallow surface of sophistication in some rich primitive soil of humanity. . . . A thrilling, a remarkable book. There is a fire at the heart of it."

The controversy over his novel did not diminish Van Vechten's pleasure in Harlem's brilliant night life. He not only continued to bring his Harlem friends downtown, but he expanded New York's nighttime boundaries by introducing his downtown friends to the glittering uptown pleasure spots. Spending the wee hours in Harlem soon became all the rage, as much a part of twenties' revelry as a pocket flask. Taxis and expensive private cars left Times Square any time after midnight and traveled uptown to Lenox Avenue, pulling up in front of resplendent nightclubs like Small's Paradise, the Nest, and the Cotton Club. People without private transportation poured out of the subway until dawn, moving along the streets in laughing groups, going from one rollicking establishment to another.

If, like Carl Van Vechten, you had been invited by an "insider," you could visit the Vaudeville Comedy Club, a private club in a huge basement room of the Savoy Building. From four or five in the morning on, after their shows had ended around town, just about all the performers from Harlem stopped by there, getting as "lowdown" as they felt like in the smoky, shadowy cavern. It might easily be ten in the morning before the horns were put away and the night was declared officially over.

Another popular Harlem activity was the elaborate costume ball for homosexuals, who came from all over the city to compete for prizes for the most beautiful female costume. Such balls were integrated and open to the public, and attracted members of the most elite downtown society, like the Astors and the Vanderbilts. Carl Van Vechten recalled with amusement how the downtown aristocrats sat "regally in boxes," during one gala, while he and the playwright Avery Hopwood served as judges.

Often, when Carl Van Vechten was returning from one of his all-night adventures, he met Paul Rosenfeld on his way to work. A neighbor who shared Van Vechten's interest in music, and also many friends, Rosenfeld led a life that was somewhat more conventional. A handsome man, about ten years younger than Carl, he was tall and well built, and carried himself gracefully. His chestnut-colored eyes could, remembered a colleague, "catch, in the matter of glances, everything there was to catch and a great deal more besides."

Rosenfeld lived at 77 Irving Place and was music editor of *The Dial*, a beautifully produced journal of ideas and letters with a long and impressive national history. The original magazine had been a transcendentalist quarterly published in Boston from 1840 to 1844, under the editorship of Margaret Fuller and Ralph Waldo Emerson. Since then, it had gone through several transformations, reflecting the philosophies of its different owners. It had moved from Boston to Cincinnati to Chicago and then, in 1918, to New York. In 1920, under the direction of Scofield Thayer, a wealthy scholar who was passionately dedicated to the arts, *The Dial* became a discriminating journal of art, literature, and ideas.

The Dial was published by intellectuals for intellectuals. Merely popular success was not important to its editors, who, at one point, coolly criticized the wildly popular work of Scott Fitzgerald as frivolous and superficial. The new *Dial* had no interest in mirroring what the public was reading and thinking about in the 1920s, but instead attempted to shape America's taste to its own high standards. The magazine's editorial column, in defense of this position, carried an essay, in June 1923, that declared, "If American letters owe us something, it is simply because we have never published anything or

Paul Rosenfeld, a sensitive, expressive, lively intellectual,
who celebrated the life of the imagination

anybody for any reason but the one natural reason: because the work
was good. It is barely possible that our greatest service to American
letters will turn out to be our refusal to praise or to publish silly and
slovenly and nearly-good-enough work."

The critic Nicholas Joost, writing about the magazine's influence
on American taste, has explained that as the twenties began, America
"possessed no magazine that . . . was trying to set free the imagination of American authors and artists and that was willing to publish
the best work available in both the accepted and the unconventional
forms of expression." While the magazine published the writings of
established American and European artists, it was very supportive of
the avant-garde.

The Dial published the work (sometimes the first appearance) of
such writers as e. e. cummings, Marianne Moore, Ezra Pound,

D. H. Lawrence, and T. S. Eliot, and reproduced paintings by, among others, Pablo Picasso and Georgia O'Keeffe. Much of this work was considered by many to be shocking. Indeed, when Paul Rosenfeld, who wrote about painting as well as music, illustrated an essay on American painting with O'Keeffe's *Black Spot*, it was the first time her art had ever been reproduced. O'Keeffe and her husband, the photographer Alfred Stieglitz, were frequent guests at Rosenfeld's Irving Place apartment, where they mixed with his musical friends, like Darius Milhaud and Aaron Copland.

The Dial's editorial staff was also present at many of Rosenfeld's gatherings. The magazine's offices were on Thirteenth Street in Greenwich Village, but contributors generally sent their work in by mail, and when they wanted to socialize with their editors, it was usually at Paul Rosenfeld's apartment. Alyse Gregory, *The Dial*'s managing editor, remembered feeling, when she stepped inside Rosenfeld's home, that she was in "an interior that might have been lifted out of some European capital — Vienna, Paris, Florence — and without disarranging a single picture, or overturning a single vase, set down on the chill, dusty sidewalk of Irving Place, New York. It was an interior both intimate and spacious, an interior for pleasures that were grave and thought that was gay, for conversation witty and civilized."

Edmund Wilson, a frequent visitor, described Rosenfeld's apartment as a place where "poets read their poetry and composers played their music . . . beneath his little collection of Hartleys and O'Keeffes . . . surrounded by his shelves full of Nietzsche and Wagner, Strindberg, Shaw and Ibsen." Despite the European atmosphere of his apartment, Paul Rosenfeld actually disliked traveling abroad. Like Robert Henri, he was totally committed to helping shape America's taste in the arts, and particularly to making the country more receptive to new writers, artists, and composers.

Born in Manhattan in 1890 to a family of means, Rosenfeld was educated at Yale and the Columbia School of Journalism. By the time his work first appeared in *The Dial*, in March 1918, he was already successful as a free-lance writer on the arts. Like Carl Van Vechten, Rosenfeld approached criticism in a lively, somewhat exaggerated manner, with what Ezra Pound, in his sly way, called Rosenfeld's "oriental splendor." Like Van Vechten too, his explanations of musical technique tended to be impressionistic rather than technical; Rimsky-Korsakov's music, for instance, was "the loveliest of picture books — but nothing more." Rosenfeld was considered by his editors at *The Dial* to be singularly valuable, precisely because he did *not* look at his material as a technician, but rather with the soul and vocabulary of a poet.

He was also able to see the connections between various art forms, and believed that the imagination could be fueled by many things. After meeting Rosenfeld in 1927, Robert Penn Warren, a graduate student at Rosenfeld's alma mater, Yale, frequently boarded the train to New York to visit the critic, who took him to see important exhibitions of modern art. "The really important thing for me, however," Warren explained, "was not the mere fact that Rosenfeld introduced me to modern painting. The important thing was that he managed to set it for me in relation to the impulse behind modern literature." It was Rosenfeld who persuaded Penn Warren to try his hand at fiction, and who published his first novella. *Prime Leaf* appeared in 1930, in an annual magazine for new writers that Rosenfeld and a friend started; *American Caravan* had its editorial offices in the living room of the critic's Irving Place apartment.

In 1927, another aspiring young writer came to Gramercy Park. The life he led was in sharp contrast to the delights found in *The Dial*'s social outpost a few streets away. Nathanael West worked as night manager of the Kenmore Hall Hotel, on East Twenty-third Street. The principal virtue of the establishment was a Gramercy Park address, and West's biographer, Jay Martin, has described it as "badly designed, with small rooms, no restaurant, and neither conference rooms nor a mezzanine. [It] was saved by its faults; in some ways, it had been planned as a kind of glorified rooming house, its small rooms renting at low rates, its lobby and drugstore, where the guests all congregated, becoming popular as unostentatious meeting places for young men and women."

West's job called for little more than his physical presence, and he was able to use the quiet late-night hours to read and write. His view of life, expressed in his writing — sardonic, pessimistic, and completely intolerant of the superficial — was hardly in step with the decade. But if Carl Van Vechten's novels so perfectly captured the mood of timeless abandon and freedom from consequence that marked the twenties, Nathanael West's voice, at least in retrospect, seemed to herald the approaching decade — when time finally ran out and the long ten-year party crashed to an end.

14

DEPRESSION
AND
RESURGENCE

⸻ ❖ ⸻

Nathanael west would, like Carl Van Vechten, write only a limited body of fiction within a ten-year period. For West, the period was the thirties; the beginning of that decade marked the end of Van Vechten's writing career.

The crash of the stock market in October 1929 signaled the demise of the manner of life that Carl Van Vechten had both written about and lived. If the twenties had been a splendid drunken party, the thirties was the painful morning after. Van Vechten was neither prepared nor willing to adjust his writing to the new decade's bleak realities.

The extremely poor critical and commercial response to his novel *Parties*, published in 1930, made it clear that Americans did not want to be reminded of their past excesses. The novel takes its central characters, David and Rilda Westlake, based on the Fitzgeralds, through a series of drunken parties with friends as aimless as themselves. Most readers and critics missed the rueful irony of Van Vechten's vision, and saw the book as just another flippant celebration of recklessness. As a man who prided himself on not looking back, without fanfare or visible regret Carl bade farewell to his career as a novelist.

Van Vechten had been relatively prudent in managing his inheritance and was able to sustain a new career in photography despite the Depression. His photographs remain remarkably insightful studies of the people he admired — Eugene O'Neill, Scott Fitzgerald, Bessie Smith, Thomas Mann, W. C. Handy, Henri Matisse, and, of course, Gertrude Stein. If he had spent the twenties in a bizarre array of evening clothes, Carl remembered the thirties as a period in which he spent "whole months, whole years" in pajamas and dressing gowns, awaiting the arrival of the famous person he had invited to sit for a portrait.

America did not want an author to remind her of her reckless past; nor did the country want to be told how foolish her optimism had been. It comes as no surprise, therefore, that Nathanael West's mocking, pessimistic voice did not attract much of an audience when his novels were first published. Two of his books, *Miss Lonelyhearts* and *The Day of the Locust*, are now considered among the finest pieces of fiction written during the 1930s, but his surrealistic treatment of the self-delusion of the American dream went largely unaccepted until 1957, when his novels were reissued as a collective body of work.

As the critic Alan Ross has suggested, "Perhaps the ruthlessness of West's portrait . . . so undisguisedly repulsive and meaningless, was too near the bone for an American audience with a mass neurosis and a guilty conscience." Certainly, if readers in the thirties were looking for reassurance that someone or something would come along to fix things up, they would find no such message in the writing of a man who declared, "There is nothing to root for in my work."

Nathanael West was born Nathan Weinstein in New York City on October 17, 1903. His parents, Max and Anna Wallerstein Weinstein, were Jewish immigrants from cultured backgrounds who had managed to achieve the dream of success in the New World. A skilled builder, Max had taken quick stock of Manhattan's growth, and become rich by constructing apartment houses above Central Park and

Nathanael West, sardonic prophet. His writing blended irony and melancholy.

Eugene O'Neill, photographed by Carl Van Vechten, who chose his subjects from among his admired and accomplished friends

along Riverside Drive. He moved his own family around the city several times as his fortune increased, ending up on Central Park West, where so many other wealthy Jewish families lived that one of West's friends nicknamed it the Gilded Ghetto.

Unlike many Jews in the still poverty-stricken ghetto downtown, the Weinsteins were a determinedly assimilated family that attended the opera far more often than a synagogue. Max and Anna also dedicated themselves to seeing that their children were readily accepted into American life. One value they shared with less successful immigrant parents was the belief that education was the key to success and social acceptance, and they actively encouraged Nathan's intellectual development. No amount of money was too great to spend on anything connected with learning, and Mr. Weinstein regularly came home after work bearing whole sets of books by Dickens, Tolstoy, or Chekhov to encourage his son's interest in important authors.

Even as a child, Nathan was a voracious reader, often absorbed in three or four books at a time. While he would willingly share any book in his collection, he taught the family bull terrier to bite anyone who tried to interrupt him after he had locked himself in his bedroom for an afternoon's reading. Occasionally he thought about putting his books away; he dreamed of becoming a sports hero. But as he grew into gangly adolescence Nathan was awkward, and his passion for baseball failed to make him proficient at the game.

In fact, Nathan was so lacking in energy that one summer when he was away at camp he was nicknamed "Pepper" to indicate how little pep he really had. All teasing to the contrary, the other boys actually liked their dreamy campmate, who captured their own foibles in witty cartoons for the camp newspaper. Nathan was not only unoffended by the nickname, he liked it so much that for the rest of his life he invited good friends to call him Pep.

For all his reading and his obvious intellectual gifts, Nathan was, at best, an indifferent student who didn't participate in any extracurricular activities at the academically prestigious De Witt Clinton High School. For the most part, he lived in his own imagination, spinning fantastic tales for friends and his beloved younger sister, Laura. To his audiences, the stories were always compelling, although they knew they weren't true. Nathan was, remembered one admiring cousin, "the master of the convincing lie."

Nathan's stories often dealt with experiences that were morbid or bizarre. Even when he was young, cruelty and violence and depravity fascinated this sheltered Jewish boy, who seemed to withdraw from the gentility his upbringing aimed at. Nathan Weinstein knew early on that he would not become a doctor or a lawyer or a banker, or even take over his father's prosperous construction business.

As he grew up, West was caught between his own indifference to formal education and his parents' fervent desire that he get as much book learning as money could buy. In 1920, at the age of seventeen, he finally left high school without graduating; but with the help of an apparently forged transcript, he managed to get accepted at Tufts University the following year. Unfortunately, he found his studies there no more engrossing than he had in high school, and he quickly lost interest in going to classes. When he failed all his courses, he was asked to withdraw, but the following semester, through an error or some sleight-of-hand, West was able to enter Brown University as a transfer student.

It will never be known whether West authored the deception or whether he was simply the beneficiary of a lucky accident. He was still using the name Nathan Weinstein, and the records department at Tufts sent to Brown a transcript that belonged to another student of the same name. That Nathan Weinstein had done extremely well at Tufts, so West was not only admitted to Brown but was granted almost two years of credits, many in the required math and science courses that had always been his downfall.

Nathanael West did much better both socially and academically at Brown. He was editor of the literary magazine, which he also illustrated, and it quickly got around that he had the largest personal library on campus and was willing to share it with friends. Thanks to an extremely generous allowance, he sported a fashionable wardrobe, complete with argyle socks and a Homburg hat. Although he was still skinny and was self-conscious about his prominent nose and protruding ears, he felt more confident about his looks when he decked himself out in impeccably tailored Brooks Brothers suits.

At Brown, West made several friends who were to be part of his life forever, among them Quentin Reynolds and a day student from Providence named S. J. (Sidney) Perelman. Both young men could always be counted on to take part in West's inventive schemes, such as the "Hanseatic League" he organized in 1923. The league members fancied themselves, according to one of the group, an intellectual elite who relentlessly mocked "what the common man was relishing." The bookplate Sid Perelman designed for West symbolizes the focus of the group; it shows a man fondly embracing a donkey, and bears a quotation from Goethe: "Do I love what others love?"

West often led the Hanseatic League in experiments with magic and in imaginary conversations between invented or mythical figures. He loved to deceive his friends by making up stories about his discovery of some wonderful writer and excitedly describing his lat-

Quentin Reynolds, distinguished journalist. From college days, he took part in "Pep" West's outrageous schemes.

S. J. Perelman, master humorist, a loving match for his friend and brother-in-law, Nathanael West

est work, concocting the intricate plots and complex characters as he went along. Pep was just as resourceful in spinning tales that might come in handy for friends who needed a way out of a problem.

When Quentin Reynolds was about to be expelled for making and selling bootleg liquor on campus, he turned to West for help. Reynolds remembers, "Pep said, 'Here — take some notes.' Handing me a pad and pencil, he began pacing. 'You will start by telling [Dean] Randall of the stroke your father had which has kept you from working for two years. Your sister is still in the hospital recovering from a serious operation.'" On and on West went with his story, finally offering a finish that he happily assured Reynolds had "a nice touch. . . . Tell him that only yesterday you went to confession and told the priest all about this. He made you promise to give it up and you agreed." When West's scheme worked, he and Reynolds celebrated with toasts of the latter's undiminished supply of illegal liquor.

On the strength of this episode, Reynolds again called on Pep when he had to write a Class Day speech a few months later. West's speech was wildly successful — convoluted, arcane, and filled with obscure off-color allusions and puns. It contained a tale about a flea named St. Puce who had been born in the armpit of Christ and died of pneumonia at the very moment of Christ's death. St. Puce would be reborn in an episode of West's first novel, *The Dreamlife of Balso Snell*, published in 1931.

Balso Snell, says the literary scholar Stanley Edgar Hyman, is "almost impossible to summarize." West's writing was surreal, and he experimented with an assortment of literary techniques that contributed to a vision of life that was essentially irrational.

Man's search for meaning, West seemed to conclude, is an exercise in the absurd. This was hardly the life view for a successful career in the construction business, and West vigorously resisted that fate when he graduated from Brown in 1924. For over two years he worked only intermittently and always reluctantly for his father, until the Weinsteins finally agreed to subsidize a trip to Paris for their son.

·   ·   ·

Before leaving for Paris, in October 1926, Nathan Weinstein legally changed his name to Nathanael West. He had experimented with an assortment of pseudonyms over the years to signal the complexity of his identity. An official name change would allow him to go to Paris as a newly created person, ready to begin an exciting new era of his life.

West adored Paris, which still held the allure for young American artists and writers it had had in the postwar years of the Lost Generation, but he was quick to recognize the pretenses of the new wave of expatriates. In an unpublished story eventually entitled "The Impostor," he wrote, "By the time I got to Paris, the business of being an artist had grown quite difficult. Aside from the fact that you were actually expected to create, the jury had been changed. It no longer consisted of the tourists and the folks back home, but of your fellow artists. They were the ones who decided on the authenticity of your madness. Long hair and a rapt look wouldn't get you to first base. . . . Even dirt and sandals and calling Sargent a lousy painter was not enough."

In fact, West did grow a long beard and experimented with a host of variations on the role of the American expatriate, making up convincing stories of his years abroad and about his past. Like so many young traveling would-be artists, he actually got little writing done, and at the end of three months he bowed to his family's urgent requests that he come home and go to work. By the time West arrived home in January 1927, he no longer had to resist taking a job in the family business; there was little business left to join. Despite the top song of the day, Irving Berlin's "Blue Skies," the skies were darkening over Manhattan. Max Weinstein's business, like so many others, was foundering as less and less of his property was rented and had to be taken over by banks and receivers.

Since West had no interest in any career but writing, working as a night clerk at the Kenmore Hall Hotel was as good a job as any. He found the Gramercy Park neighborhood appealing, and was quite pleased that his $35-a-week salary was supplemented by free room and board. Most important, the work allowed him free time for reading and writing. By now, West owned about five hundred books, and he would pore over old favorites by Chekhov and Stendhal, delight in the mixture of fantasy and melancholy in Gogol, or analyze the exciting new experiments of Aldous Huxley and the lethal intellectual humor of James Joyce. "He idolized Joyce," remembered S. J. Perelman, "considering him . . . the foremost comic writer in the language." Yet Pep was not above mocking his idol by parodying certain scenes from Joyce in his own writing as a kind of secret, literary joke.

Nathanael West made the Kenmore Hall Hotel a cost-free center of social life for his friends. Sid Perelman, Quentin Reynolds, and Maxwell Bodenheim regularly came by for lunch and a swim in the hotel swimming pool, or stopped in at night to have a drink and talk about books and their own attempts at writing. The Brown alumni grapevine quickly spread the word that a visit to Gramercy Park could get you a free room at the Kenmore Hotel if you were willing to take one that hadn't yet been cleaned after the previous night's guest.

For his closest friends, West was even more generous with the Kenmore's facilities. The first person in West's circle to publish a story was a fellow he had met in the Village named Dashiell Hammett, whose work had begun to appear in the pulp magazine *Black Mask*. Hammett was notoriously imprudent with money, regularly racing against time to finish a story before his rent came due. It was a race he didn't always win. On one occasion, when he was halfway through a serial for the magazine and was about to be evicted from his room, Quentin Reynolds expansively suggested that he stay at the Kenmore until he finished the story. As Reynolds remembered the experience, he telephoned West about Hammett: "'Register him under a phony name. . . . When he finishes his serial he can run like a deer and you can say he was some skip artist who just blew the joint.' There was silence at the other end of the line. 'What is it, Pep?' I asked anxiously. 'I was just trying to think of a good name to register him under,' Pep said mildly. 'How do you like "T. Victrola Blueberry"?'"

Reynolds said he would be right over with Mr. Blueberry and a bottle of gin bought on credit from a sympathetic bootlegger to stimulate Hammett's productivity. That night the three stayed up late in the finest suite in the hotel, talking of the kind of things young writers talked about in the 1920s.

"'You got a title for the serial?' Pep asked. 'I think I'll call it *The Maltese Falcon*,' Dash said."

West often did his own writing in his hotel office, and one evening he looked up to see Sid Perelman, who had come by to invite him to dinner with a new acquaintance. Perelman was now not only West's closest friend but, to their mutual delight, was also engaged to West's sister, Laura. Perelman had begun writing for a successful new magazine, *The New Yorker*. Its brand of sharp skepticism was completely congenial with Perelman's satiric gifts, and it adeptly captured the twenties' mood of lighthearted cynicism. The young woman the two men dined with that evening wrote an advice-to-the-lovelorn column for the *Brooklyn Eagle* under the pseudonym of Susan Chester, and had been shocked by the strange letters she received from readers. It occurred to her that Perelman might be able to turn the letters into a funny piece for his magazine.

A quick reading showed Perelman that while they were naïve and wildly comic, they were far too sad and desperate for his use. Nathanael West, however, found them riveting. Perelman explained that he "saw in them and their recipient the focus of the story he called *Miss Lonelyhearts*," which, from its conception in the Greenwich Village restaurant, would take West four years to write. Into the tale of *Miss Lonelyhearts*, West worked his own version of pleas for help often sent by the friendless to newspaper columnists. One, from a sixteen-year-old girl who signed herself "Desperate," requested advice on how to have a social life, because "I would like to have boy friends like the other girls and go out on Saturday nites but no boy will take me because I was born without a nose — although I am a good dancer and have a nice shape and my father buys me pretty clothes."

Miss Lonelyhearts is a complicated allegorical novel about a young man who writes a newspaper advice column. He treats the job as a lark, but as the tragic letters accumulate, he becomes depressed and haunted by his own need for salvation. Although the book, which was published by Horace Liveright in 1933, was much better received critically than *Balso Snell* had been in 1931 when it was published by a small press, the Depression ruined any chance of financial success. The Liveright Company suddenly declared bankruptcy, and the printer of *Miss Lonelyhearts* refused to release the books to the stores because he hadn't been paid. By the time the legal difficulties had been straightened out and a new contract drawn up with Harcourt Brace, the reviews were generally forgotten, and *Miss Lonelyhearts* sold only a few hundred copies.

The novel's aborted success mirrored the general upheaval of the Depression. It was a time of national bewilderment that West, despite his cynicism, found "brutal and heartbreaking." The horror of the stock market crash had begun a cycle of despair that touched every aspect of life in the nation and made New York almost unrecognizable to those who remembered its glory of just a few years earlier.

A visiting member of the British government, Mary Agnes Hamilton, who had made several trips to Manhattan during the 1920s, recorded her impressions when she returned to the city in December 1932. New York's newest wonder, the Empire State Building, stood unoccupied, its owners meeting expenses only by charging sightseers who wanted to go up to the roof for the astonishing view. When Miss Hamilton went to the theater, she was shocked by the changes that had taken place in Times Square. Instead of the crowds of elegantly dressed revelers, now, "at any hour of the day and late into the evening . . . it is packed with shabby, utterly dumb and apathetic-looking men . . . waiting for the advent of the coffee wagon run by Mr. William Randolph Hearst of the *New York American.* . . . At every street corner . . . men try to sell one apples, oranges. . . . On any day, rows of them line every relatively open space, eager to shine one's shoes."

Nathanael West experienced this despair every day as he presided over the domestic life of the hotel, and it profoundly confirmed his personal and literary view of the grotesque, pitiful truth of the human condition. Man's need to dream, and the inevitability of his disillusionment, were West's constant themes, and in that sense the Depression contributed to his creativity. Indeed, W. H. Auden would describe the thirties as a time when the country suffered from "West's disease," which he defined as "a disease of consciousness which renders it incapable of converting wishes into desires."

Looking out from his office into the hotel lobby, West saw the "shabby, lonely men and women killing time by reading pulp magazines," feeding their need to invent "elaborate daydreams," and he wondered how long it would take before they admitted how bleak and hopeless their lives really were. The question became even more poignant when West went to work at a larger hotel, of higher quality, on East Fifty-sixth Street. The Sutton was an apartment hotel; it had a great many luxurious suites and well-decorated rooms located on separate floors for male and female guests. (Despite this "sop to respectability," remembered S. J. Perelman, "the elevator men did not regard themselves as housemothers, and for the frisky, a rear stairway offered ready access or flight.") The young professionals or older men and women with some private income struggled to stay on rather than admit defeat and move someplace where their money might hold out a little longer.

That fewer and fewer people could afford the Sutton allowed Pep once again to offer lodging to his friends, assuring them that it was better to have the hotel's windows lit up so that it didn't look as if it were dying. As a consequence, the Sutton Club Hotel is remembered as an important literary center of the 1930s. Before the new Mr. and Mrs. Sidney Perelman moved to an apartment on Washington Square, they spent several months at the Sutton, as did Norman Krasna, Quentin Reynolds, Erskine Caldwell, James Farrell and his wife, Edmund Wilson, and Lillian Hellman, who buried herself in her room trying to write her first play, *The Children's Hour*. Still reckless with money, Dashiell Hammett once arrived from a stay at the Hotel Pierre, gleefully showing Pep that he had put on all of his clothing in layers to escape from the glamorous hotel without paying his bill. As S. J. Perelman appreciatively recalled, his brother-in-law once again put the writer "on the cuff and staked him to a typewriter and a bottle of beer a day. The upshot, the best-seller called *The Thin Man*, clinched Hammett's reputation."

In 1931 alone, twenty thousand people committed suicide because of economic despair, and at least half a dozen were guests of the Sutton Club Hotel; they jumped from the hotel's upper terrace. One evening, as the night manager looked on in fascinated horror, a guest aimed his fall badly, and though he managed to end his life, he did so by crashing through the glass ceiling of the hotel dining room just as the other guests were arriving for dinner. To West, the Sutton, like the Kenmore, seemed a microcosm of the outside world, where people battled continually with false hope and an omnipresent sense of disaster. Occasionally, he and Lillian Hellman would steam open guests' mail, not so much from curiosity as to get a closer look at their individual stories and the sources of their particular tragedies.

Even Gramercy Park was not immune to loss; some long-time residents had to give up homes they had expected to live in for a lifetime. Paul Rosenfeld's inherited income was drastically reduced, and he was forced to leave his splendid Irving Place apartment, taking only a few of his lovingly acquired possessions to a tiny new apartment in Greenwich Village.

Still, by the standards of the day, Rosenfeld was lucky. For, although before 1930 few Americans were really poor, over the next few years some forty million people would experience genuine poverty. By 1933, industrial output was less than half what it had been before the crash, 25 percent of the labor force was unemployed, and those who held jobs were earning 60 percent less than they had in 1929. Prices for every conceivable item dropped to an unheard-of low, but almost no one could afford to purchase anything new. A fur coat cost $92 and a cloth coat $7.00, a double bed and mattress sold for $14.95, a large kitchen stove, $23.95.

On March 4, the final day of Herbert Hoover's presidency, the banking system collapsed completely. "We are at the end of our string," the beleaguered President said. "There is nothing more we can do." Of course, most Americans blamed Hoover's administration for their terrible plight. The newspapers that homeless men covered themselves with as they slept on park benches were called "Hoover blankets," and the "Hoover flag" was a pocket turned inside out. In Central Park, a village of shacks made of packing boxes and pieces of scrap metal sprang up; called Hoover Valley, it was duplicated in every city in the country.

The country's new President, Franklin D. Roosevelt, took office on the day of the bank closing, beginning a career that would make him a hero to some, a villain to others. Whatever one's camp, Roosevelt's voice was the first to offer some hope to Americans, in 1933, that things would indeed get better, and to take measures to see that they did. The glimmer of promise encouraged the fantasies that everyone seemed so desperate to cling to, and they sought the stuff of myth and dream to distract them from the continuing bleakness of real life.

During the Depression, library circulation figures increased by 40 percent, with people borrowing primarily historical novels, in which handsome men and women dressed in period costumes and engaged in breathtaking, romantic adventures. Dance marathons, where one could dance long past thinking, were extremely popular, and young men and women spent as many nights as they could dancing with furious abandon. Undoubtedly a metaphor for those who felt that their lives had fallen apart, jigsaw puzzles became the rage; the craze for doing them swept through the city. The thirties also saw a dramatic increase in the memberships of fraternal organizations. It was estimated that almost half the adults in the country belonged to some organization with an exotic name — Pharaohs, Owls, Odd Fellows — where, in some "den" or "grotto" or "nest," people got together under a clearly defined set of rules that would never surprise them by changing or disappearing the following week.

Gambling was widespread. In 1934, the largest salary in the United States was earned by a man named Moe Annenberg, who owned the *Racing Form*. People took what few dollars they still had and tried to recoup their losses by betting on a horse. More often than not, they lost even more. Movie theaters instituted their own forms of gambling, with nightly games of Banko, Keno, or Screeno. The audiences who flocked to the movies in record numbers not only lost themselves in the fantasies on the giant screen, but dreamed of winning the jackpot when the movie was over and the theater manager came on stage to spin the big, bright wheel of fortune.

Even without the games of chance, the movies proved to be the Depression's major antidote. Those immigrants from the ghetto who had recognized the lure of the short "flicks" and opened their nickelodeons had moved to Hollywood. There, with big budgets, they made pictures that helped Americans forget what waited for them outside the movie palaces. During the thirties, some eighty-five million people a week went to the movies, where, for twenty-five cents (ten cents for children), one could watch a lavish musical extravaganza with Fred Astaire and Ginger Rogers dancing to choreography by Busby Berkeley, or grow flush with romantic sentiment as heiress Bette Davis gave up "everything" to run off with the man she loved.

Many in New York's writing community found their way to Hollywood during the thirties, Nathanael West among them in 1936, although he always made it clear that he had nothing but contempt for the "pants pressers" who ran the big studios. As Budd Schulberg put it, few writers escaped the need to "refill their larders against the long cold winters of the Depression." At any given time, in the Stanley Rose Book Store on Hollywood Boulevard, which served as a home away from home for displaced writers, one might find John O'Hara, Scott Fitzgerald, Erskine Caldwell, Dashiell Hammett, Sid Perelman, Dorothy Parker, William Faulkner, or William Saroyan. Schulberg has recalled that while Rose had his favorites among the writers, West, who was far less known than many of the others, always "enjoyed the highest perch in Stanley's aviary of rare literary birds."

While employed as a screenwriter of low-budget pictures for the Republic Studios, West was working away at what Schulberg has called "Pep's terrifying little masterpiece," *The Day of the Locust.* West's Hollywood friends eagerly awaited his new book, which had as its backdrop the garish experiences of the Hollywood community. The novel tells the story of a young painter working at a Hollywood studio as a set and costume designer and the people he meets in what Schulberg described as a series of "madhatter vignettes that start with a laugh and end with a gasp of pain and regret." The novel, whose title stems from the plague of locusts that attacked the Egyptians in the Book of Exodus, concludes with a savage murder and a riot at a movie première.

Like West's earlier novels, the book did very poorly. A few

months after its publication by Random House in 1939, he wrote to his loyal supporter F. Scott Fitzgerald, "So far the box score stands: Good reviews — fifteen percent, bad reviews — twenty-five percent, brutal personal attacks — sixty percent." *The Day of the Locust* would not earn its author more than $500. It is clear in retrospect that another reason for West's lack of commercial success in the thirties was that he went against the era's literary grain. The Depression years were a time when writers became intensely involved with politics, almost exclusively the politics of the left. Books on radical themes were prominent: "strike novels" and gritty stories of poverty and capitalistic oppression. Critics as well as readers were oriented to the writing of "social realism."

As a result, explained Budd Schulberg, "The same kind of critical thinking that clobbered Scott Fitzgerald for his affinity with wealth and decadence in *Tender Is the Night* had its knives out for West and his novels of grotesque or black humor that refused to pay proper obeisance to positive collective action." It would take a country weary from its largest war and embittered by failed dreams of glory to appreciate West's black-comedy approach to pessimistic themes. When his collected works were published in 1957, people newly discovered the man whose writing had so early anticipated the absurdist authors of later generations, from Samuel Beckett to Kurt Vonnegut to Jules Feiffer and Joseph Heller.

West, of course, would never know this renaissance. In 1940, married only a few months to a girl named Eileen McKenney (celebrated in the play by Ruth McKenney, *My Sister Eileen*), he was killed, with his bride, in a fiery automobile crash on the way home to Los Angeles from a rollicking trip to Mexico. F. Scott Fitzgerald had died the day before, and before both bodies were shipped home for burial, they were laid out in the same Hollywood funeral home.

By the time of the death of these two writers, whose careers were marked by the Depression, the country seemed to have largely recovered from the Depression's economic destruction. As if to celebrate its rebirth, in 1939 New York City put on the largest, most expensive exposition ever known. The New York World's Fair opened on April 30, 1939, on over a thousand acres in Flushing Meadow in Queens. Although rumblings of war could be heard from abroad, fairgoers flocked in huge numbers for a giddy glimpse of America's miraculous future. New inventions, from television to nylon stockings, promised untold delights to those who could pay the fifty-cent entrance fee to the World of Tomorrow.

In the city itself, the bread lines and beggars had disappeared, Broadway was glittering with new shows, and people were dancing to big bands in fancifully designed supper clubs. There were some people, of course, whose fortunes were so great or who were sufficiently foresighted that they managed to escape economic catastrophe during even the depths of the Depression. Many of these survivors of what had once been high society mixed with the current cultural darlings of the social scene, the movie stars, to create something called "café society." When Prohibition was repealed, in 1933, the city's leading speakeasies became fashionable restaurants, where the rich and glamorous played. The Stork Club, "21," and El Morocco were the luxurious settings for members of the traditional social elite, like the Astors, the Vanderbilts, and the Whitneys, as well as Douglas Fairbanks, Jr., Bruce Cabot, and a few questionably titled but very charming expatriates.

Perhaps influenced by the publicity-hungry movie stars, what mattered to café society, even more than the party or the people or the fun, was knowing that the world would read about their exploits. Their ultimate thrill was publicity, and the ultimate achievement was getting one's photograph published in the new picture magazine, *Life*. The quintessential achievement of a thirties' press agent was the caption that ran under the portrait of an obscure society matron in *Life* magazine: "Mrs. Orson D. Munn, who won fame in a limited circle by wearing a foxtail for a hat at the Colony Restaurant, drops in at El Morocco several times a week, is known for the spirited way she dances the rumba with her remarkably agile husband."

Undoubtedly, the public's desire for vicarious excitement also influenced the growth of the publicity profession. In much the same way that people escaped to the movies, they devoured intimate bits of gossip about movie stars and the people who lived like movie stars.

At the same time, the privileged group recognized the value of good public relations and were careful not to flaunt too much good fortune when so many people had been so recently suffering. In 1939, the newspapers still made much of the fact that the coming-out party of Brenda Frazier, the season's leading debutante, had cost $60,000. The reports of such extravagance were followed by a series of denials by Brenda's mother, who assured the public that the party had cost only $16,000. From this hunger for attention, mixed with the need for a positive public image, the industry of public relations was born, and, as with every profession, there soon appeared a man who seemed destined to rule it from the start.

Benjamin Sonnenberg was nine years old in 1910, when he arrived on Ellis Island with his mother and two sisters. After five years alone in New York, his father had finally saved enough money from his clothing stand on Grand Street to bring his family from Russia to New York. Ben grew up in the teeming streets of the Jewish ghetto, and found his only recreation at the Henry Street Settlement House, where, under the tutelage of its founder, Lillian Wald, ghetto children could learn about art and theater and get a taste of what life offered beyond mere survival.

Miss Wald took young Ben Sonnenberg under her wing, allowing him to live at the settlement house while he attended high school, and helping him win a scholarship to Columbia University. She even recommended him for a job doing field work for a relief agency, which took him to Europe in 1922. The months in Europe gave Benjamin Sonnenberg his first sense of what it would be like to be rich. "You could live like a Lord in Europe for thirty or forty dollars a week then," he remembered. "I stayed in first-class hotels, bought books, went to the theater and ballet, had some suits made to order and acquired a cane, a black Homburg and a Burberry. And," he added seriously, "the significance of having a man draw your bath and lay out your clothes burst upon me like a revelation. I took a tintype in my mind of the way I wanted to be a bon vivant, a patron of the arts, a man who could mix Picasso with Dun and Bradstreet."

Back home in New York, Ben recognized the potential of a busi-

Ben Sonnenberg, the quintessential inventor of public images,
whose greatest creation was himself

ness that made other people feel important. In 1924, after marrying Hilda Caplan, whom he had met at a Henry Street dance when
he was sixteen years old, Ben — sporting "my cane, my Homburg
and my Burberry" — worked as a free-lance press agent for plays
and moderately successful nightclub performers. Gradually, he
moved up to working with bigger stars and was able to persuade the
managers of the stars' hotels to hire him to send out stories about
their more glamorous guests, augmenting their establishments' reputation through the reflected publicity.

By the 1930s, Ben Sonnenberg had only the biggest stars as
clients; most of his business came from large corporate clients who
wanted his services to enhance both their corporate and personal im-

ages. When a member of a major family was caught acting up in café society and got his name in the paper for all the wrong reasons, Ben would come to the rescue. He explained, "The family escutcheon . . . once a wondrous shiny object . . . now has become slightly tarnished. . . . What I do for him is simple: I breathe on the family escutcheon — and he polishes while I breathe."

Even for a person whose reputation was unsullied, hiring Benjamin Sonnenberg meant acquiring a public persona that was sometimes more interesting than the real one. When asked to define the business of public relations, Sonnenberg often replied, "I'm the builder of bridges into posterity," or, with a mischievous smile, "Building large plinths for little men to stand on."

The watering places of café society became Ben Sonnenberg's turf. He made sure to get the best tables at "21," El Morocco, and the Stork Club, where he was certain to be noticed by a style of dress that most resembled that of an Edwardian dandy. His standard costume was a four-button suit, a stiff shirt with a starched, detachable collar, a bowler hat in winter or a boater in summer, and, when the mood hit him, a walking stick. "I knew that wherever I went, people would say, 'Who in God's name is that?' It didn't matter what they said afterward." In fact, there was another reason behind Sonnenberg's choice of wardrobe; the grace and solidity of the past countered the "flim-flam, fly-by-night" reputation of his recently born and, to many eyes, suspect profession. The time Ben spent in Europe, especially in England, had given him a taste for history, tradition, stability, and the kind of personal power that comes from knowing that you are comfortable and completely in control of your environment.

It was because of these aspirations that Benjamin Sonnenberg moved to Gramercy Park, first to live in a small apartment, and then to the extraordinarily beautiful red brick house that stands at the corner of Twentieth Street and Irving Place. The home had been originally constructed in 1845, the same year that George Templeton Strong was building his own "palazzo." In 1888, it was purchased by Mr. and Mrs. Stuyvesant Fish, who hired their neighbor Stanford White to do extensive renovations. When Sonnenberg moved in, in 1931, many of White's luxurious touches remained and were eventually restored to their original splendor, such as the center hall's magnificent white marble staircase and the beautiful fireplace in the perfectly proportioned oak-paneled room just off the hall.

By the time the Sonnenbergs moved in, the house had been converted into apartments, as had the adjacent building, once the site of the Fishes' stable. At first, Ben and Hilda could afford to live only in a duplex apartment on the first floor, and rented out the rest of the house, but the thirty-year-old entrepreneur knew that he would be master of all the property before too long. And, to be sure, in the ensuing years, he turned the house into the finest privately owned residence in the city. When he had finished expanding and renovating, Benjamin Sonnenberg was master of a home with thirty-seven rooms, including a top-floor ballroom with a bank of windows overlooking the park.

From the moment he moved in, Ben Sonnenberg used his home for entertaining. Mrs. Fish had been a famous if somewhat eccentric hostess — she had once given an elegant sit-down dinner for her dogs and their canine friends from the neighborhood — and Benjamin Sonnenberg would, during his own tenancy, become the city's most celebrated party giver. A Sonnenberg party did not have the free-form abandon of those wild parties that went on around the corner on Irving Place during the 1920s. Indeed, although Sonnenberg's parties were sparkling gatherings of twenty to two hundred guests who were the absolute leaders in the arts, professions, and politics, the events were controlled by the host. "I love to own things," Ben explained. "Being a host is part of ownership, since in a way, you own your guests. I hate being a guest myself; I like to control the menu, both as to food and people. I suppose it's the philosophy of a man of property." Ben Sonnenberg furnished his property with a vast, highly personal collection of art, furnishings, and decorative objects. In his housekeeping staff, which always numbered at least six, there was one person who did nothing but polish his extensive brass appointments and objets d'art. His close friend Alistair Cooke would later describe Ben's indefatigable and idiosyncratic collecting:

"For over forty years he roamed through England [mostly] plucking a Sargent . . . here, an Ingres or an Old Master drawing there, combining them in his head with . . . an Irish hunt table, a Welsh dresser, a Caroline silver tankard, a set of Chippendale . . . to bring them home to their proper setting."

There was no neighborhood in New York that could offer Ben Sonnenberg the sustenance that he found in Gramercy Park. His appreciation of the neighborhood's British overtones was as strong as Samuel Ruggles's attempts to create that atmosphere a hundred years earlier. And Sonnenberg's ability to mix people from the arts, politics, business, and society at his parties carried on the cross-fertilization that had marked life in the park since its beginnings. Thus, while Benjamin Sonnenberg lived by twentieth-century illusions, in many ways he seemed the appropriate person to reign over the neighborhood from its grandest nineteenth-century house.

When the 1940s did bring a new war to New York City, its marks were less visible than during the Civil War and First World War. Still, many patterns of life were altered, and the contrasts in the ways people lived once again dramatically sharpened. During and after the Second World War, social and physical change transformed the city that surrounded Samuel Ruggles's carefully designed enclave, but Benjamin Sonnenberg's instincts were correct. In Gramercy Park, harmony rather than change and contrast continued to prevail. No matter what new wonder or disaster occurred outside the graceful square with the little park at its center, the Gramercy Park neighborhood would always resound softly with what Henry James called "the incomparable tone of time."

EPILOGUE

---◆---

EVEN ON AN AFTERNOON in late winter, joggers circle Gramercy Park. Their quick pace is as appropriate to our time as the nineteenth-century residents' easy stroll was to theirs. Yet, as we have seen, those quieter times bore the seeds of tremendous urban change.

Today, the area's residents rush from converted brownstone condominiums to hail passing taxis. Along Park Avenue South, chic new restaurants spring up almost daily in buildings that once housed merchants and manufacturers. They are filled with young communications executives whose offices have moved to the desirable downtown address. New supermarkets and service stores on Third Avenue give testimony to the neighborhood's rapidly expanding population, much of it housed in luxury highrises.

Inside the peaceful, graceful square, a visitor would not sense the dense population that surrounds him. Yet even in this protected enclave, homes are equipped with alarm systems to ward off burglars, and a homeless person with her belongings collected in a grocery wagon slumps against the stately gates of Samuel Ruggles's park.

The clause in Samuel Ruggles's deed stipulating that the neighborhood must prohibit "anything that is dangerous or offensive" to the community is frequently challenged by entrepreneurs who want to open a restaurant or put up a new hotel, and the owner of the Gramercy Park Hotel (once the site of Stanford White's home) often battles with area residents over his choice of guests, such as noisy rock groups given to late-night reveling.

The Gramercy Park Association holds fast to the wishes of the founder, however, and has updated the meaning of his provision to "preserve and maintain the residential character of the neighborhood of Gramercy Park and . . . promote the interests and comfort of the property owners and residents of the neighborhood."

Since 1966, landmark status has helped the association to honor Samuel Ruggles's goals. The Gramercy Park Historic District includes the square's original homes, its turn-of-the-century apartment houses, and parts of Irving Place, Eighteenth Street, and Nineteenth Street — the "block beautiful." No alterations can be made to these buildings without the Landmark Commission's approval, and, as various developers have discovered, owners of non-landmark buildings in historic districts cannot alter their property if the changes will adversely affect the appearance of the neighborhood. Through these means, the area's nineteenth-century character has been kept largely intact. Its venerable buildings are mellow with time and meticulously maintained, and the square exudes the secret charm of a richly storied past.

Thus, despite the intrusions of modern reality, Gramercy Park is an oasis of quiet and serenity. Although few struggling artists can afford to live there, established members of the arts have continued through the decades to call Gramercy Park home. Scores of others faithfully frequent the Players' and National Arts clubs, so the mixture of talents in a fraternal setting happily endures. John F. Kennedy lived here as a boy before his father moved the family to London to take up his post as United States ambassador to the Court of St. James's.

Most of all, Gramercy Park continues to share a strong sense of place with both residents and visitors. In the late 1940s, the world-renowned architect and artist Le Corbusier wrote about how much Manhattan changed between his relatively frequent visits. No sooner does a building go up, he commented, "than the city decides it wants something even grander." Consequently, he concluded, New York is never more than twenty years old, because it is constantly being re-shaped "on the scale of the new times."

Happily, enough of Gramercy Park remains more than twenty years old to hold at bay the invasions of progress. To return to the neighborhood after a day in the impersonal world "outside" is to come home to a bastion of civility, and the relationship of the park to the great city that flourishes around it also remains unaltered. Samuel Ruggles's vision was prophetic when, nearly 150 years ago, he pleaded the need for urban retreat: "Come what will, our open spaces will remain forever imperishable. Buildings, towers, palaces may molder and crumble beneath the touch of time, but space . . . glorious, open space, will remain to bless the city forever."

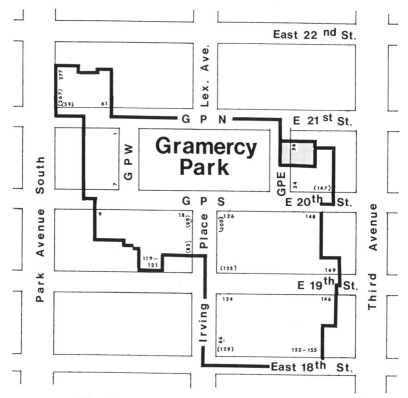

The efforts of devoted traditionalists are rewarded:
Gramercy Park is declared a historic district.

Notes

Bibliography

Index

NOTES

---◆---

For complete references to all sources cited in the Notes, please see the Bibliography.

CHAPTER 1

Many of the sources used in this chapter served as a background for the entire book, because they chronicled the beginnings and growth of New York City. The works I relied on are those by Batterberry, Boyer, Van Wyck Brooks, Evans, Fairfield, Garrett, Hirsch, Hone, Hughes, Jefferson, Kouwenhoven, Lamb, Nye, Pine, Pivar, Todd, Wecter, and Wolfe.

The book compiled by Bayrd Still, *Mirror for Gotham*, which introduced me to the letters of John Pintard, is a unique and valuable reference work. It draws on more than six hundred commentaries about Manhattan, made by visitors from all over the world between the years 1774 and 1950. These descriptions are in the form of articles, book entries, letters, and diary excerpts. The comments of John Pintard, who was born in New York City in 1759 and worked as a city inspector and clerk in the Common Council, are in a collection of letters published by the New-York Historical Society, which owns the Pintard manuscripts. *The Diary of Philip Hone*, edited by Allan Nevins, in two volumes, provides a vivid portrait of the city in the early part of the nineteenth century and introduces many people who will be met again in the diary of George Templeton Strong. The principal collection of papers concerning Samuel Ruggles is in the Rare Books and Manuscript Division of the New York Public Library. Some papers are also at Yale University Library and the New-York Historical Society.

CHAPTER 2

The major source for this chapter was the first volume of the remarkable diary kept by George Templeton Strong. According to Nevins, Strong's friends never knew he was such a dedicated diarist. It was Nevins's belief that this accounts for the honesty and vividness of Strong's writings, for "if a man is known to be keeping a journal, his friends and acquaintances may play up to it; if he wishes it published in his own time, he must be over-discreet in his entries." The diary is in four volumes; the original manu-scripts are owned by the Red Cross in Washington, although Columbia has a full set of photostats. Other writings used in this chapter are by Batter-berry, Boyer, Henry Collins Brown, De Leeuw, Ellington, Headly, Hone, Hughes, Jenkins, Lockwood, Moody, Nye, Pelletrau, Pessen, Schermerhorn, Stansell, Still, Thompson, Todd, and Wecter.

CHAPTER 3

The principal sources for this chapter, besides Strong's diary, were Van Wyck Brooks, Carter, De Leeuw, Ditzion, Hewitt, Lamb, Lynn, Mack, Pine, Spann, and Wyllie. Lamb's historical study of New York City is a full and comprehensive work. Professor Wyllie's treatise on the myth and reality of the self-made man is a provocative work.

CHAPTER 4

Sources for this chapter were Armstrong, Boynton, Crapsey, Harper, Lehmann-Haupt, Maurice, Strong, James Wilson, Wyllie. Lehmann-Haupt and Boynton give the background for the story of the house of Har-per. Strong's diary entries about the Harper fire are vivid and moving reading.

CHAPTER 5

Sources were Crapsey, Ellington, Headly, Mack, Pessen, Reigel, Simpson, Spann, Stansell, Strong, and *The 1866 Visitors Guide*. The work by Crap-sey on poverty and vice contrasts dramatically with Pessen's study of wealth and power before the Civil War. The dichotomy of prewar society clearly laid the groundwork for the social change that took place after the war. Stansell's study focuses on women in New York in a period when "the di-alectic of female vice and virtue was a central issue."

CHAPTER 6

Sources for this study were Atkinson, Campbell, Hughes, Hornblow, Jen-kins, McCabe, Moody, Lloyd Morris, Nevins, Pique and Kretsch, and Eleanor Ruggles. The Booth papers are in the Walter Hammond–Edwin Booth Theatre Collection and Library of the Players' Club, which has a distinguished store of books and writings about the theater. James McCabe was a minister who became a journalist; he wrote extensively about every aspect of New York life during the 1870s and 1880s. His articles, which are collected in guidebooks, cover politics, "virtues and vices," geography and architecture, morals and manners.

CHAPTER 7

Sources were Amory, Baldwin, Bouton, Boyer, Henry Collins Brown, Eliot Clark, Harris, Jenkins, Larkin, Lynn, Miller, Moore, George Morris, Platt, Roth, Saint-Gaudens, Stansell, Tharp, and Wilkinson. Boyer, an architectural preservationist and city planner, paints a clear picture of the physical changes in New York City in the second half of the nineteenth century. Saint-Gaudens's reminiscences, discreet in certain of their revelations, nonetheless presents an intimate view of the sculptor and his views on art and life. Tharp and Platt provide a view of the ever-more Gilded Age.

CHAPTER 8

Sources were Ames, Baldwin, Britt, Henry Collins Brown, Campbell, Crane, Dolan, Durso, Ellington, Gernsheim, Gipson, Kolodin, Krehbiel, Lloyd Morris, Mount, Platt, Pivar, Riegel, Eleanor Ruggles, Smith, Stansell, Stern, Tharp, Wecter, Wilkinson, and White. Many of these books cover social and architectural material that enhances the view of White gained through his letters; they also give fascinating facts about the Metropolitan Opera, Madison Square Garden, and the rich salon life of the period. The best view of the oppressed woman in the dark shadows of New York life is found in Crane's novel *Maggie*. Mount's biography of Sargent remains the definitive source on that artist.

CHAPTER 9

Sources were Crane, Davis, Dolan, Edmiston and Cirino, Gilder, Henderson, Hillway, Howells, Leacock, Lehmann-Haupt, Maurice, Melville, Metcalf, Lloyd Morris, Smith, and Rufus and Otilie Wilson. Rosamund Gilder, herself a writer, provides a warm and insightful commentary to her father's letters. I was fortunate to supplement this material by interviews with Ms. Gilder before her recent death at the age of ninety-nine. She lived till the end of her life in the Gramercy Park apartment her father had commissioned for his family.

CHAPTER 10

Asbury, Britt, Cerf, Current-Garcia, Gernsheim, Gilder, Long, Maurice, Stansell, Wharton, Williams, Rufus and Otilie Wilson, and Wolff were sources used here in addition to the work of O. Henry himself, which of course is the most valuable study of the writer. The book by Williams provides an intimate view of a very private man. Wolff's erudite biography of Edith Wharton is fine reading.

CHAPTER 11

Sources were Arnason, Braider, Milton Brown, Eliot Clark, Dolan, Henri, Larkin, George Morris, Perlman, Pope, Sochen, Ward, Wecter, and Wyllie. Ward's study of the immigrant illustrates the world that George Bellows drew on for many of his paintings. Robert Henri's writings on art illustrate why he was such a remarkable teacher. They are invaluable for anyone wanting to understand the philosophy as well as the technique of art.

CHAPTER 12

Sources were Braider, Emily Clark, Kellner, Kolodin, Krehbiel, Kunitz, Lueders, Lloyd Morris, and the writings and reminiscences of Van Vechten. Once again, the writings by the chapter's principal subject, Van Vechten, present the most comprehensive view of the man and cover the range of his many careers.

CHAPTER 13

Sources used were Batterbury, Emily Clark, Edmiston and Cirino, Joost, Kellner, Lloyd Morris, Munson, Rosenfeld, Sochen, and Van Vechten. Munson's study of the twenties is an important memoir-history of the postwar period, concentrating on its literary life and accomplishments. Joost writes comprehensively of the history and changes in the life of *The Dial* magazine.

CHAPTER 14

Sources were Anderson, Comerchero, Edmiston and Cirino, Holdberger, Light, Martin, Munson, Perelman, Schulberg, Ross, Spender, and West. Schulberg and Perelman wrote of warm memories of West. Ben Sonnenberg allowed very little to be written about him and destroyed all his papers before his death. However, I was able to interview a number of his employees and colleagues, who gave a fascinating glimpse of a very controversial man.

BIBLIOGRAPHY

Ames, Mary Clemmer. *Alice and Phoebe Cary.* New York: Hurd & Houghton, 1873.

Amory, Cleveland. *Who Killed Society?* New York: Harper & Brothers, 1960.

Anderson, Jervis. *This Was Harlem, 1900–1950.* New York: Farrar, Straus & Giroux, 1982.

Armstrong, Maitland. *Day Before Yesterday.* New York: Charles Scribner's Sons, 1920.

Arnason, H. H. *History of Modern Art.* 2nd edition. Englewood Cliffs, N.J.: Prentice-Hall, 1978; and New York: Harry N. Abrams, 1978.

Asbury, Herbert. *The Gangs of New York.* New York: Alfred A. Knopf, 1927.

Atkinson, Brooks. *Broadway.* New York: Macmillan, 1974.

Baldwin, Charles C. *Stanford White.* New York: Dodd, Mead & Co., 1931.

Batterberry, Michael, and Ariane Batterberry. *On the Town in New York: From 1776 to the Present.* New York: Charles Scribner's Sons, 1973.

Bogardus, Ralph, and Fred Hobson. *Literature at the Barricades: The American Writer in the 1930s.* University, Ala.: University of Alabama Press, 1982.

Bouton, Margaret. "The Early Works of Augustus Saint-Gaudens." Unpublished dissertation, Radcliffe College, 1946.

Boyer, M. Christine. *Manhattan Manners.* New York: Rizzoli International Publications, 1985.

Boyer, M. Christine, and Jessica Scheer. "The Development and Boundaries of Luxury Neighborhoods in New York: 1625–1890." Working Paper #1, Center for Preservation Planning, Columbia University, 1980.

Boynton, Henry W. *Annals of American Bookselling, 1638–1850*. New York: John Wiley & Sons, 1932.

Braider, Donald. *George Bellows and the Ash Can School of Painting*. New York: Doubleday & Co., 1971.

Britt, Albert. *Turn of the Century*. Barre, Mass.: Barre Publishers, 1966.

Brooks, Gladys. *Gramercy Park Memories of a New York Girlhood*. New York: E. P. Dutton, 1958.

Brooks, Van Wyck. *The World of Washington Irving*. New York: E. P. Dutton, 1944.

———. *An Autobiography*. New York: E. P. Dutton, 1965.

Brown, Henry Collins. *Fifth Avenue Old and New, 1824–1924*. New York: Fifth Avenue Association, 1924.

———. *In the Golden Nineties*. New York: Valentine's Manual, Inc., 1928.

Brown, Milton. *The Story of the Armory Show*. New York: New York Graphic Society, 1963.

Campbell, Helen Stewart. *Darkness and Daylight: Lights and Shadows of New York Life*. Hartford: A. D. Worthington & Co., 1892.

Cerf, Bennett, and Van H. Cartmell. *The Best Short Stories of O. Henry*. New York: Modern Library.

Clark, Eliot. *History of the National Academy of Design, 1825–1953*. New York: Columbia University Press, 1954.

Clark, Emily. "Carl Van Vechten," in *Innocence Abroad*. New York: Alfred A. Knopf, 1931.

Comerchero, Victor. *Nathanael West: The Ironic Prophet*. Syracuse: Syracuse University Press, 1964.

Crane, Stephen. *Maggie, A Girl of the Streets*. New York, 1893.

———. *The Red Badge of Courage*. New York: D. Appleton & Co., 1895.

Crapsey, Edward. *The Nether Side of New York: Or the Vice, Crime and Poverty of the Great Metropolis*. New York: Sheldon & Co., 1872.

Coates, Robert M. "Messiah of the Lonely Hearts." *The New Yorker*, April 15, 1933.

Current-Garcia, Eugene. *O. Henry*. New York: Twayne Publishers, 1965.

Dana, Nathalie. *Young in New York*. New York: Doubleday & Co., 1962.

De Leeuw, Rudolph. *Both Sides of Broadway: From Bowling Green to Central Park*. New York: De Leeuw Riehl Publishing Co., 1910.

Dictionary of American History. New York: Charles Scribner's Sons, 1976.

Ditzion, Sidney. "Mechanics and Mercantile Libraries." *The Library Quarterly* X (1940).

Dolan, Anne M. "The Literary Salon in New York, 1830–1860." Unpublished dissertation, Columbia University, 1957.

Durso, Joseph. *Madison Square Garden.* New York: Simon & Schuster, 1979.

Edmiston, Susan, and Linda Cirino. *Literary New York.* Boston: Houghton Mifflin Co., 1976.

Ellington, George. *The Women of New York: Or Social Life in the Great City.* New York: The New York Book Co., 1870.

Evans, Meryle R. "Knickerbocker Hotels and Restaurants, 1800–1850." *New-York Historical Society Quarterly* 36 (1952).

Fairfield, Francis Gerry. *The Clubs of New York: With an Account of the Origin, Progress, Present Conditions and Membership of the Leading Clubs.* New York: Henry L. Hinter, 1873.

Field, Henry M. *The Story of the Atlantic Telegraph.* New York: Charles Scribner's Sons, 1892.

Ford, Ford Madox. *Memories and Impressions.* Reprint. Harmondsworth: Penguin Books, 1979.

Garmey, Stephen. *Gramercy Park.* New York: Balsam Press, Inc., Rutledge Books, 1984.

Garrett, Thomas M. "A History of Pleasure Gardens in New York City: 1700–1865." Unpublished dissertation, New York University, 1978.

The Gentleman's Directory of New York City. New York, 1870.

Gernsheim, Alison. *Victorian and Edwardian Fashion.* New York: Dover Publications, 1963.

Gilder, Richard Watson. *The Letters of Richard Watson Gilder.* Ed. by Rosamond Gilder. Boston: Houghton Mifflin Co., 1921.

Gipson, Richard McCandless. *The Life of Emma Thursby.* New York: The New-York Historical Society, 1940.

Goldberger, Paul. "The Last Town House." *Esquire* 13 (March 1979).

———. "Gramercy Park." *New York Times,* June 1975, C:23.

Harper, Henry J. *The House of Harper*. New York: Harper & Brothers, 1912.

Harris, Neil. *The Artist in American Society: The Formative Years, 1700–1860*. New York: George Braziller, 1966.

Headly, Joel T. *The Great Riots of New York, 1712–1873*. Indianapolis and New York: Bobbs-Merrill Co., 1970.

Henderson, Helen W. *A Loiterer in New York*. New York: George H. Doran Co., 1917.

Henri, Robert. *The Art Spirit*. Philadelphia: J. B. Lippincott Co., 1923.

Hewitt, Edward R. *Those Were the Days*. New York: Duell, Sloan & Pearce, 1943.

Hillman, Geoffrey T. "A House on Gramercy Park." *The New Yorker*, April 8, 1950.

Hillway, Tyrus. *Herman Melville*. New Haven: College and University Press, 1963.

Hirsch, Leo H., Jr. "The Negro and New York, 1783 to 1860." *Journal of Negro History* 3 (1963).

Hone, Philip. *The Diary of Philip Hone*. Ed. by Allan Nevins. 2 vols. New York: Dodd, Mead & Co., 1936.

Hornblow, Arthur. *A History of the Theatre in America*, 2 vols. Philadelphia: J. B. Lippincott Co., 1919.

Howells, William Dean. *Literary Friends and Acquaintances: A Personal Retrospect of American Authorship*. New York and London: Harper & Brothers, 1900.

Hughes, Glenn. *A History of the American Theater, 1700–1950*. New York: Samuel French, 1951.

James, Edward T. *Notable American Women, 1607–1950*. Cambridge: Belknap Press of Harvard University Press, 1971.

Jefferson, William. *The American Hotel*. New York: Alfred A. Knopf, 1930.

Jenkins, Stephen. *The Greatest Street in the World: Broadway*. New York: G. P. Putnam's Sons, 1911.

Joost, Nicholas. *Scofield Thayer and The Dial*. Carbondale: Southern Illinois University Press, 1964.

———. *The Dial, 1912–1920*. Barre, Mass.: Barre Publishers, 1967.

Judson, Isabella Field. *Cyrus W. Field, His Life and Work*. New York: Harper & Brothers, 1899.

Kellner, Bruce. *Carl Van Vechten and the Irreverent Decades*. Norman: University of Oklahoma Press, 1968.

Kolodin, Irving. *The Metropolitan Opera, 1833–1966: A Candid History*. New York: Alfred A. Knopf, 1966.

Kouwenhoven, John A. *The Columbia Historical Portrait of New York*. New York: Harper & Row, 1972. (Originally published by Doubleday & Co., 1953.)

Krehbiel, Henry. *Chapters of Opera*. New York: Henry Holt, 1908.

Kunitz, Stanley J., ed. *Twentieth-Century Authors*. 1st supplement. New York, 1955.

Ladies Shopping Guide and City Directory. New York: G. P. Putnam's Sons, 1981.

Lamb, Martha J. *History of the City of New York, Its Origins, Rise and Progress*. Vol. 3. New York: A. S. Barnes & Co., 1896.

Langford, Gerald. *Alias O. Henry, A Biography of William Sydney Porter*. New York: Macmillan, 1957.

———. *The Murder of Stanford White*. Indianapolis: Bobbs-Merrill Co., 1962.

Larkin, Oliver. *Art and Life in America*. New York: Rinehart & Co., 1949.

———. *Samuel F. B. Morse and American Democratic Art*. Boston: Little, Brown & Co., 1954.

Leacock, Stephen. *Essays and Literary Studies*. New York: Dodd, Mead & Co., 1916.

Lehmann-Haupt, Hellmut. *The Book in America*. New York: R. R. Bowker Co., 1952.

Light, James F. *Nathanael West: An Interpretive Study*. Evanston: Northwestern University Press, 1971.

Lockwood, Charles. *Bricks and Brownstones*. New York: Harper & Row, 1975.

Long, E. Hudson. *O. Henry: A Biographical Study*. Philadelphia: University of Pennsylvania Press, 1947.

———. *O. Henry: The Man and His Work*. Philadelphia: University of Pennsylvania Press, 1949.

Lovett, Robert Morss. *All Our Years: The Autobiography of Robert Morss Lovett*. New York: Viking Press, 1948.

Lueders, Edward. *Carl Van Vechten and the Twenties*. Albuquerque: University of New Mexico Press, 1955.

————. *Carl Van Vechten*. New York: Twayne Publishers, 1965.

Lynn, Kenneth. *The Dream of Success: A Study of the Modern American Imagination*. Boston: Little, Brown & Co., 1955.

Mack, Edward C. *Peter Cooper, Citizen of New York*. New York: Duell, Sloan & Pearce, 1949.

Martin, Jay. *Nathanael West: The Art of His Life*. New York: Farrar, Straus & Giroux, 1970.

Maurice, Arthur Bartlett. *The New York of the Novelists*. New York: Dodd, Mead & Company, 1916.

————. *O. Henry*. New York: Doubleday, Page & Co., 1925.

McCabe, James, Jr. *Lights and Shadows of New York Life*. New York: Farrar, Straus & Giroux, 1970.

————. *New York by Gaslight*. New York: Greenwich House, 1984.

The McGraw-Hill Encyclopedia of World Biography. New York: McGraw-Hill, 1973.

Melville, Herman. *Billy Budd and Other Prose Pieces*. London: Constable & Co., 1924.

————. *The Letters of Herman Melville*. Ed. by Merrill Davis and William Gilman. New Haven: Yale University Press, 1960.

Metcalf, Eleanor Melville. *Herman Melville: Cycle and Epicycle*. Cambridge: Harvard University Press, 1953.

Miller, Michael. *The Bon Marché: Bourgeois Culture and the Department Store, 1869–1920*. Princeton: Princeton University Press, 1981.

Moody, Richard. *Edwin Forrest: First Star of the American Stage*. New York: Alfred A. Knopf, 1960.

Moore, Truman, and Margaret Moore. "End of the Road for Ladies' Mile?" Pamphlet. New York: The Municipal Arts Society and the Historic Districts Council, 1985.

Morgan, Charles Hill. *George Bellows, Painter of America*. New York: Reynal, 1965.

Morris, George. *The National Academy of Design: A Century and a Half of American Art*. New York: National Academy of Design, 1975.

Morris, Lloyd. *Incredible New York*. New York: Random House, 1951.

————. *Curtain Time*. New York: Random House, 1953.

Mount, Charles Merrill. *John Singer Sargent*. London: The Cresset Press, 1957.

Munson, Gorham. *The Awakening Twenties*. Baton Rouge: Louisiana State University Press, 1985.

New York Panorama. Federal Writers' Project. New York: Pantheon Books, 1984. (Originally published by Random House, 1938.)

Nye, Russell B. *Society and Culture in America, 1830–1860*. New York: Harper & Row, 1974.

O. Henry. *The Voice of the City*. New York: Doubleday, Page & Co., 1919.

Oppel, Frank, ed. *Tales of Gaslight New York*. Secaucus, N.J.: Castle, 1985.

Pelletrau, William. *Early New York Houses*. New York: Francis P. Harper, 1900.

Perelman, S. J. *The Last Laugh*. New York: Simon & Schuster, 1981.

Perlman, Bennard B. *The Immortal Eight*. Cincinnati: North Light Publishers, 1979.

Pessen, Edward. *Riches, Class, and Power Before the Civil War*. Lexington, Mass.: D. C. Heath & Co., 1973.

Pine, John B. "Gramercy Park," in Henry C. Brown, *Valentine's Manual of Old New York*. New York: Valentine's Manual, Inc., 1920.

Pintard, John. *Letters from John Pintard to His Daughter Eliza Noel Pintard Davidson, 1816–1833*. The New-York Historical Society, Collections, LXX–LXXIII (1937–1940).

Pique, Jean Pierre, and Robert W. Kretsch. "The Prince of Players' Legacy." *American Review of Art and Science*, Summer 1965.

Pivar, David Jay. *The New Abolutionism: The Quest for Social Purity, 1876-1900*. Michigan: University Microfilms, 1965.

Platt, Frederick. *America's Gilded Age*. New York: A. S. Barnes & Co., 1979.

The Players After 75 Years. Ed. by George Woodbridge Stewart. New York: The Players, 1968.

Pope, Jesse E. *The Clothing Industry in New York*. Columbia: University of Missouri Press, 1905.

Proceedings of the Chamber of Commerce of New York State, 1859–1881.

Riegel, Robert Edgar. *American Women*. Rutherford, N.J.: Fairleigh Dickinson University Press, 1970.

Rosenfeld, Paul. *The Boy in the Sun*. New York: The Macaulay Co., 1938.

Ross, Irwin. *The Image Merchants*. Garden City, N.Y.: Doubleday & Co., 1959.

Roth, Leland M. *McKim, Mead and White, Architects*. New York: Harper & Row, 1983.

Ruggles, Eleanor. *Prince of Players*. New York: W. W. Norton, 1953.

Ruggles, Samuel. "Vindication in 1849 of the Canal Policy of New York of 1838." Pamphlet. New York, 1849.

————. "Semi-Centennial Address to the Alumni of Yale and Graduates of 1814." Speech. New York, 1864.

————. "The Memory of De Witt Clinton." Speech. New York, 1875.

————. "Importance of Open Squares in the City of New York." Pamphlet. New York, 1878.

————. "Freedom of Ocean Telegraphs." Speech. New York, 1886.

————. Tribute of the Chamber of Commerce of the State of New York to the Memory of Samuel Ruggles. New York, 1881.

Saint-Gaudens, Augustus. *The Reminiscences of Augustus Saint-Gaudens*. Ed. and amplified by Homer Saint-Gaudens. New York: The Century Co., 1913.

Schermerhorn, Gene. *Letters to Phil: Memories of a New York Boyhood, 1848–1856*. New York: New York Bound, 1982.

Schulberg, Budd. *Writers in America*. New York: Stein & Day, 1983.

Shaw, Ronald E. *Erie Water West: A History of the Erie Canal, 1792–1854*. Lexington: University of Kentucky Press, 1966.

Smith, Herbert. *Richard Watson Gilder*. New York: Twayne Publishers, 1970.

Smith, Jane. *Elsie de Wolfe: A Life in the High Style*. New York: Atheneum Publishers, 1982.

Sochen, June. *The New Woman in Greenwich Village, 1910–1920*. New York: Quadrangle Books, 1972.

Spann, Edward K. *Ideals and Politics: New York Intellectuals and Liberal Democracy, 1820–1880*. Albany: State University of New York Press, 1972.

Spender, Stephen. *The Thirties and After*. New York: Random House, 1978.

Stansell, Christine. *City of Women: Sex and Class in New York, 1789–1860*. New York: Alfred A. Knopf, 1986.

Stern, Robert A. M. *Pride of Place*. Boston: Houghton Mifflin Co., 1986.

Stern, Robert A. M., Gregory Gilmartin, and John Massengale. *New York*

1900: Metropolitan Architecture and Urbanism, 1890–1915. New York: Rizzoli International Publications, 1983.

Still, Bayrd. *Mirror for Gotham.* New York: New York University Press, 1956.

Street Commissioners Report, April 1, 1811. New York: The New-York Historical Society.

Strong, George Templeton. *The Diary of George Templeton Strong.* 4 vols. Ed. by Allan Nevins and Milton Thomas. New York: Macmillan, 1952.

Tharp, Louise Hall. *Saint-Gaudens and the Gilded Era.* Boston: Little, Brown & Co., 1969.

This Fabulous Century. Vols. 3 and 4. New York: Time-Life Books, 1969.

Thompson, D. G. Brinton. *Ruggles of New York.* New York: Columbia University Press, 1946.

Todd, Charles Burr. *In Olde New York.* New York: Ira J. Friedman, 1907.

Van Vechten, Carl. *Music After the Great War.* New York: G. Schirmer, 1915.

———. *Interpreters and Interpretations.* New York: Alfred A. Knopf, 1916.

———. *Peter Whiffle: His Life and Works.* New York: Alfred A. Knopf, 1922.

———. *The Blind Bow-Boy.* New York: Alfred A. Knopf, 1923.

———. *Nigger Heaven.* New York: Alfred A. Knopf, 1926.

———. Introduction to James Weldon Johnson, *The Autobiography of an Ex-Colored Man.* New York: Alfred A. Knopf, 1927.

———. *Parties.* New York: Alfred A. Knopf, 1930.

———. *Sacred and Profane Memories.* New York: Alfred A. Knopf, 1932.

———. Introduction to Gertrude Stein, *Three Lives.* New York: Modern Library, 1933.

———. *Fragments from an Unwritten Autobiography.* 2 vols. New Haven: Yale University Library, 1955.

———. "The Reminiscences of Carl Van Vechten, A Rudimentary Narration." Typescript of tape-recorded interviews for the Oral History Research Office of Columbia University. New York, 1960.

———. "The Dance Criticisms of Carl Van Vechten." *Dance Index* 1 (September, October, November 1942).

———. *The 1866 Visitors Guide to New York City.* Reprint. New York: Schocken Books, 1975.

Ward, David. *Cities and Immigrants.* New York: Oxford University Press, 1971.

Wecter, Dixon. *The Saga of American Society: A Record of Social Aspirations, 1607–1937.* New York: Charles Scribner's Sons, 1937.

West, Nathanael. *The Dream Life of Balso Snell.* Paris and New York: Contact Editions, 1931.

———. *Miss Lonelyhearts.* New York: Liveright, 1933.

———. *The Day of the Locust.* New York: Random House, 1939.

Wharton, Edith. *Old New York.* 4 vols. New York: D. Appleton, 1924.

———. *The Collected Short Stories.* Ed. by R. W. B. Lewis. New York: Charles Scribner's Sons, 1968.

———. *A Backward Glance.* New York: Appleton-Century, 1934.

White, Norval, and Elliot Wilensky. *AIA Guide to New York City.* New York: Collier Books, 1978.

———. "Intimate Letters of Stanford White." *The Architectural Record,* XXX, No. 3 (September 1911).

Who Was Who in America, Vol. 2, 1943–1950. Chicago, 1950.

Widmer, Kingsley. *Nathanael West.* Boston: Twayne Publishers, 1982.

Wilkinson, Burke. *Uncommon Clay.* New York: Harcourt Brace Jovanovich, 1985.

Williams, William Wash. *The Quiet Lodger of Irving Place.* New York: E. P. Dutton, 1936.

Wilson, James G. *Thackeray in the United States, 1852–53, 1855–56.* 2 vols. New York: Dodd, Mead & Co., 1904.

Wilson, Rufus Rockwell, and Otilie Wilson. *New York in Literature.* Elmira: The Primavera Press, 1947.

Wolfe, Gerard R. *New York: A Guide to the Metropolis.* New York: McGraw-Hill Co., 1983.

Wolff, Cynthia Griffin. *A Feast of Words: The Triumph of Edith Wharton.* Oxford: Oxford University Press, 1977.

Wyllie, Irvin G. *The Self-Made Man in America.* New York: The Free Press, 1954.

INDEX

Page numbers in italics refer to illustrations.

ABOUT THE AUTHOR

Carole Klein is the author of *The Single Parent Experience* (1973); *The Myth of the Happy Child* (1975); *Aline* (1979), the biography of Aline Bernstein, stage designer and the lover and mentor of Thomas Wolfe; *Mothers and Sons* (1984); *Gramercy Park: An American Bloomsbury* (1988); and *Overcoming Regret: Lessons from the Road Not Taken* (1992). Her articles and book reviews have appeared in magazines, newspapers, and literary journals, such as the *New York Times, Reader's Digest, New Woman, Biography*, and *Confrontation*.

Ms. Klein holds two degrees from Goddard College: a bachelor's in English and women's studies, and a dual master's in sociology and psychology. She has taught English, creative writing, and women's studies courses at Goddard, State University of New York, and New York University and lectures regularly on writing, women writers, women's issues, and cultural history. She is a member of the writing faculty of New School University of New York City, PEN, the Author's League, and the Biography Seminar of the New York Institute for the Humanities.

Library of Congress Cataloging-in-Publication Data

Klein, Carole.
    Gramercy Park : an American Bloomsbury / Carole Klein.
        p.   cm.
    Originally published: Boston : Houghton Mifflin Co., 1987.
    Includes bibliographical references and index.
    ISBN 0-8018-6297-3 (alk. paper)
        1. Gramercy Park (New York, N.Y.)—Intellectual life.   2. Gramercy Park
    (New York, N.Y.)—Social life and customs.   3. New York (N.Y.)—
    Intellectual life.   4. New York (N.Y.)—Social life and customs.   I. Title.
    F128.68.G77K43   2000
    974.7′1—dc21
                                                            99-38638